Classical and Christian Ideas
of World Harmony

CLASSICAL
and
CHRISTIAN
IDEAS
of
WORLD HARMONY

*Prolegomena to an Interpretation
of the Word* Stimmung

LEO SPITZER

Edited by Anna Granville Hatcher
Preface by René Wellek

Angelico Press

For information, address:
Angelico Press, Ltd.
169 Monitor St.
Brooklyn, NY 11222
www.angelicopress.com

paper 978-1-62138-760-2
cloth 978-1-62138-761-9

Cover design
by Michael Schrauzer

PREFACE

THE LATE LEO SPITZER (1887–1960) has a deservedly high reputation as a philologist whose multitudinous contributions to etymology, the study of word-formation and syntax, range over all the Romance languages.   He is, of course, best known for his extensive work in stylistics.   The finesse with which he interpreted passages and whole poems by means of a close examination of their linguistic surface, his sure grasp of a text, his sense of history, his feeling for the minutest shades of diction, the steady focus on the aesthetic fact make his studies models of "close reading." Spitzer never falls into the traps of mere sensitive impressionism, extravagant ingenuity, anachronistic speculation or irrational mysticism of much of the recent, not only American and not only new, criticism.   The posthumous collection of his *Essays on English and American Literature* (Princeton University Press, 1962) should demonstrate how fruitful his methods were, even outside his speciality.   They should carry his name far beyond the confines of those interested in the Romance world.

Less well known, however, is the fact that Spitzer was not only a philologist and student of stylistics but also practiced what he liked to call "historical semantics," an activity persuasively exemplified by the present treatise on *Classical and Christian Ideas of World Harmony*.   It was originally published in two instalments in the review *Traditio* (Vols. II, 1944, pp. 409–64, and III, 1945, pp. 307–64) and appears now in a revised and considerably expanded version prepared for republication by Anna Granville Hatcher, Professor of Romance Philology at The Johns Hopkins University.

"Historical semantics" is Spitzer's term for a peculiar combination of lexicography and history of ideas. He either starts with a
particular word, *e.g.*, "mother tongue," and traces its meaning in
different cultural and temporal settings, or he starts with a concept
given in a particular civilization and shows the variety of word-
material attracted by this concept as in this treatise on *World
Harmony* or in the closely related paper on *Milieu* and *Ambiance*
(reprinted in *Essays in Historical Semantics*, New York, 1948).
Spitzer focusses always on the learned key-words of our civilization
and ranges freely over the history of theology, philosophy, music,
literature, the fine arts, science and superstition. His "historical
semantics" is not just lexicography, not even etymology (though he
does speculate about derivations), but it is rather, word history
within a general history of thought. The word is studied primarily
for its meaning, its reference in a cultural context which includes
the meaning of other words related etymologically or in their
conceptual field. Conceptual field is a term referring to the
"ensemble of synonyms existing at a certain time in a certain
language" (*Essays in Historical Semantics*, p. 303). In looking at a
word, we see other words nearby, or in the background as we would
see other objects in looking at any object. Spitzer moves from one
word to the other, from a concept to similar or contrasting concepts
with the ease of a master who surveys the whole tradition of the
West in its totality. He wryly commented about his turning from a
"specialist" to a "universalist" late in life, as obviously such studies
cannot be carried out within the limits of one linguistic family.
Spitzer, though often highly critical of the limitations of traditional
"comparative literature," constantly reminds us that "our depart-
mentalized organization of philology rests on an artificial basis.
There is no such thing as 'modern philology,' or modern philologies;
they all naturally tend to merge into one unified Western philology
which would have as its aim to trace the developments of the two
and a half millennia of Western cultural life" (*Essays*, p. 303).
Obviously such a study cannot be done without a knowledge of
many languages. Spitzer cannot "understand how one could read
a philosopher properly without recourse to the text in its original
language," and we may surely add that a poet cannot be properly

read in translation either. Spitzer follows this injunction consist-
ently and he can do so as he knows all the relevant languages, and
learned or relearned what he needed for his purposes. He is
constantly accumulating evidence for "the European solidarity that
has existed throughout: solidarity in word material (which was
exclusively that of the ancients) and solidarity in the semantic
developments which, through the ages, have made their contributions to the original material." (*Essays*, p. 303.)

Spitzer is anxious to distinguish his own method from that of two
related disciplines: the "history of ideas" in the sense in which it
was defined and practiced by his colleague, A. O. Lovejoy, and
Geistesgeschichte as it flourished in the time of Spitzer's teaching
career in Germany. In several places and particularly in an article
directed against Lovejoy's attempt to trace some of the key concepts
of Hitlerism to German romantic thought (cf. "Geistesgeschichte
vs. History of Ideas applied to Hitlerism," in *Journal of the History
of Ideas V* (1944), pp. 191–203 and "History of Ideas versus Reading
of Poetry," in *Southern Review VI* (1941), pp. 584–609), Spitzer has
argued against what he considers the atomism and excessive
intellectualism of Lovejoy's method. He doubts the possibility of
isolating "unit-ideas" and questions the assumption of an un-
emotional idea for which only "affective concomitants" are allowed.
For Spitzer "important ideas are from the start passionate responses
to the problems which agitate their period." "The assumption that
an idea in history is a completely separate element" is inconceivable
to Spitzer. "In any movement, with any individual one idea is
ever ready to merge with another." Lovejoy's closely reasoned and
somewhat hair-splitting reply (*Journal of the History of Ideas V*
(1944), pp. 204f.) shows that Spitzer was not fully aware that
Lovejoy was conscious of all these problems; but surely Spitzer put
his finger on the differences between Lovejoy's and his own method
when he emphasized totality, unity, climate of an age, emotional
atmosphere, the links and transitions between words rather than the
distinctions between unit-ideas and a rationalistic criticism of their
implied "metaphysical pathos" which were Lovejoy's peculiar
forte.

While Lovejoy's method seemed to Spitzer too atomistic and

rationalistic, German *Geistesgeschichte* seemed to him too irrational-istic, too verbalistic in its reliance on a completely unified "spirit of the time." Spitzer, however, prefers the term *Geist* to "intellectual history" or "history of ideas" but *Geist* is to him "nothing ominously mystical or mythological but simply the totality of the features of a given period or movement which the historian tries to see as a unity" (*ibid.*, p. 202). *Geist* suggests the unity of feeling and thought, the atmosphere, the climate of opinion for which he is searching.

Classical and Christian Ideas of World Harmony is thus not merely a chance example of the method. The very topic: "world harmony" is almost an emblem of Spitzer's *Geist*: his conception of the unity of the European spirit, the old world's feeling for an ordered, even musically ordered universe. The treatise is a demonstration of the growth of European cultural solidarity, and at the same time a study of its breakdown since the Enlightenment. Spitzer treats "the case of world harmony as a signal example of the expansion of the concept of music to fields, which, in other civilizations, would seem entirely remote from music" (*Essays*, p. 6), and he shows also the "demy-thologizing" of the world, its disenchantment, its loss of harmony. John Hollander has since called this process "The Untuning of the Sky" using a striking phrase from Dryden's "Ode on St. Cecilia's Day" in a brilliant study centered on English poetry of the sixteenth and seventeenth centuries. (*The Untuning of the Sky: Ideas of Music in English Poetry* 1500–1700, Princeton, 1961). On a larger scale, Spitzer depicts this same disintegration of the old world concepts with a certain tone of nostalgia. "The world-embracing metaphysical cupola that once enfolded mankind disappeared, and man is left to rattle around in an infinite Universe" (*Essays*, p. 300). But later in his life, Spitzer treated this nostalgia as a mere phase in his development, as something he had to leave behind. On one of his last pronouncements, the Preface to *Romanische Literatur-studien* (Tübingen, 1959) he speaks of the changes in his outlook. "From an intellectual half regretting the loss of faith and the coming of the Renaissance" he has again become a "determined friend of light and clear form," of "la belle lumière du monde" in the words of Ronsard. While Spitzer's regret or half regret for the destruction of the old belief in world harmony faded, as no illusion cŏuld long keep his allegiance, he surely preserved his aesthetic admiration for the old world-picture, his historical interest in understanding it and his feeling for its survivals in our time and in our languages. *Stimmung* is such a survival as he shows convincingly, and so is "mood" as moods preserve ancient feelings. The *musica humana*, the well-tempered man, was or tried at least to be in harmony with the great *musica mundana*, while *musica instrumentalis* was a means of reconciling microcosm and macrocosm, man with nature—the work or even the composition of God. Without succumbing to superstition or sentimentality we may feel this even today in our deepest experience of music and poetry.

Spitzer has a very personal method of getting at things: he believes in "mass strategy," in the accumulation of quotations, in the marshaling of evidence, in what may appear at first sight only "chaotic enumeration," the name he gave to the method of poets like Whitman and Claudel. But then he suddenly shifts focus, takes a poem, even a well-known poem such as Milton's "On a Solemn Music," or a sonnet of Shakespeare's, and subjects it to close scrutiny commenting on many details and correcting misinterpretations by even famous scholars. Karl Vossler, Karl Young, David Masson, Fernand Baldensperger, Friedrich Gundolf and many others are not spared if they fail in imaginative sympathy with the medieval point of view or introduce biographical or historical irrelevances. But then suddenly Spitzer can drop the preoccupation with the concrete and soar to generalizations about our civilization, about Rome, Greece, the Middle Ages, the Renaissance, the Baroque, or about the differences between the nations, the characters of their languages and the traditions of their scholarship. The vistas are often breathtaking, the shifts possibly too abrupt: some intermediate stages of development seem to be missing as we realize that behind the concern for the mass of details there is a passionate desire for unity and harmony in Spitzer. That is why *Classical and Christian Ideas of World Harmony* is not merely an immensely learned treatise in historical semantics, but also a memorial to the man and to his ideal of scholarship. It is a stupendous display of world harmony as a creed, a demonstration that "all is all," that everything is related to everything: the planets and the lute, colors heard and sounds seen, rhyme and nature in Spring, echo and birds' song, *The Merchant of Venice* and *Tristan und Isolde*. All this and much, much more is pulled together, drawn into a concert, a "unity in variety" and even a "unity in discord," which is after all the central theme of the treatise: world harmony.

Christmas, 1962   RENÉ WELLEK

EDITOR'S NOTE

In its original version, Professor Spitzer's historical study of the concept of World Harmony appeared in *Traditio* II (1944) and III (1945); as its sub-title indicated ("Prolegomena to a Study of the Word *Stimmung*"), it was intended to serve as an introduction for the subsequent treatment of a single German word: a word whose many connotations could be fully appreciated only when seen against the conceptual background of many centuries and many literatures.

For several years after the completion of his study on World Harmony, Professor Spitzer continued to collect material concerned with this concept, at the same time that he was working on his analysis of *Stimmung*: he had hoped to bring out together in one volume both this word-study and the expanded version of World Harmony. By 1948, he abandoned the project because of certain practical difficulties, the main one being that of publishing a book written half in English and half in German. The two manuscripts were found among his papers after his death in 1960; since the first was practically complete, and since the already-printed version had become one of his most widely-read studies, it seemed desirable to make accessible (if still without the companion-piece with which it had been conceived) the present version.

In the original form, many of the quotations were lacking in bibliographical indications, and a number of misprints had crept in, often involving a corruption of the page references that had been given. In the preparation of this volume for the press, every effort was made to locate all passages quoted (whose number had been almost doubled by the new material) and to make any corrections and additions necessary; though complete success cannot be claimed, still the results of this labor should have made the present volume much more practically useful for consultation.

CONTENTS

CLASSICAL AND CHRISTIAN
IDEAS OF WORLD HARMONY

INTRODUCTION

Die Sonne tönt, nach alter Weise
In Brudersphären Wettgesang . . . —Goethe, *Faust*

Und so ist wieder jede Kreatur nur ein Ton, eine Schattierung einer
grossen Harmonie, die man auch im Ganzen und Grossen studieren
muss, sonst ist jedes Einzelne nur ein toter Buchstabe.—Goethe to
Knebel, November 17, 1789

IN THE FOLLOWING STUDY I propose to reconstruct
the many-layered occidental background for a German word: the
concept of world harmony which underlies the word *Stimmung*.
This task implies a survey of a whole semantic "field," as it was
developed in different epochs and literatures: the concept and the
words expressing it have to be brought face to face, and in the words,
in turn, the semantic kernel and the emotional connotations with
their variations and fluctuations in time have to be considered.
A "Stimmungsgeschichte" of the word *Stimmung* is necessary. I
hope that this historical development will spontaneously, if gradually,
emerge from the mosaic of texts to which I wish my running text
to be subordinated: the consistency of the texture of verbal and
conceptual associations and motifs through the centuries seems to
me to be herewith established. "Avez-vous un texte?" was the
insistent question which the famous positivist Fustel de Coulanges
was wont to address to his pupils when they made a historical
statement. The student in historical semantics must ask: "Have
you *many* texts?," for only with a great number of them is one
enabled to visualize their ever-recurrent pattern. I realize that the

I

medieval art of tapestry (which Péguy has revived in literature), with its possibility of showing a constant motif along with the labyrinth of interwoven ramifications, would be a more adequate medium of treatment than is the necessarily linear run of the words of language. And, in any case, I shall be obliged, in the notes, to anticipate or recapitulate the events which cannot be treated at their historical place.

I came across the problem of *Stimmung* (which has been quite inadequately treated by Germanists) when working on that of *"Milieu* and *Ambiance"*—to which I consider it to be a parallel; it has been necessary, in some cases, to discuss the same expressions in both studies, though I have sought to avoid as much as possible any duplication. Here, as in the companion study, I "take the word seriously": the development of thought is always shown together with the development of word usage; in fact, it is development of thought which, I believe, provokes linguistic innovation while, on the other hand, preservation of thought betrays itself in linguistic conservatism. In both studies stress is laid more on preservation of word material than on its renewal: *Stimmung* ultimately echoes Greek words, just as *ambiente, ambiance* echo the Greek περιέχον; these equations are no more astonishing than are those of French *il est – ils sont* = Indo-European **esti – *sonti*, although scholars in linguistics have hitherto shown more interest in the latter type, that is, in the morphological patterns into which the ideological contents of occidental civilization have been poured, than in the expressions for the contents themselves. It is a fact that most current abstract words have a Greco-Latin philosophical and religious background, though they may look thoroughly German—a background which has not always been investigated as was done in the case of ἐλεημοσύνη > *misericordia* > *Barmherzigkeit*.

About the concrete linguistic-historical continuity from ancient Greece and Rome via the Christian Middle Ages to our modern secularized civilization, one can rather learn from historians of religion and philology than from "system-minded" linguistic comparativists who are little interested in the philosophical and religious ancestry of modern thinking. I shall always remember the words of a colleague of mine, a German historian of art, who had atheistic convictions: one day, striding up and down his room as he discussed with his students the Christian elements of our civilization, he stopped short and, looking down at the antique rugs on which he had been treading, he confessed, with bad grace, "Christianity is like these good old rugs: the more you trample them the less they fade." And somewhat similar must be the experience of a linguist devoted to historical semantics: he will always discover an ancient "religious tapestry" of Greco-Roman-Christian origin.

Now, the procedure of continuously rediscovering the same pattern of thought recurring in so many manifestations of linguistic and cultural life throughout the centuries may strike the reader as banal and tedious. It would be possible, perhaps, for me to sum up the lengthy study which is to follow in these words: The Pythagorean concept of world harmony was revived in modern civilization whenever Platonism was revived; and the German word *Stimmung* is the fruit of one of these revivals. Thereby the thousand or more texts which I have chosen as illustrating this development would be dispensed with. That I have preferred the long way round is due to my belief that the most important requirement for historical understanding is the philological re-enactment of such world-embracing concepts, which must be sought out in all the nooks and corners of our languages and our civilization. It is not the fact that a certain concept was paramount in a certain civilization that matters most, but the way in which it was present at various times: the way in which its influence made itself felt in details. To state a historical truth about a philosophical concept is not enough. Indeed, such summary statements all too often tempt one to brush aside the concept, to avert its impact, to cause it to evaporate. The concepts must be taken seriously—as I am obviously attempting to do in the following chapters. The reader will be invited to dwell on one idea, continuously reworked over scores of pages, without asking impatiently, "So what?," but rather wondering, "So, how?" He will be invited to meditate, not to tabulate, or, as Goethe says, to "think again what has once been thought"; "to recognize the once-cognized," in the words of the philologian Böckh.

It is true that the treatment of the particular subject of world harmony involves a special danger: the harmonizing habit of thought which historically underlies this concept, may encroach upon the mental processes of the historical semanticist who seeks to study the conception, and who, as he follows the track of the words, may be tempted to assume semantic developments to be *already*, or *still*, present at a particular moment—only because he knows the whole curve, the before and the after, of the development. To diagnose the vitality, the emotional force in a conception at a particular historical moment is not easy (the words may be petrified reminiscences). A historical analyst such as Professor Lovejoy, for example, would perhaps tend to distinguish many more *differences* in word usage than I have been able to see, who would, by natural habit, rather emphasize the bridges connecting the seventeen meanings of "nature" in the eighteenth century, than the abysses between them. I readily admit that the synthetic attitude may be a serious danger, and doubly so in a study on *musica mundana* to which no mortal ear can ever boast to be coldly objective; for world music is, perhaps, what a German coinage could express: *der Seelenheimatlaut*, the music of man's nostalgia yearning home-ward—heavenward! And yet, too intellectual an attitude toward one of the most heart-inspiring cosmic conceptions ever imagined would be an unnecessary, if not an impossible, sacrifice to scholarly impassivity. We have in our republic of letters too many scholars whose abstract coolness is due largely to their lack of belief in what they have chosen to study, and I feel that the scholar cannot adequately portray what he does not love with all the fibers of his heart (and even a "hating love" would be better than indifference): I side with Phaedrus in the *Symposium*, speaking of Eros: ὁ γὰρ χρὴ ἀνθρώποις ἡγεῖσθαι παντὸς τοῦ βίου.

In addition to the different scholars who have contributed to this study, I want to thank Dr. Anna Granville Hatcher (who first sensed that what originally was a note in my article, "*Milieu* and *Ambiance*" should rather become an article in its own right) for the keen criticism which is for her a necessity and for the criticized a marvelous help.[1]

CHAPTER I

IT IS A FACT that the German word *Stimmung* as such is untranslatable. This does not mean that phrases such as *in guter (schlechter) Stimmung sein* could not easily be rendered by Fr *être en bonne (mauvaise) humeur*, Eng *to be in a good (bad) humor, in a good (bad) mood; die Stimmung in diesem Bilde (Zimmer)* by *l'atmosphère de ce tableau (cette chambre)*,[1] or *l'ambiance* . . . ; *Stimmung hervorrufen* by *to create, to give atmosphere, créer une atmosphère; die Stimmung der Börse* by *l'humeur, le climat de la bourse; für etwas Stimmung machen* by *to promote; die Seele zu Traurigkeit stimmen* by *disposer l'âme à la tristesse*, etc. But what is missing in the main European languages is a term that would express the unity of feelings experienced by man face to face with his environment (a landscape, nature, one's fellow man), and would comprehend and weld together the objective (factual) and the subjective (psychological) into one harmonious unity. The oft-quoted saying of the French-Swiss Amiel, "Le paysage est un état d'âme,"[2] rather reveals by analysis than succeeds in bridging the fundamental dualism prescribed to him by his Romance language and which his Germanic pantheistic soul wished to overcome: for a German, *Stimmung* is fused with the landscape, which in turn is animated by the feeling of man—it is an indissoluble unit into which man and nature are integrated. The Frenchman can neither say **l'humeur d'un paysage* nor **mon atmosphère* (at least not without expressed justification),[3] whereas the German has at his disposal both "the *Stimmung* of a landscape" and "my *Stimmung*." And there is also in the German word a constant relationship with *gestimmt sein*, "to be tuned," which, with its inference of a relative solidarity or agreement with something

5

more comprehensive (a man, a landscape, is tuned *to* "something"), differentiates it from *state of mind, état d'âme, Gemützsustand,* and presupposes a whole of the soul in its richness and variability; when Hegel, in his *Vorlesungen über Ästhetik,* III, 424, defines the contents of lyric poetry, in the statement: "Die *flüchtigste Stimmung des Augenblicks,* das Aufjauchzen des Herzens, die schnell vorüberfahrenden Blitze sorgloser Heiterkeiten und Scherze, Trübsinn und Schwermuth, Klage, genug *die ganze Stufenleiter der Empfindung* wird hier in ihren momentanen Bewegungen oder einzelnen Einfällen über die verschiedenartigsten Gegenstände festgehalten, und durch das Aussprechen dauernd gemacht," the word *Stimmung* evokes the most fugitive of moods, but within the framework of the "whole scale of feelings."[4] Similarly, Schopenhauer (*Die Welt als Wille und Vorstellung,* I, 3, 51) may write: "die Stimmung des Augenblickes zu ergreifen und im Liede zu verkörpern ist die ganze Leistung dieser poetischen Gattung" (i.e., of lyric poetry); again (I, 3, 38), when ascribing the feeling of harmony to the elimination of man's *Wille* and its replacement by *Erkennen,* he uses the same word to denote a general *Gestimmtsein*: "Innere Stimmung, Übergewicht des Erkennens über das Wollen, kann unter jeder Umgebung diesen Zustand hervorrufen ... aber erleichtert und von aussen befördert wird jene rein *objektive Gemüthsstimmung* durch entgegenkommende Objekte."[5]

Such is the range of the German word: from fugitive emotionalism to an objective understanding of the world. Moreover, there is a constant musical connotation with the word, due to its origin, as we shall point out, which can be revived at any moment in modern writing: E. R. Curtius, writing in his *Frankreich,* p. 152, on Paris, will say: "Alle diese Kontraste sind ... befasst in einer *Einheit von Atmosphäre und Stimmung,* worin die Anmut heiterer Gärten, das naive Kleinleben der Strasse, die geschwungene Folge der Seinebrücken, ... die so verschiedene Eigenart der einzelnen Stadtviertel *zusammenklingen.* Paris ist nicht nur eine Stadt, es ist auch eine *Landschaft* aus Wasser, Bäumen, Rasen, und sie hat ihren eigenen Himmel, dessen zart *abgetönte* Farben mit den blassen grauen und gelblichen *Tönen* der Häuser *zusammenstimmen.*" The potential musicality in the word family is like a *basso ostinato* accompanying the intellectual connotation of "unity of the landscape and feelings prompted by it."

If we are to delve now into the historic foundations of *Stimmung*, we find the surprising fact that the German word, however individual may be its use today, and however wide its semantic range, is simply and clearly indebted to the all-embracing ancient and Christian tradition which is at the bottom of all the main European languages. The German has made his original talent (in the biblical sense) fructify in an individual manner, but the talent itself which he has inherited is identical with that of the other peoples of the Occident. It is significant that *Stimmung* in its current meaning of "changing mood of the moment" is most easily translatable into other languages (Eng *mood, humor, temper*, etc.), whereas the *Stimmung* which extends over, and unites, a landscape and man, finds no full equivalent: it is precisely the latter, the so "specifically German" semantic development which originates in the all-embracing and international European tradition. Originally the word did not suggest a changing, temporary condition, but rather a stable "tunedness" of the soul, and in this meaning—although neither S. Singer (*Zeitschrift für deutsche Wortforschung*, III and IV) nor F. Mauthner (*Wörterbuch der Philosophie*, preface) mentions it in their lists, nor does the *Deutsche Wörterbuch* in its treatment of *Stimmung*—it was evidently a loan translation (*Bedeutungslehnwort*) from Latin words such as *temperamentum* (*temperatura*) and *consonantia* (*concordia*), which mean a "harmonious state of mind." We have to deal here with an ancient semantic texture consisting mainly of two threads; in the following lines we shall try to unravel what in ancient and medieval thought was woven together: the ideas of the "well-tempered mixture" and of the "harmonious consonance," which fuse into the one all-embracing unit of the world harmony.

It is to the harmonizing thought of the Greeks (which, instead of being blamed by modern critics as a lack of analysis impeding progress in natural sciences, should be understood in its poetic quality, in its power of making the world poetic) that we owe the first picture of the world seen in a harmony patterned on music, a world resembling Apollo's lute—*seen* because ἰδέα and εἶδος,

Denken and *Anschauung* were one for the Greek; this, of course, was
in contrast to the imagination of the Jews as expressed in the
Scriptures: there, though things seen abound, they are immediately
put into the service of the invisible God Himself. It was probably
not only the "so-called Pythagoreans" (to use the expression
which E. Frank, in his book, *Plato und die sogenannten Pythagoreer*
[Halle, 1929], borrowed from Aristotle to designate later scientists
of about 400 B.C. who attributed their scientific discoveries to the
mythical Pythagoras), but Pythagoras himself who assumed a
fourfold harmony in the world. This had to be fourfold, since
the "holy τετρακτύς" pervaded his thinking: the harmony of the
strings (and of the string), of the body and soul, of the state, of the
starry sky; and this idea has been alive wherever the influence of
Pythagoras was felt, from Plato, Ptolemy, and Cicero to Kepler,
Athanasius Kircher, and Leibniz. Less than the other thinkers of
the earliest age of Greek philosophy and science (sixth–fifth
centuries B.C.) did the Pythagoreans keep science clear of mythology,
and it is this "theological" approach which later endeared their
speculations to the Christian age. It has been suggested that the
cult of Apollo, the god with the lute as his attribute, inspired the
musical simile of Pythagoras, and that the "real Pythagoreans"
were probably an Orphic sect. Observing the wondrous regularity
of the movement of the stars, they may have come to imagine a
musical harmony in them: the seven planets were comparable to
the seven strings of the heptachord of Terpander (*ca.* 644 B.C.) and
the (assumed) sounds of the spheres revolving around the center at
different distances to the seven intervals of this lute; the distances
between the spheres themselves were "tones." World harmony
appeared as a musical harmony, inaccessible to human ears, but
comparable to human music and, since reducible to numbers
(τὸν ὅλον οὐρανόν ἁρμονίαν εἶναι καὶ ἀριθμόν), to some degree
accessible to human reason. In spite of the fact that the simile,
world harmony – musical harmony, was derived (historically
speaking) from a human instrument,[6] the Pythagoreans inverted
the order by admitting that the human lute (as imagined in the
hands of the god Apollo) was an imitation of the music of the stars;
human activities had to be patterned on godly activities, i.e., on

the processes in nature: human art, especially, had to be an imitation
of the gods, i.e. of reasonable nature. Thus we will witness a
continuous flow of metaphors from the human (and divine) sphere
to nature and back again to human activities, which are considered
as imitating the artistic orderliness and harmony of nature. A
clearly idealistic conception of the world, opposing the materialism
of Ionian natural philosophy, had taken hold of a visual (and
acoustic) symbol in order to make itself understood.

In a system such as that of Heraclitus, the visual symbol was
complicated by the dialectics of integrated contrasts, παλίντροπος
(var. παλίντονος) ἁρμονίη ὅκωσπερ τόξου καὶ λύρης; harmony
dominates, but a harmony which comprehends strife and antagonism
as a synthesis is beyond thesis and antithesis (an idea for which
Hegel is indebted to Heraclitus). The lute and the arrow are alike
in form; this fact, and the fact that both are attributes of Apollo,
are for Heraclitus symptomatic of the ease with which strife (the
arrow)[7] can turn into harmony: for the name of the bow (βιός) is
life (βίος) and its work, death.[8] The Greek mind has been able to
see harmony in discord, to see the triumph of "symphony" over
the discordant voices. A sentence such as Philolaos' (Diels, n° 32,
B 10), ἁρμονία δὲ πάντως ἐξ ἐναντίων γίνεται, ἔστι γὰρ ἁρμονία
πολυμιγέων ἕνωσις καὶ δίχα φρονεόντων συμφρόνησις is
typical in its theme of control imposed upon the discordant;
the paradoxical expression δίχα φρονεόντων συμφρόνησις, "the
making concordant of the discordant" confronts us with the
two antagonistic forces of harmonious unification and discordant
manifoldness, but the συμψρόνησις, the "thinking-together" is
triumphant, the discordant is made subject thereto (the linguistic
expression itself portrays the wrestling with chaos and the triumph
of cosmos). Small wonder that this felicitous linguistic analysis of
cosmic life has been retained in the following centuries. With the
Romans we find expressions of the type concordia discors (Pliny),[9]
said of heat and humidity; rerum concordia discors (Ovid, Horace),
dissimilium concordia quam vocant ἁρμονίαν (Quintilian); things
are made to "feel" also with the pupils of Greece. Nor are these
isolated examples of the tendency to endow the universe with
human feelings: sympathy (the human capacity of suffering with

one's fellow man) is attributed to the stars in a kind of cosmic empathy ("kosmische Einsfühlen" which Max Scheler, *Wesen und Formen der Sympathie*, p. 95, has termed characteristic of occidental thought). With Posidonius, if we are to believe K. Reinhardt (*Kosmos und Sympathie*, p. 54), sympathy (expressed in later writers by συμπάθεια, συγγένεια, σύμπνοια) becomes a cosmic principle of world-cohesion; and Dion of Prusa, in a political oration, the ideas of which have gone over to Augustine (cf. H. Fuchs, *Augustin und der antike Friedensgedanke*) contrasts the ὁμόνοια, the concord of the elements, of nature, and the animals with the egotism (πλεονεξία) of petty man and his communities.

In a universe thus animated by human feelings (patterned on godly ones), music seemed to express best the inner depths of human and cosmic nature. The central position of music in Greek thought (an art much neglected by students in the antiquities in comparison with the plastic arts of the Greeks, of which so many remnants have come to us), has been described by E. Frank: the ποιητής was for the Greeks the type of the Creator, who was poet and composer (i.e. musician) at the same time, whereas the sculptor was merely a δημιουργός, an artisan, dangerously close to the mere technician, the βάναυσος. Frank gives the history of Greek music from its liturgic, classically measured period of *melos* (linear development of melody) and enharmonic (the distinction of fourth-tones, a refinement which our ears, trained only for diatonic music, can no longer appreciate) to chromaticism, later diatonicism, and to absolute music, i.e., music without words that is descriptive of human emotions. After Damon (fifth century), a mathematician and states-man, had recognized in music the main pillar of the state (any musical innovation can shake it from top to bottom), the first philo-sopher to take note of the increased importance of music is Democritus (*ca.* 430–400), who, by placing it as a separate discipline together with arithmetic, astronomy and geometry, became, so to speak, the founder of the medieval quadrivium. Democritus expressed the feeling of his time when he stated that the essence and the happiness of mankind consists in "harmony." Archytas, Plato's Pythagorean friend, sought (after 400 B.C.) to find the essence of the individual soul, as of the world soul, in the tones of music, and to establish the exact physical laws underlying this art (the relationship between the length of strings and the pitch of tones: the proportion 2 : 1 gives the octave, 3 : 2 the quint, 4 : 3 the quart, etc.). In his theory we find an explanation not only of the difference of sounds but also of the movement, determined by mathematics, of quantitative celestial bodies; it originated, according to Frank, not with Pythagoras or the older Pythagoreans, but with the "so-called Pythagoreans," probably from Archytas himself, who, like any modern scientist, *proved* his mathematical harmony of the celestial bodies.[10] Though inspired originally by theology, this constitutes one of the greatest among scientific discoveries; centuries later it was exhumed by Kepler, who, in 1618, found it in the *Harmonice* of Ptolemy, that is, in a late re-elaboration ("a Pythagorean dream," as he says) of the Archytan ideas compiled 1500 years before him and corroborating his own independent research of twenty-two years. Plato evidently knew and appreciated the greatness of this find, which had been realized probably at his time: at the end of *Nomoi* he states the two basic principles that the immortal soul is prior and superior to all bodily developments and that there is a Noῦς in the constellations: "man must therefore appropriate to himself the rigorous mathematical sciences whose close relationship with music he must have apprehended in order to learn their use in the harmonious education of his character, and of the moral and juridical conscience."

Plato, in the *Timaeus*, uses the exact schemes of Archytas to a purely speculative end, building a new cosmogony around these numerical speculations. How the world soul (a religious concept), the regulation of the cosmos (a concept of physics), world harmony (a musical concept) and the soul of man (a psychological concept) are fused, can perhaps best be seen in this dialogue (cf. A. Rivaud's introduction to the *Association Budé* edition, X). According to this, since the soul is in general the cause of life and life manifests itself by regular movements ordered in view of a purpose, so the world soul, the first and oldest creation of the Demiurgos, is the principle of orderly movement in the universe; thus the world soul guarantees the order of the skies—and from theology we have gone forward to astronomy and physics. This world soul, identified with the heavenly sphere and its moving force, is itself the result of a mixture, at the hands of the Demiurgos, of an indivisible, eternally stable essence (the One; the World of Ideas or Eternal Forms), and of the divisible and visible, transitory essence—a mixture of elements, to which has been added, in a second mixture, the very product, containing divisible and indivisible elements, of the first mixture: the three elements (they are three for Plato) are mixed in a proportion

$$A, B, C. \left(= \frac{A}{2} + \frac{B}{2} \right)^2$$

in which the divisible has been joined "forcibly" by the Demiurgos with the indivisible to form a *harmony*. The compound thus formed was divided by him into seven parts which have to each other the relationship either $1 : 2 : 4 : 8$ or $1 : 3 : 9 : 27$—by now we have turned from metaphysics to mathematics.[11] Out of the two progressions the Demiurgos has formed the series of seven members: $1,2,3,4,8,9,27$; this is the "great tetraktys" which the ancients figured as the two branches of a lambda:

$$
\begin{array}{cc}
8 & 27 \\
4 & 9 \\
2 & 3 \\
& 1
\end{array}
$$

The intervals between these members have been filled by applying two μεσότητες, the arithmetic and the harmonic mean. In order to define the interval between two consecutive members, Plato now uses music: every member is a sound (φθόγγος) of the scale. The higher number does not correspond to the number of vibrations as in modern acoustics, but to the location in the lute: the highest string (ὑπάτη) gives the lowest tone. The problem of harmony consists, then, of "unifying" or "filling" the intervals of the scale by terms which have definite relationships with the original series. This operation is called ἁρμόττειν, harmonization, and the result is a ἁρμονία. The choice of the numbers determining the intervals is effected, not by observation, but by a priori reasoning. This series so deduced, and comprehending all possible scales, is much longer than the one used in the musical scale—it must be so since it represents the world soul which surpasses in harmony all the limited scales produced by imperfect human instruments. The ἁρμονία or διὰ πασῶν, the octave interval of five tones and two λείμματα (residues), representing two tetrachords, uses only the proportion 1 : 2, whereas the celestial harmony goes up to 27. These a priori constructed intervals are not, let us remember, tones susceptible of sensuous apperception, but absolute numerical consonances (cf. also *Republic* 531c). Thus the element of numbers, guaranteeing beauty, order, and measure to the cosmos, is the one important and lasting element of the world soul, and consequently of the human soul: a beauty hidden to mortal man, though graspable by the mathematically trained philosopher and musicologist. Man must regulate his senses to the *nous* underlying the revolutions of the celestial spheres and make straight the irregularity and disorder in the view of attaining harmony. "Harmony, having movements akin to the periodic revolutions (περιόδοις) of the soul, is, for him who has an intelligent relationship with the Muses, not useful for unreasonable enjoyment as it appears today, but has been given by the Muses as an ally of the soul for the order (εἰς κατακόσμησιν καὶ συμφωνίαν) and unison in the periodic revolution of the soul which has become unorderly (ἀνάρμοστον)" (*Tim.* 47d).

One must, in order adequately to grasp the full meaning of such sentences, realize the cosmic overtones of the key words used by Plato to describe the musical harmony: περίοδοι are the periods in the life of the soul that are comparable to those celestial revolutions which produce the harmony of the spheres; συμφωνία is the order introduced into the soul by music, an order which re-establishes the order of the cosmos; ἁρμονία is the result of being well joined, well fitted together ("Ebengesang" is Goethe's equivalent in *Satyros*); and the soul which really understands music, does not "enjoy" hedonistically alone, but understands the *nous* of the Muses, the beauty of order. The whole cosmos is based upon numbers: the four elements are bound together in friendship by numbers ordained by God (32b-c). The forms are connected with numbers, since the four elements originate from triangles numerically determined: the corporality characteristic of matter is based on limitation of planes; from the triangles originate the geometrical forms which correspond to the elements (the cube to the earth, the pyramid to the fire, etc.). The numerical beauty of the creation, and its origin, could not fail to appeal to Christians, who could read in the *Liber sapientiae* (itself influenced by Greek thought): "Sed omnia in mensura, et numero, et pondere disposuisti" (11, 21).

In *Gorgias* 507e, Socrates makes his own the Pythagorean theory that heaven and earth, God and man, are bound together by a geometrical proportion and "therefore" the universe is called a cosmos. In the *Republic* 617b, we find the harmony of the spheres poetically explained by their revolving on the spindle of Necessity.[12] On each of the spheres there is a Siren who utters her own sound (φωνὴν μίαν . . . ἕνα τόνον); and by the voices of the eight Sirens singing together[13] harmony is produced (μίαν ἁρμονίαν ξυμφωνεῖν). Though Plato, in a passing remark in the *Cratylus* (405d), which was intended to illustrate the technique of etymological procedure, connects the individual and traditional god Apollo with world harmony (his etymological example being, Apollo = ἁ− "together" + πόλος, πόλησις "turn," "rotation" [of the spheres; since Apollo ἁρμονία τινὶ πολεῖ ἅμα πάντα, i.e., he presides over world harmony]), in his serious cosmological speculations he speaks only in terms of a world soul as a general principle (a concept which was not found before him and which was rejected by Aristotle; cf. Frank), a principle that is outside of the particular corporal beings and has its seat in the midst of the universe which it pervades and embraces (thus it is the περιέχον from which *ambiente* originates; cf. my "*Milieu* and *Ambiance*," passim). This world soul is also identifiable with light and with the good (ἀγαθόν); hence, later, the emanationistic theories of the Neoplatonists. With these theories a new myth is created, a myth resting on a scientific basis, but not identifiable with science; as Goethe has said (*Farbenlehre*, quoted by Frank, p. 15), "Plato verhält sich zur Welt wie ein seliger Geist, dem es beliebt auf ihr einige Zeit zu herbergen. Es ist ihm nicht sowohl darum zu tun sie *kennen zu lernen*. . . . Er dringt in die Tiefen, mehr um sie mit seinem Wesen auszufüllen, als um sie zu *erforschen*."

The myth prompted the identification of world soul and world harmony: a harmony not to be found in the elements of the bodies (this would have been Democritean philosophy, which Plato opposes in the *Phaedo*), but incorporeal, mathematical harmony. The human soul could be patterned only on the world soul, in this philosophy which projects human qualities into the cosmos only to have the cosmic forces guide things human: the regression from the macro- to the micro-cosmic was typical in Greek philosophy (Frank, p. 319); consequently, the human soul, too, must be based on numbers. Aristotle, in his *Politics*, seems to attribute to the Pythagoreans the idea that the soul either is, or has, harmony (Boyancé, *Le culte des Muses chez les philosophes grecs* [Paris, 1937] p. 117). The Pythagorean Simmias, in Plato's *Phaedo* (85e)—and in this case he is refuted by Socrates—states that the soul is harmony: it has the same relation to the body as harmony, likewise invisible, has to the lute. The concept of "the lute of the soul" which we will find so often is here imminent.[14]   In those fragments of Philolaus which are based on Plato (Diels, n° 32, B 6–11; 22) we find such sentences as: "The soul is fitted to the body by number and by the immortal incorporeal harmony. . . . The soul loves the body because without it, it could not use the senses; separate from the body it leads an incorporeal life in the world" (this fragment is preserved only in the Latin of Claudianus Mamertus: "anima inditur corpori per numerum et immortalem . . . convenientiam"). The word *convenientia* is the equivalent of "harmony" (which we shall find in Cicero). Number obtains within the human soul and "fits together all things with the perception thereof"; and all things divine, demoniac and human, more specifically human deeds, words, technical practices and music, are under the influence of that ἁρμονία in which there is no trace of deceit and envy, as there is in the unlimited and the unreasonable. It was logical to transfer this mathematico-harmonic approach to the life of man in the community.   Archytas, after mathematical and musical speculations, came to see a "canon" of life in the finding of a (mathematical) yardstick: a way to prevent dissension and to increase concord between rich and poor.   The transition to the life of the state is herewith achieved (Diels, n° 35, B 3).   Friendship is also a musical performance which consists of the tuning of two souls. Aristotle, in general so opposed to Platonism and Pythagoreanism (he refutes Plato's theory of world harmony in *De coelo* ii. 291), had to yield to the vogue of music and to use the musical simile: he thinks that the perfect friendship is with one other person rather than with two, and that real friendship rests on the accord of souls and minds. This teaching will go over to the Church Fathers (e.g., John Chrysostom, in his praise of friendship, explains the cithara as love, the sounds produced by it as the words of friendship, the musician who brings about the ἁρμονία and συμφωνία as the power of love;[15] cf. L. Schrade, VII, 249), later to the Renaissance thinkers such as Castiglione and, finally, to the eighteenth-century enthusiasts of the cult of friendship, who dwelt on the tuning (*sich stimmen*) of two brother souls.[16]

It was only logical that music was considered by the Pythagoreans to have a curative effect on body and soul. According to Boyancé the Pythagorean conception was centered on the effect of musical incantation (particularly that of religious music) on the cathartic processes in man. The magic song of Orpheus offered in itself aesthetic and philosophic catharsis; art and philosophy, too, with the Pythagoreans, were seen as musical (Plato, *Phaedo*: ὡς φιλοσοφίας μὲν οὔσης μεγίστης μουσικῆς; cf. Boyancé, p. 262), and hence capable of healing and of appeasing the excess of passions (therefore the Muses were called upon by the Greeks to preside over all παιδεία, i.e., Greek culture). As L. Edelstein writes in the *Bulletin of the History of Medicine*, Supplement I, p. 23-4:

> It is clear that in such a theory bodily and psychic factors are blended in a peculiar way. At the same time there is a moral element involved: unhealthy desire is uncontrolled desire. . . . The same considerations for body and soul, the same combination of precepts and prohibitions seem to be characteristic of the Pythagorean treatment of diseases. . . . If health, the retention of the form, changes into disease, the destruction of the form, the body needs purification through medicine just as the sick soul needs purification through music.

With his concept of holy purity and harmony (which must have appealed later to the Christians), the Pythagorean physician cured the soul as well as the body; health to him was harmony, the proper "attunement" of body and soul. Theophrastus states that gouty pains in the hip, as well as snakebites, are cured by playing the flute;

to Democritus the flute is the remedy for many of the ills that flesh
is heir to. Gellius, who reports these statements, adds: "So very
close is the connection between the bodies and the minds of men,
and therefore between physical and mental ailments and their
remedies." Diocles holds that one has to understand friendly
consolation as incantation (επαοιδή), for it stops the flowing of
the blood when the wounded man is attentive and, as it were,
connected with the man who speaks to him (cf. Edelstein, op.
cit., vol. V, p. 235). It is by such theories that we may understand
the frequent scenes in Shakespeare or Lope, where a sad mood
(melancholy) is consoled through the efficacy of music arranged
by an understanding friend or servant.

The healthy soul is "symphonic," i.e., harmonious. Stobaeus
explains the ὁμολογουμένως τῇ φύσει ζῆν of the stoic Zeno: τοῦτο
δ' ἔστι καθ' ἕνα λόγον καὶ σύμφωνον ζῆν, ὡς τῶν μαχομένως
ζώντων κακοδαιμονούντων, which is translated by Cicero:
"convenienter naturae vivere"; cf. Arnim, Stoicorum veterum
fragmenta, I, n° 179.

In the Republic ix. 591d, Plato establishes the parallel: individual
body—individual soul—polis, all three being predicated on order
and temperance. There is in man himself a πολιτεία, which bids
him attune his body to the harmony of his soul, "if he has true
music in him" (the expression "to have music in oneself" will
concern us later): τὴν ἐν τῷ σώματι ἁρμονίαν τῆς ἐν τῇ ψυχῇ
ἕνεκα ξυμφωνίας ἁρμοττόμενος φανεῖται ... ἐάνπερ μέλλῃ τῇ
ἀληθείᾳ μουσικὸς εἶναι. In the Republic iv, all innovation in music
is forbidden; one cannot alter the laws of music without shaking the
foundation of the state.[17]

The Pythagorean theory of the harmony of the spheres was
retained by the Romans and, by their mediation, transmitted to the
Christians; the most important document in this connection is the
one so dear to Dante (cf. Par. I, 18): the Somnium Scipionis of
Cicero, which contains the following dialogue between Scipio
Aemilianus and Scipio Africanus (v. 18–19):

Quid ? hic . . . quis est, qui complet aures meas tantus et tam dulcis sonus ?
Hic est . . . ille, qui intervallis coniunctus imparibus, sed tamen pro rata
parte, ratione distinctis, impulsu et motu ipsorum orbium efficitur et acuta

cum gravibus *temperans* varies aequabiliter *concentus* efficit . . . Illi autem octo cursus, in quibus eadem vis est duorum, septem efficiunt distinctis intervallis sonos, qui numerus rerum omnium fere nodus est. Quod docti homines nervis imitati atque cantibus aperuerunt sibi reditum in hunc locum, sicut alii, qui praestantibus ingeniis in vita humana divina studia coluerunt. Hoc sonitu oppletae aures hominum obsurduerunt. Nec est ullus hebetior sensus in vobis, sicut ubi Nilus ad illa, quae Catadupa nominantur, praecipitat ex altissimis montibus, ea gens, quae illum locum accolit, propter magnitudinem sonitus sensu audiendi caret. Hic vero tantus est totius mundi incitatissima conversione sonitus, ut eum aures hominum capere non possint, sicut intueri solem adversum nequitis eisque radiis acies vestra sensusque vincitur.[18]

Similarly, Quintilian, *Institutio* i. 10. 12, says: ". . . cum Pythagoras et eum secuti acceptam sine dubio antiquitus opinionem vulgaverint, mundum ipsum ratione esse compositum quam postea sit lyra imitata, nec illa modo contenti dissimilium *concordia* quam vocant ἁρμονίαν, sonum quoque his motibus dederunt."

And now passages on the musical world soul and its cohesive and sympathetic power from Cicero, *De deorum natura* ii. 7. 19 (commented by Reinhardt, p. 111, who speaks of a "Weltsensorium"):

Quid vero? tanta rerum *consentiens, conspirans, continuata*[19] cognatio quem non *coget* ea quae dicuntur a me, *comprobare*? possetne una tempore florere, dein vicissim horrere terra aut tot rebus ipsis se immutantibus solis accessus discessusque solstitiis brumisque cognosci, aut aestus maritimi fretorumque angustiae ortu aut obitu lunae commoveri aut una totius coeli conversione cursus astrorum dispares conservari? haec ita fieri omnibus *inter se concinentibus* mundi partibus profecto non possent, nisi ea uno divino et continuato spiritu continerentur. [iii. 11. 28]: Itaque illa mihi placebit oratio *de convenientia consensuque* naturae, quam quasi *cognationem continuatam conspirare* dicebas . . . illa vero *cohaerent* et permanent naturae viribus . . . estque in ea iste quasi consensus, quam συμπάθειαν Graeci vocant.

One is struck by the accumulation of alliterations (*co-*) and of formations with the prefix *con-* (rendering such Greek terms as συμπάθεια, συγγένεια, σύμπνοια), whereby Cicero would impress upon us the cohesion of the world by sympathy.[20] And, in such expressions as *convenientia consensuque*, we may note the same fact pointed out in my study on "milieu": Where the Greeks used *one* firmly established, circumscribed term at a time, the Romans resorted to *copia verborum* and the accumulation of assonant terms.

In these passages I have underlined particularly (along with *temperans* of which we shall speak later) *concentus* (*concinere*), *convenientia, consensus* (*consentiens*) because of the anthropomorphic terminology. And now the reader may listen to the broad sweep of a Ciceronian period which is itself a picture of the balance and the harmony of the world, a world built on the equation: the well-balanced, just state = life = harmony (*De re publica* ii. 42):

> Ut enim in fidibus aut tibiis atque ut in cantu ipso ac vocibus, *concentus* est quidam tenendus ex distinctis sonis, quem immutatum aut discrepantem aures eruditae ferre non possunt; isque concentus ex dissimillarum vocum moderatione *concors* tamen efficitur et *congruens*; sic e summis et infimis et mediis et interiectis ordinibus, ut sonis, moderata ratione civitas *consensu* dissimillorum *concinit*; et quae *harmonia* a musicis dicitur in cantu, ea est in civitate *concordia*, artissimum atque optimum in omni re publica vinculum incolumitatis, eaque sine iustitia nullo pacto esse potest.[21]

The idea of musical world harmony gained favor in Christian Latin literature. The Pythagorean harmony of the spheres could be inferred also from the Scriptures (Job 38, 7): "cum me laudarent simul astra matutina et jubilarent omnes filii dei"; Erigena applies this interpretation to "Et concentum caeli quis mirefaciat," where cosmic music becomes angelic choirs.[22] Again, in the *Liber sapientiae* 19, 17, we have a comparison between the cosmic elements and musical instruments: in order to show how the elements, though changing their form in obedience to God's designs of retributive justice, retain their essence, the author offers the following simile: "in se enim elementa dum convertuntur, sicut in organo qualitatis sonus immutatur, et omnia suum sonum custodiunt" (Luther translates: "wie die seiten auf dem psalter durch einander klingen und doch zusammen lauten"—ἔρις καὶ φιλία). But more characteristic, perhaps, of the Christians than their interest in the dogmatic harmonizing of ancient and Christian thought, was their emphasis on *feeling*, particularly the feeling of *caritas*. The text par excellence that illustrates the correspondence between music and Christian love is 1 Cor. 23, 1 : "si linguis hominum loquar, et Angelorum caritatem autem non habeam, factus sum velut aes sonans, aut cymbalum tinniens." Only through charity can man reach true music. According to the

Pythagoreans, it was cosmic order which was identifiable with music; according to the Christian philosophers, it was love. And in the *ordo amoris* of Augustine we have evidently a blend of the Pagan and the Christian themes: henceforth "order" is love. The *tam dulcis sonus* of other spheres which Scipio Aemilianus heard in his vision, the Christian believer in God could also hear in the universe. Some of the earliest Greek Christian writers coupled the intuition of the monotheistic God with Platonic supernaturalism and the vivid feeling of the Greeks for natural science—and this to a degree that at times casts doubt upon their orthodoxy. When Origen (*Comm.* to John 5, 5) wishes to state that God is transcendent, not immanent to His creation, and that He is incorporeal and, consequently, is not to be identified with either a part or the whole of the world, he says: οὐδαμοῦ γὰρ ἡ μόνας καὶ οὐδαμοῦ τὸ σύμφωνον καὶ ἕν (quoted by Gilson-Böhner, *Geschichte der christlichen Philosophie*, p. 51). The One, the Monad, is the σύμφωνον, the in itself Harmonizing Consonant. The "world soul," or God, holds the different created minds together as the soul within us holds together the different parts of our body. He is enthroned above all the created beings whose different movements He has tuned in such a way as to fit into the harmony of the world: since the ones need help, the others are able to offer help, while others again offer to the "forward developing" ones an opportunity for struggle and rivalry (= ἔρις καὶ φιλία; *De principiis*, ii. 1. 2; Gilson-Böhner, p. 64–65). Gregory of Nyssa states that the soul of man is present everywhere in the body "just as an artist is present in his musical instrument"; the soul informs the different organs like a musician eliciting different tones from different strings. The soul living in, and endowing with life, the whole of the body is the microcosmic analogy to the soul of God in the world; this is everywhere present as is shown by the all-binding, invisible harmony of the contrasting elements in this world (*De hominis opificio* 12; dialogue with Macrina, *loc. cit.* p. 95). Below we have an explicit and doubtless orthodox Christian version of the idea of world harmony as treated by Ambrose in his *Hexaemeron* (iii. 5, 21–3; Migne, 14, 177–8: concerning the creation of the sea by God on the third day):

Et vidit Deus quia bonum (Gen. I, 10) ... Vidit ergo Deus quia bonum mare. Etsi pulchra sit species hujus elementi, vel cum surgentibus albescit cumulis ac verticibus undarum, et cautes nivea rorant aspergine, vel cum aequore crispanti, clementioribus auris et blando serenae tranquillitatis purpurascentem praefert colorem, qui eminus spectantibus frequenter offunditur quando non violentis fluctibus vicina tundit littora, sed velut pacificis ambit et salutat amplexibus, *quam dulcis sonus,* quam jucundus fragor, quam *grata et consona resultatio* ["echo"], ego tamen non oculis aestimatum creaturae decorem arbitror: sed secundum rationem operationis judicio operatoris *convenire,* et *congruere* definitum. Bonum igitur mare, primum quia terras necessario suffulcit humore. ... Bonum mare, tanquam hospitium fluviorum, fons imbrium, derivatio alluvionum, invectio commeatuum, ... subsidium in necessitatibus, refugium in periculis, gratia in voluptatibus, salubritas valetudinis, separatorum conjunctio, itineris compendium [through the islands, in which man may find refuge from the *intemperantiae saecularis illecebris*]. ... Mare est ergo secretum temperantiae, exercitium continentiae, gravitatis secessus, portus securitatis, tranquillitas saeculi, mundi hujus sobrietas, tum fidelibus viris atque devotis incentivum devotionis, ut cum undarum leniter alludentium *sono certent cantus psallentium,* plaudant insulae *tranquillo motu fluctuum sanctorum choro, hymnis sanctorum personent.* Unde mihi ut omnem pelagi pulchritudinem comprehendam quam vidit operator? Et quid plura? Quid aliud ille *concentus undarum* nisi quidam *concentus est plebis?* Unde bene mari plerumque comparatur Ecclesia, quae primo ingredientis populi agmine totis vestibulis undas vomit: deinde in oratione totius plebis tanquam undis refluentibus stridet, cum responsoriis psalmorum, cantus virorum, mulierum, virginum, parvulorum, *consonus undarum fragor* resultat. Nam illud quid dicam, quod unda peccatum abluit, et Sancti Spiritus aura salutaris aspirat?

In this prose hymn, where theological exegesis gives way, first slowly and then resoundingly, to lyricism, the Greek concept of world harmony is rejuvenated by the enthusiasm and awe at the wonders of the creation; this Christian knows how to weave into the "goodness" of the biblical text the Greek καλοκαγαθία without letting his community forget the Creator: indeed this beautiful and good world leads toward the transcendental God. Ancient ideas are everywhere in this text, ready at hand: the sea which *velut pacificis ambit et salutat amplexibus* reflects the Oceanus and the περιέχον (v. above); with the picture of the sea nourishing the earth with its waters and thereby fostering the harmony of the elements, we have the Greek idea of the κρᾶσις to which we shall return later; the substantial epithets of praise, which seem the more deserved because of the adverse conditions to which they are related (*subsidium in necessitatibus, refugium in periculis*, etc.), could have been taken from panegyrics or *exempla* extolling the moral integrity and poise of ancient sages in adversity; and, last but not least, in every line there is the presence of world harmony and of the harmonizing tendency (and the Ciceronian reminiscences are patent everywhere). The peculiarly Christian trend in this passage is the upward striving from the visible world harmony to the invisible will of the Creator, which only reason, not the senses, can grasp: "ego tamen non oculis aestimatum creaturae decorem arbitror." The description of the sea in its manifold aspects and in its pictorial richness culminates first in a musical world harmony ("*sonus* . . . grata et *consona* resultatio"); then the "harmonious echo" answers to the reasonable will of the Creator-Artist ("secundum rationem operationis judicio operatoris *convenire*, et *congruere* definitum"— the echo of the creation to the Creator is also marked by the repetition of the word stem of *operare*). The creation is good and beautiful as is the Creator-Artist, and now the *bonum* of the biblical text is expanded into a picture of moral behavior, of temperance ("mare est ergo secretum temperantiae"). E. K. Rand, *Founders of the Middle Ages* (1928), p. 98, who quotes this passage in an abbreviated form, recognizes the transition to allegory ("there is a spiritual sea, which the eye of allegory can behold"), but the moral implications reach farther back in our text (i.e., not only to *subsidium in necessitatibus*, but to the very text glossed *Et vidit Deus quia bonum*), and we glide almost imperceptibly from the visible to the transcendental. Indeed, the sea does not "mean something else," as Mr. Rand would have us believe: it *is* at the same time a visible and an invisible sea: the numerous equations characteristic of allegory ($a = \alpha$, $b = \beta$, $c = \gamma$) are missing here. How much Ambrose, not only interprets, but *sees*—with Greek eyes! In one glance he embraces the sea and its island; only in seeing sea and islands as a unit can he unite the contrasting ideas of the Infinite, in which we can lose ourselves, and of the harbor, which is temperance and retreat from the *saeculum*. Once his glance has taken in the islands, he can discern the Christian sanctuaries there established (island churches? one who has travelled in Southern Europe may be reminded of Palma de Mallorca, or of Byzantine island sanctuaries in the Black Sea).[23]   Nature and man meet and unite in a concert of softly singing waves and pious songs ("cum undarum leniter alludentium sono certent cantus psallentium")—both of them "sacred."

At this point Ambrose, with his innate *sobria ebrietas*, seems to feel that the Christian beauty of the scene has become so far beyond expression that only God, the *operator*, might really describe it; a human simile (*plerumque comparatur*) can give but a slight reflection of the consonance of the *concentus undarum* with the *concentus plebis*; the *concentus*, "harmony," is one, and in it Nature and community are fused.   The "waves" of the flocking believers and the "waves" of the responses are again unified by one simile which points to the purification by grace, wrought through the Holy Ghost: the waters of baptism wash away the stain of sin.   We have been led, imperceptibly, with a Horatian *suavitas*, from one picture (and concept) to another, from the musical harmony of the sea to the harmonious agreement between Creator and creation, to the harmony between sacred nature and pious mankind, to the harmony of the divine service, of grace, of purification from sin: the first phrase *consona resultatio* contained potentially already the "consonant response"; the last, *consonus undarum fragor*, only repeats it after its whole content has been unveiled.   The "poetic" flavor of the passage had been felt by the sensitive scholar that Professor Rand is (although I can but find his definition of Ambrose as "a mystic" rather vague); but I would say that his poetry rests precisely in the imperceptible transformation of one picture into the other, as in a "transparency."   It is the essence of the poetic to free us from the one accepted and firmly aggregated reality of the world we believe we live in, opening up before us multivalent relationships and other worlds (possible even if evanescent).   With Ambrose the convergence of the different pictures is only symbolic of the true beauty of God; the Christian world harmony makes possible the shift from one picture to the other, since they all converge in the transcendental.   In Christian art, earthly images may easily appear, to melt away and vanish, since to the Christian no single phenomenon has the importance that it did to the pagan.   Here we have not the dualistic device of the Ciceronian simile, but metaphoric fusion. We are offered a parallel with the modern "poetics by alchemy," exemplified by the practice of a Góngora, who may lead us by metaphors from - a maid adorning herself for marriage to Egyptian tombstones. Or we may think of the famous passage in which Proust, by the use of metaphors, transforms lilac into fountain; or of Valéry's *Cimetière marin*, that "sea cemetery" reminiscent of the Ambrosian landscape which becomes successively a roof covered with white pigeons, a temple of Time, a flock of sheep with a shepherd dog, a multicolored hydra; all this is based on the same Christian poetics of kaleidoscopic transformation of symbols. Synesthetic apperception always bears witness to the idea of world harmony as we shall repeatedly state in the following chapters: all the senses converge into one harmonious feeling.

It is easily understandable—though nonetheless forever a subject of admiration—that Ambrose, who thought world harmony to be reflected by earthly music, was logically led to invent the Christian hymn: for what else is the hymn but a response in sounds and thoughts to divine grace? In the most famous of the Ambrosian hymns (Migne, 16, 1474): "Aeterne rerum conditor, / . . . Hoc [by the cock's crowing] excitatus Lucifer, / Solvit polum caligine, / Hoc *omnis errorum chorus* / Viam nocendi deserit. // Hoc nauta vires colligit, / Pontique mitescunt freta, / Hoc ipse petra Ecclesiae [sc. Peter] / Canente, culpam diluit . . . . / Te nostra vox primum sonet, / Et vota solvamus tibi," we have the same fusion of images as in the *Hexaemeron*: Night and day are the evil and the good which sing choruses; the sea is calmed when the cock crows (in Latin it "sings" harmoniously), heralding the light of day; the sound has "universal repercussions"; there is action and reaction, a musical echo to sin and purification—and the latter brings world harmony. The time factor is transformed into a synchronic singing of nature and man and grace.   Vossler, *Hist. Jahrbuch* 1940, p. 623, describes the "revolutionary restauration" involved in the Ambrosian creation: a restoration insofar as language, which had become rhetorical, polemic, aggressive, propagandistic with the earlier Fathers (Tertullian, etc.), was forced back again into the inwardness of the soul ("Innerlichkeit des Gemüts")—or, what is here the same, into

the inwardness of the community. The absence of rhyme, the
nobility of the words, the fixed metrical scheme were conservative
features with the Ambrosian hymns, while the introduction of a
bizarre, Oriental music (which must have inspired the words) was
a revolutionary deed. We can understand now that the idea of
world harmony asked for representation in sounds echoing like the
rock of the Church to the waves of the sea under the "applause of
Nature." Ambrose, whom Professor Rand has humorously
described as an efficient "executive," had the productive idea of
having world harmony "performed," as it were, *hic et nunc*, in his
Milan community, which would thus become representative of the
whole of Christianity responding to God: each community hymn
henceforth becomes thus an active proof of that harmony of grace
which embraces man and nature. It is the immortal merit of
Ambrose to have assigned to Christian music the task of embodying
the Greek world harmony; music's assignment henceforth is to
perform what is in its very nature to express, the praise of the
Creator of musical world harmony. The Psalms were full of
musical elation in praise of God, but the idea of world harmony was
only potentially present; their radiant and resounding similes were
symbolic only of the inner wealth of a religious feeling: pictures
conjured up to figure the unspeakable. Renan in his *Histoire du
peuple d'Israël* has characterized the Jewish spirit as that of inward
meditation: "Cet esprit se résume dans les nuances diverses du mot
siah, signifiant à la fois méditer, parler bas, parler avec soi-même,
s'entretenir avec Dieu, se perdre dans les vagues rêveries de l'infini"
—there was no sound but that of the soul.[24] The Greeks, on the
other hand, ascribed to music the highest place in the universe
(cf. the *Timaeus*); and yet, though we are indebted to them for
much philosophical speculation about music, it could be said that
they have left us comparatively little of the music which should
illustrate their philosophy. But in the hymns of Ambrose, we
have a "performance," an "incarnation"[25] of that world harmony
about which the Greeks had speculated; and the Church, which
was represented in his hymns as echoing the music of the universe,
served, actually, as the theater for the performance of these hymns
(as it was to serve later as the original stage of medieval drama).

Ambrose called upon music to be the perennial affirmation of, and response to, world music. The triumph of this achievement continues undiminished to this day; when Renan, the skeptical humanist, pays homage, before the Acropolis, to the spirit of pure reason of the Pallas Athene, one thing makes him hesitate to accept the Hellenic creed: the hymns he had heard in his childhood in the land of the Cymmerians (Brittany), those songs which had been imported by "foreign Syriac priests" (an allusion to the Syriac music introduced by Ambrose): "Tiens, déesse, quand je me rappelle ces chants, mon cœur se fond, je deviens presque apostat. Pardonne-moi ce ridicule, tu ne peux te figurer le charme que les magiciens barbares ont mis dans ces vers. . . ."

The visible in grace, the θέατρον in the literal sense of the word, and the all-accessible "catholic" in the mysteries of faith, are what the "Greek eye" of Ambrose, combined with an insistence on the practical and liturgic, was able to demonstrate; these truths can be *shown* to *all* people: "Veni, redemptor gentium, *Ostende* partum virginis, *Miretur omne saeculum*: Talis decet partus deum." Note the expressions of totality,[26] reaching to the outmost boundaries of the world, in the hymn attributed to Ambrose, *A solis ortus cardine* (Migne, 17, 1210):

A solis ortus cardine | Et usque terrae limitem | Christum canamus principem, | Natum Mariae Virginis. || Gaudete *quidquid gentium |* Judaea, Roma et Graecia | Aegypti, Thrax, Persa, Scytha, | Rex unus *omnes* possidet. || Laudate vestrum principem | *Omnes* beati ac perditi . . . | Fit porta Christi *pervia |* Referta plena gratia | Transitque rex et permanet | Clausa ut fuit per saecula . . . || Lapis de monte veniens | *Mundumque* replens gratia . . . || . . . *Patens* excepit Dominum | Terra salutem generans. || . . . Exsultet *omnis* anima, | Nunc redemptorem *gentium | Mundi* venisse Dominum . . . || Creator *cuncti* generis | Orbis quem *totus* non capit | In tua, sancta Genetrix, | Sese reclusit viscera" [the birth of the Savior from the narrow womb of the Virgin is opposed to the world-wideness of this praise].[27]

Just as there is, in the hymns of Ambrose, a union of conservative traits of style with innovations, so, in his handling of world harmony we find the pagan idea combined with a new Christian enthusiasm; the Christian Church has thus become a stage for the "Gesamtkunstwerk" of the hymn, in which music, words, the echo of the stone, perhaps even gesture and dance, collaborate. All the colorfulness and opulence of paganism is contained therein, but forced into the will of the one God. There is *in nuce* the aesthetics of Jesuit art: *omnia ad majorem Dei gloriam.*[28] I insist on dance being virtually included in this art. In Ambrose we have seen nature give "applause" to the hymns like an audience to a theater performance; from this, it was only a step to include in the performance gestures, mimics, and dance expressing supernatural beauty; the ritual dance of the priests and, consequently, a rhythmic response by the audience, is as logical in early Christian impersonations of world harmony as is the χορεία in the Platonic music of the spheres.[29]

In this connection we may note a passage which Diels, *Elementum*, p. 59, claims to be a *not clear* translation "from some Greek": " . . . ignis quoque cum sit calidus et siccus natura, calore aeri adnectitur,[30] siccitate autem in communionem terrae ac societatem refunditur atque ita sibi *per hunc circuitum et chorum quendam concordiae societatisque conveniunt*: unde et graece στοιχεῖα dicuntur quae latine elementa dicimus, quod sibi *conveniant et concinant*." Evidently we change here from Polyhymnia to Terpsichore: the harmony between the four elements is revealed by qualities which every two of them have in common (e.g., fire with earth, etc.), and in this passage dancing is introduced. The Greek source is, in fact, Basil (fourth century) who, in his homilies on the *Hexaemeron* (Migne, *Patr. Gr.*, 29, 92), states of the elements which dance together (συστοιχούντων) that their name στοιχεῖα is well chosen (στοιχεῖα is the Greek word for "elements" and "letters"; κατὰ στοιχεῖον, "in order, in step"; the poet Alcman speaks of girls dancing in order as ὁμοστοίχους: fragment 117, ed. A. Garzya, Naples, 1954). But, when faced with remnants of Greek thought, we should rather think of the words engendered by a sensuous picture than the reverse: as the Greeks heard the ἁρμονία in the universe, they saw the χορεία of the elements. The Christians will replace the dance of the spheres by the dances of angels; and thus it was logical, especially in the case of the Greek Fathers, that ritual dances were introduced into the Church: the apocryphal *Acta Johannis*[31] represents Christ, after the Last Supper, inviting the apostles to form a circle around him, joining

hands; then he sings to them a hymn with lines such as "Grace
leads the chorus . . . I will play the flute [the pagan instrument!],[32]
dance ye all!"[33] Basil writes: "Quid itaque beatius esse poterit
quam in terra tripudium angelorum imitari"; Clement of Alexandria:
"Idcirco et caput et manus in coelum extendimus et pedes excitamus
in ultima acclamatione orationis"; and St. Paulinus, likewise:
"Ferte Deo, pueri, laudem; pia solvite vota, / et pariter castis date
festa choreis" (though Augustine castigated the liturgic dances of
the neophytes for their pagan implications). Thus the dance, in
the oldest Church, was a means of proclaiming, by imitation, the harmony of the world; had not David sung and danced in praise of God?

  The feeling of world harmony is conceived quite differently with
Augustine; whereas it is the practice of Ambrose to show the ordered
richness and plenitude of the world, and his choirs are the polyphonic
responses of a spatially immense universe filled with grace, with
Augustine the emphasis is on the monodic, on the one pervading
order of the richness as it reveals itself in the linear succession of
time. Borrowing the laws of numbers (*numeri*)[34] from the Pythagoreans, he, experienced as he was in the succession of civilizations
which he himself had seen rise and fall, thought in terms of a
creation created in a certain time and developing in time: his
creation has a beginning, a middle, and an end,[35] it moves on the
line of history. Who thinks of time thinks of memory, as we see it
again in Bergson; over a millennium before Bergson had given his
explanation of the *durée intérieure*,[36] which can be grasped as a
whole only by the simile of a poem, Augustine showed the part
played by memory in the rhythm or musical apperception of the
unit of a poetic line: his example is the characteristic Ambrosian
line *Deus creator omnium* with its indication of space and world-
wideness; sensitive as he is to succession in time, he shows how the
understanding of the line is conditioned by memory (since the
syllables in the moment are still retained by memory after they
have ceased to sound). The laws of numbers are important to
Augustine because only by their objective, mathematical certainty
can we demonstrate the certainty of God—and by applying the
numbers to a stretch of time he succeeds in making man conscious
of himself as a being living in time. Man can find only in his soul

the *numeri* testifying to the existence of God; numbers and their laws are higher than human reason.[37] Music (and metrical poetry)[38] is based on numbers and develops in time; how could music not bear witness to God?[39] In one of his letters (Migne, 33, 527) Augustine speaks of world harmony, of the *universi saeculi pulchritudo*, the *magnum carmen creatoris et moderatoris*, as conceived in terms of time; it is a hymn scanned by God, since God allots the convenient things to the convenient time. No wonder that he expresses the continuous "moderations" or interventions of God by a series of verbs, the "Zeitwörter" par excellence:

> [God] qui multo magis quam homo novit quid cuique tempori accomodate adhibeatur; quid quando impertiat, addat, auferat, detrahat, augeat, minuatve, immutabilis mutabilium sicut creator, ita moderator, donec universi saeculi pulchritudo, cujus particulae sunt, quae suis quibusque temporibus apta sunt, velut *magnum carmen* [variant: *musicum carmen*] cujusdam ineffabilis modulatoris[40] excurrat, atque inde transeant in aeternam contemplationem speciei qui Deum rite colunt, etiam cum tempus est fidei.

"Debout dans l'ère successive!": this ending of Valéry's *Cimetière marin* is nothing else but the consciousness of modern European man of his Augustinian time-conditioned nature.

How can the *numeri* that rule over man in history be brought into contact with God? By showing that the history of man and the history of the God-man agree through "numbers": There is the one historical fact, the death and resurrection of Christ, which is in "musical" harmony with the parallel event in the history of men. "Simplum eius [Christ's death and resurrection] congruit duplo nostro [death and resurrection of the two elements of which man consists, body and spirit]".

And now let us watch the well-known Ciceronian *con-* pattern expand its synonyms in the expression of Augustinian world harmony determined by numbers (*De trinitate*, 4. 2. 4 and 4. 3. 6):

> Haec enim *congruentia*, sive *convenientia*, vel *concinentia*, vel *consonantia*, vel si quid commodius dicitur, quod unum est ad duo, in omni *compaginatione*, vel, si melius dicitur, *coaptatione* creaturae, valet plurimum. Hanc enim *coaptationem*, sicut mihi nunc occurrit, dicere volui, quam Graeci ἁρμονίαν vocant. Neque nunc locus est, ut ostendam quantum valeat *consonantia* simpli ad duplum, quae maxima in nobis reperitur, et sic nobis insita naturaliter (a quo utique, nisi ab eo qui nos creavit?), ut nec imperiti possint eam

non sentire, sive ipsi cantantes, sive alios audientes: per hanc quippe voces acutiores gravioresque *concordant*, ita ut quisquis ab ea dissonuerit, non scientiam, cujus expertes sunt plurimi, sed ipsum sensum auditus nostri vehementer offendat. . . . ipsis autem auribus exhiberi potest ab eo qui novit in regulari monochordo . . . Huic ergo duplae morti nostrae Salvator noster impendit simplam suam: et ad faciendum utramque resuscitationem nostram in sacramento et exemplo praeposuit et proposuit unam suam. . . . [He was no sinner] indutus carne mortali, et sola moriens, sola resurgens, ea sola nobis ad utrumque *concinuit*, cum in ea fieret interioris hominis sacramentum, exterioris exemplum.

The cithara of Augustine is a monochord, i.e. an instrument with one string—everything tends toward mono-theism (*De civitate Dei*, XVII, xiv): "Erat autem David vir in canticis eruditus, qui harmoniam musicam non vulgari voluptate, sed fideli voluntate dilexerit. . . . Diversorum enim sonorum rationabilis moderatusque *concentus concordi varietate compactam* bene ordinatae civitatis insinuat unitatem." In the *cum*-prefix Augustine sees more than the "togetherness" of the manifold (as does Ambrose); he sees rather the convergence, the *Übereinstimmung* in one proposed aim: *cum*- is to him, grammatically speaking, perfective (cf. the nuance of Latin *conficere=perficere*); *consonare, concinere* mean "to arrive at harmony, unity."[41]   The treatise *De musica* mounts upward like a gradual psalm in steep consistency and imperturbability toward the Oneness (6. 17. 56–58):

Numerus autem et ab uno incipit, et aequalitate ac similitudine pulcher est, et ordine copulatur.   Quamobrem quisquis fatetur nullam esse naturam, quae non ut sit quicquid est, appetat *unitatem*, suique similis in quantum potest esse conetur atque ordinem proprium vel locis vel temporibus, vel in corpore quodam libramento salutem suam teneat: debet fateri *ab uno principio* per aequalem illi ac similem speciem divitiis bonitatis eius, qua *inter se unum et de uno unum* charissima, ut ita dicam, charitate junguntur, omnia facta esse atque condita quaecumque sunt, in quantumcumque sunt, . . . ipsa species qua item a caeteris elementis terra discernitur, nonne et *unum* aliquid quantum accepit ostentat, et nulla pars eius a toto est dissimilis, et earumdem partium *connexione atque concordia* suo genere saluberrimam sedem infimam tenet ?

All numeral relationships, for example the *parilitas* in walking, eating, etc., turn our understanding toward awareness of the One: "idipsum est judiciale nescio quid, quod conditorem animalis insinuat Deum: quem certe decet credere auctorem omnis *convenientiae*

atque *concordiae*" (*De musica* 6. 8. 20). The Augustinian
hierarchy is a pyramid like the Platonic: at the bottom are the
bodies which "tanto meliora sunt quanto numerosiora talibus
numeris"; then come the souls which "divinis sapientiae numeris
reformantur," if they turn away from earthly sin toward the
Creator. We may remember the Augustinian sentence, "de vitiis
nostris scalam nobis facimus, si vitia ipsa calcamus" and the scale of
souls in *De animae quantitate* (a title explainable only by the awareness
of *numeri* in things psychological). Self-improvement happens in
time: "Ita coelestibus terrena subjecta, orbes temporum suorum
numerosa successione quasi *carmina universitatis associant.*" The
poem of the world, like any poem, can only be understood in
time by a soul which endeavors to understand the action of
Providence, which itself unfolds in time (*De ordine*, II, xix, 50–1);
only the "ordinate soul" (the soul which is aware of the *numeri*)
can understand the harmony of God:

> Cui numerorum vim atque potentiam diligenter intuenti nimis indignum
> videbitur et nimis flendum, per suam scientiam versum bene currere cithar-
> amque concinere, et suam vitam seque ipsam quae anima est, devium iter
> sequi et dominante sibi libidine, cum turpissimo se vitiorum strepitu dissonare.
> Cum autem se composuerit et ordinaverit, ac concinnam⁴² pulchramque
> reddiderit, audebit jam Deum videre, atque ipsum fontem unde manat omne
> verum, ipsumque Patrem Veritatis. Deus magne, qui erunt illi oculi!

The God-Artist, creating in time, realizes his *idea*, his providential
decisions, like a musician:

> ... musica, id est scientia sensusve bene modulandi, ad admonitionem
> magnae rei, etiam mortalibus rationales habentibus animas Dei largitate
> concessa est. Unde si homo faciendi carminis artifex novit quas quibus
> moras vocibus tribuat, ut illud quod canitur decedentibus ac succedentibus
> sonis pulcherrime currat ac transeat; quanto magis Deus, cujus sapientia, per
> quam fecit omnia, longe omnibus artibus praeferenda est, nulla in naturis
> nascentibus et occidentibus temporum spatia, quae tanquam syllabae ac
> verba ad particulas hujus saeculi pertinent, *in hoc labentium rerum tanquam
> mirabili cantico*, vel brevius, vel productius, quam modulatio praecognita et
> praefinita deposcit, praeterire permittit! Hoc cum etiam de arboris folio
> dixerim et de nostrorum numero capillorum; quanto magis de hominis ortu
> et occasu, cujus temporalis vita brevius productiusque non tenditur, quam
> Deus dispositor temporum novit universitatis moderamini *consonare*! (*Epist.*
> 166, 13.)

Even the hair and the foliage, generally images of luxuriant, willful, undisciplined growth, are subjected to Augustine's intuition of a preordained unitarian Platonic idea of God which realizes itself in time! God takes the shape of the *archimusicus*, who considers his subject matter under the aspect of rhythm and time (or of the history-minded philologian). Apart from the impetus given to history by the author of *De civitate Dei*, we must note that the self-consciousness of man rests on temporal-rhythmical grounds; music with its *durée réelle* becomes the field of investigation for the inner senses by which, and by which alone, world harmony and God can be intuited; that the parts *aliqua copulatione ad unum rediguntur*, is to be understood only by the spiritual senses of a *vir intrinsecus oculatus et invisibiliter videns*, for seeing itself is foremost a mental, not a sensuous operation, *"mente* igitur . . . *videmus"* (*De relig. vera* 32, 59–60).

Different from Ambrose with his world choirs, Augustine forges the human soul together to a firm unit and hammers out of it the consciousness of the monotheistic God. There is less of a universal theater of the world before our eyes than a universal drama progressing to the end, appealing to the spectator's "time sense." There is no widening of the keyboard as with Ambrose, there is only the spiritualization of the instrument of the soul. The *lied* that rises from the Augustinian soul is linear and strives straightforward up to God: more of the lonely struggle of the soul ridding itself from the earth as in a Beethoven *largo*, than of the world-embracing Jesuitic baroque. Wherever Christians shall live in the cell of meditation (Pascal, Kierkegaard, Rilke), the "one clear harp of divers tones" of Augustine (to quote Tennyson) will resound; wherever, on the contrary, the "great theatre of the world" is displayed, in baroque or romantic art (Calderón,[43] Hofmannsthal, Wagner,[44] the opera in general) we will meet with Ambrosian choirs and synesthetics. Augustine, the encyclopedist, who, in all branches of human knowledge worked toward unity, is one Christian possibility; the width and fullness of Ambrose, another. Two ways open to Christianity: the one, inherited from Plato, turning its back on the *saeculum*, aspiring toward monotheistic monody; the other transforming pantheistic fullness into Catholic polyphony. When Norden writes, "Augustine was the greatest poet of the old Church, in spite of his having written as little verse as Plato," the lower rank which, by implication, he ascribes to Ambrose, strikes me as unjust, as being, perhaps, inspired by a too "Protestantic" definition of the poetic by the otherworldly; it would fit the aesthetics of the Jansenistic meditations of a Pascal, but not the Gallican baroque of a Bossuet, who sees and comprehends the world and whose poetry is not at a lower rung of the aesthetic ladder. Should poetry conform only to the poetic of the ear and not also include that of the eye? It seems to me wiser not to delimit poetry too narrowly, not to weaken the vigor of the basic polarity Augustine—Ambrose.

If, indeed, we think now of our problem of historical semantics, "World Harmony > Stimmung," we discover that Ambrose has done relatively more for the concept of world harmony, Augustine for that of *Stimmung*—but without the former the latter is unthinkable. The dualism suggested by my title reflects indeed a historical and cultural succession: The (ancient) fullness of the world had to be present to the human soul before it could proceed toward its unification, a unification of richness, not of poverty. The spatial *cum-* had to be visualized before the perfective *cum-* could be conceived. On the other hand, *Stimmung*, with its stress on innerworldliness, has derived the most from Augustine; and the worldharmonic overtones, still present at the time of Luther, will fade out in modern times in German. It is no chance that the eighteenth century, when German *Stimmung* was lexicologically constituted, was among other things the period of a pietism of the *schöne Seele* which ultimately harks back to Augustinianism. Nor is the Ambrosian world harmony dead today: if the man of the nineteenth century leaves behind the cell of his *Stimmung* he may perhaps see a *Stimmung* on the top of a mountain, at a seashore, or when he bathes in the waves of music (in Wagner), only the immediate life around him, his environment, has become unpoetic; it is only *ambiente*, a *milieu*, an *Umwelt*, spatial, yes, but narrow and not pervaded by the Idea of God; this is the situation which I studied in my article devoted to these words.

CHAPTER II

THE AUGUSTINIAN TREND was continued into the Middle Ages by one of the "founders" of this age (as Rand calls them), Boethius. In regard to the problem discussed by the ancient Greeks—whether differences of sound are due to the physiological perception of the ear, of the senses (Aristoxenos), or to the *ratio* and *proportio*, i.e., to mathematical data (Pythagoras)—Boethius, like Augustine, sides more with the latter school of thought: "Consonantiam vero licet aurium quoque sensus diiudicet, tamen ratio pependit"; "*consonantia* dissimilium inter se vocum in unum redacta *concordia*"[1] (and he coined the word *unisonus* after the pattern of *unanimis*, etc.); "acuti soni gravisque mixtura suaviter uniformiterque auris accidens" (this is the *temperatura* of Aristoxenos who speaks of a mixture of two halftones in any tone). The four strings of the tetrachord reflect the "music of the world," i.e., world harmony as portrayed in Plato's *Timaeus*: "ad imitationem [=μίμησις] musicae mundanae quae ex quattuor elementis constat"; Boethius emphasizes Plato's saying "*mundi animam musica convenienda fuisse coniunctam*": the world-soul is a musical, harmonious soul, and to this our human soul is tuned: "musicam naturaliter nobis coniunctam"; the *musica humana* sings the accord of body and soul and, with the application of the concept of καλοκαγαθία, we come easily to the influence of music on human morals ("non solum speculationi, verum etiam moralitati coniuncta").[2] The purely speculative character of this musicology is revealed by the fact that vocal art is missing from the consideration of human music.[3] The *musica instrumentalis* tends to stress the mechanical and acoustic aspects of music; the study of these different aspects is not reserved for the musical artist but is the concern of any man that reflects about music—of the philosopher: hence the high place assigned to music in the medieval educational system of the quadrivium. The patterning of human and instrumental music upon the *musica mundana* and the *musica elementalis*, that is, upon the music of the world, had as a consequence the development of earthly music—to speak in Miltonian terms: "with heav'nly touch of instrumental sounds / In full harmonic number join'd."

The idea of world harmony, in which music is seen as symbolizing the totality of the world, is an idea which was ever present to the mind of the Middle Ages. Thus we will not be surprised to find Gregory the Great identifying the Greek music of the spheres with angelic concerts, since, according to him, the angels echo heavenly music (a similar thought is found in Dante, *Purg.* XXX, 92–4). Again, Honorius of Autun, continuing Augustinian concepts, represents God the Maker as playing on a world cithara: "Summus opifex universum quasi magnam citharam condidit in qua veluti varias chordas ad multiplices sonos reddendos posuit" (quoted by Allers, p. 375). The simile anticipates many a purple passage of the Renaissance and Baroque periods. Bukofzer, *Speculum*, XVII, 165–80, in his treatment of the influence of speculative thought on music in the Middle Ages, quotes (p. 180) from the *Speculum musicae* (fourteenth century) the impressive sentence: "Musica generaliter sumpta *objective* quasi ad omnia se extendit"[4]—*objective*: music is objective, world-representative (and -embracing). And, just as the world is full of mystery, so also is music. Divine providence has "mix'd" the tones in such a manner that man cannot guess the result: thus, music, although rational, is mysterious (as Plato had said): "Cur namque aliqua tam dulci ad invicem *commixtione consentiant,* alii vero soni sibi misceri nolentes, insuaviter discrepent, profundioris divinaeque est rationis et in aliquibus inter abditissima naturae latentis" (*Musica enchiriadis,* ninth century, *apud* Bukofzer, p. 173). Mankind has no insight into the arcana of the God-ordained, pre-established musical harmony (Remigius of Auxerre: *veram musicam non potest mundana musica imitari*). But there always remains a tie between musical harmony and the harmony in nature; Dana B. Durand sums up as follows the ideas of Nicholas of Oresme (fourteenth century): "Precisely as some musical intervals are more consonant than others, so the pattern of natural qualities within a given species is susceptible of intension and remission in the degree of pulchritude and nobility. . . . Configurations of consonance, harmony and concord determine the pattern of joy and delectation eternally experienced by the blessed angels, precisely as the disposition of particles determines the degree of receptivity to heat in a tin basin."

The doctrine of the *Musica enchiriadis*, according to which God alone knows the secret why certain musical configurations are harmonious, will finally lead to Leibniz' idea (*Letters*, ed. Kortholt, n° 154): "musica est exercitium arithmeticae *occultum nescientis se numerare animi*"; it is to the *numeri* in music that we subconsciously respond, though the soul of the listener does not know about its own (unconscious) arithmetical operations. This is aesthetics of the *je ne sais quoi* brand, ultimately of mystical origin and consonant with Augustine's idea of the "inner senses"—though we should never forget that music in the Middle Ages was intended not as an appeal to man's subjective irrationality but as an objective reminder of laws ultimately inaccessible to the human mind.

One aspect of the *musica mundana* of the world lute, as handed down by the Pythagoreans to the Middle Ages, was the idea of the completeness of the "instrument of the world," in which no string could be missing without impairing the whole harmony. Here we recognize the medieval idea of the finite, unified *summa*; thus it is hardly surprising to find the musical scale, or the totality of the strings of an instrument, considered as representative of the totality of the soul (the world soul or the human soul), by which it is reflected: by means of the octave and of the two other main intervals, the quint and the quart, totality could be figuratively represented.[5] The Middle Ages preserved the Greek names of the octave, which had been transmitted by Vitruvius (Du Cange, s.v. Diapason): "Concentus quos natura hominis modulari potest, Graeceque συμφωνίαι dicuntur, sunt sex, Diatessaron, Diapente, Diapason, Diapason cum Diatessaron, Diapason cum Diapente, Disdiapason" (similar statements in Martianus Capella, *v.* Du Cange and ThLL; diapason = ἡ διὰ πασῶν [συμφωνία], diatesseron = ἡ διὰ τεσσέρων, etc.). The Greeks, in line with their harmonizing thought, also used *diapente* and *diatesseron* in reference to mixtures in medicine of five or four elements, respectively; *diatesseron*, in addition, was the name of an order of columns in architecture. Modern musicologists will note that the third is missing from this list of intervals; E. Frank, *loc. cit.* p. 18, shows that this omission goes back to the Platonic numerical speculation, which, though attacked by Aristotle and his pupil Aristoxenos, was finally triumphant and became accepted as the "canonic" system. Plato could not accept the proportion 6 : 5, which had been discovered by Archytas, because 5 was an "unharmonic" number; and because of this metaphysical whim of Plato, the third was missing from the medieval scale, as determined by Boethius, and was explained away as dissonant. It was not until about 1200 that it was rediscovered— by Welsh musicologists, probably aided by the evidence of the Archytas fragment; this was a "renaissance" as important as was Kepler's rediscovery of the heliocentric system of Greek origin, and a triumph of the natural over the speculative; as a result the triple chord was made possible. Further developments took place in the fifteenth–sixteenth centuries (in 1482 by the Spaniard Bartolomaeus Ramis; 1518 by Franchinus Gafurius, *De harmonica musicorum instrumentorum*; 1529 by Ludovico Fogliani, *Musica theoretica*); the triple chord was defended against Pythagorean authority—and modern music, based upon this chord, arose. Later Descartes was to insist on the harmoniousness of the major triple chord, and Rameau to discover the "conversion" of the chord.[6]

In the meantime medieval music was content with the three Platonic intervals, and medieval descriptions of religious music will insist upon them as guaranteeing an image of completeness: the "complete" music of the religious service is in unison with the completeness of God and his creation. In the *Cambridge Songs* (tenth century) we find a poem *Vitae Dator* (n° 12, ed. Strecker) in which the discovery of music is attributed to a Greek who, listening to the busy hammers in a blacksmith's shop, discerned, *per acumen mentis*, that hammers of different weight give forth different sounds (evidently Archytas' discovery is here attributed to Pythagoras): "Ad hanc [artem] simphonias [intervals] tres / *subplendam* istas fecit: / *diatesseron, diapente, diapason,* / infra *quaternarium;* / que *pleniter* armoniam sonant; / . . . et siderum motus / iussit continere, *ma ten tetradem* [cf. Mart. Cap. on μὰ τὴν τετράδα, *perfectae rationis numerum*], et nomine suo vocavit" (cf. also n° 45); in the same collection, n° 21 consists of the one single prose sentence: "Diapente et diatesseron simphonia et intensa et remissa pariter consonantia diapason modulatione consona reddunt." In Deguille-ville's French poem *Trois pelerinages* (thirteenth century, *v.* Godefroy s.v. *diapenté*) we read: "Souvent estoit repris sanctus / Devotement et sus et jus / *Musique de rien oblié* / N'y avoit son [= the becoming, the necessary] *diapanté,* / Non, n'y aussi *son diapason* / Ne *le doulx dyaptesseron*"; and in Pierre's *Roman de lumere* the completeness of God is openly revealed by the musical accord He has engineered in the world: "Que *Deus acorde* en diapason / E *deus* en diatessaron / E *deus* aussi en diapenté / Od semitonus e toens complenté": the idea of God's presence in the completeness of the world is hammered into the reader's brain as well by the anaphoric repetition of His name as by the enumeration of the chords[7] (I fail to understand the last two words of this quotation).

Furthermore, the verse from the thirty-second Psalm: "Confite-mini Domino in cithara: in psalteriis *decem chordarum* psallite illi," suggested the idea of a *moral* world of harmony and complete-ness (Augustine and other Fathers had seen in the *psalterium* a symbol of the Corpus Christi).[8] Thus we find the inference, applied to the *psalterium decem chordarum,* that, just as every string of the psaltery must be in place, so, not a single law of the moral code (or of the Decalogue) may be missing (this serves to explain the title of Joachim del Fiore). In Alanus ab Insulis, "Distinc-tiones," s.v. *chorda* (Migne, 210, 738) we find: " . . . Isaias: *Venter meus de Moab sicut cithara clamabit.* Sicut cithara sonum composi-tum non emittit si una chordarum rupta fuerit, sic spiritualis venter prophetae dulce melos non resonabit si una chorda virtutum defuerit. Philosophorum quoque sententiae confirmant virtutes cohaerere, ut, si una defuerit, omnes deessent."

Curtius, "Die Musen im Mittelalter," ZRPh, LIX, 129–88, quotes (p. 143) the much earlier text of Fulgentius, *Fabula de novem musis,* in which Apollo and the nine Muses appear as allegories of the ten *modulamina* of the human voice; they are evidently meant to harmonize ancient mythology with the ten-stringed psalter of David. The importance, for the problem of *Stimmung*, of all these attempts to allegorize the strings of the lute and to compare man's soul (and the world soul) with a tuned instrument is evident. With the fourteenth-century Italian mystic Catherine of Siena, we find a comparison of the forces of the mind with the major strings, and those of the senses with the minor; if all these forces are used in the praise of God and in the service of our neighbor, "producono un suono simile a quello di un organo armonioso." Bertoni, *Lingua e pensiero* (Florence, 1932), pp. 91–2, who mentions this passage, points out Catherine's predilection for understatement (she will use the epithet "small" when she really means "great," e.g.: *con una santa piccola tenerezza*) which corresponds to her feeling that all virtues, great or small, concord "in the rhythm of an infinite symphony." It is as though the complete world organ of the harmonious soul included the soft pedal of modest self-improvement. In such sentences we are not far from the "tuning" of the soul, or from *Stimmung*. The importance of such passages lies in the resolute unification of the human soul; it was thus conceived of as a firmly delimited, well-circumscribed unit.[9]

In this same Catherinian passage we find a mention of the polyphonic organ. From a musical apperception of the world as a polyphonic orchestra (an idea underlying Ambrose' and Augustine's feeling) to the modern symphony orchestra was no easy step: the yoke imposed by Greek monody upon the Middle Ages was not to be quickly shaken off. That a feeling for the orchestral was present at the time, however, would seem to be borne out by the fact that (according to Groves) the organ made its appearance (in the Occident) in the fifth century (it had already been known to the Greeks). In the description of the organ given by Julian Apostata in the *Greek Anthology* (quoted by Du Cange, s.v. *organum*), there is an emphasis on the fitness of this instrument, with its manifold stops and the variety of its sounds, for expressing the grandeur of the universe (the συμφράδμονες κανόνες = *concordes calami* indicate "collaboration" to a musical effect); we find the same insistence on variety in the description of the organ sent by the

Emperor of Byzantium to Charlemagne: "rugitu quidem, tonitrui boatum, garrulitatem vero lyrae vel cymbali, dulcedine coaequabat." The most interesting passage in this connection is found in August-ine's *Enarratio in psalmum CL*, an exegesis of the most "musical" of David's psalms; he questions the use of the word *organum* in the verse *laudate eum in chordis et organo*: why does the psalmist point to strings when speaking of the *organum*, just as he had in the pre-viously mentioned *psalterium* and cithara spoken of strings? *Organum*, according to Augustine, may have two meanings: it is either, in the Greek sense, the designation of any musical instrument, or else, in a more genuinely Latin sense, it may refer to the "organ." Thus the psalmist has added *organum* to *chordae* because he had in mind, not a stringed instrument, but a concordance as of organ strings: "non ut singulae sonent [chordae], sed ut *diversitate concordissima consonent, sicut ordinantur in organo*" (Migne, 37, 1964).

There is still, according to Augustine, another implication in this passage, which was preceded by the verse, *Laudate Dominum in sanctis ejus* [*sancti* = "the Just" at the time of resurrection]: "Habebunt enim etiam tunc sancti Dei *differentias suas consonantes, non dissonantes, id est, consentientes, non dissentientes*: sicut fit *suavissimus concentus ex diversis* quidem, sed non inter se adversis sonis." Handschin, in his article "Die Musikanschauung des Johannes Scotus [Erigena]" in *Deutsche Vierteljahrsschr.* V, 316–41, at 323–4, insists on the theme *concentus ex diversis . . . non inter se adversis sonis*. Whereas the Stoics (like Heraclitus) had thought of harmony as forcing together the inimical, Augustine has in mind rather the ability of harmony to smooth out apparent discord—as the "inner ear" of the believer hears the unity underlying diversity. Thus the *concordia discors* foreshadows the differentiated harmony of the saints—and the organ is a symbol of the *discordia concors* of world music. And in his comment on verses 5–6 of Psalm 150 (*Laudate eum in cymbalis bene sonantibus*), Augustine ends by enumerating, in a kind of anticipated "Calderonian résumé,"[10] all the instruments mentioned in the Psalm: "Vos enim sancti ejus . . . virtus ejus estis, sed quam fecit in vobis; et potentatus ejus, et multitudo magnitudinis ejus, quam fecit et ostendit in vobis. *Vos estis tuba, psalterium, cithara, tympanum, chorus, chordae, et organum, et cymbala jubilationis* bene sonantia, quia consonantia. Vos estis haec omnia . . . " (*loc. cit.*, 1965–6). Here we have clearly a symphonic world orchestra of the saints celebrating the almighty nature, the *multitudo magnitudinis* of God; the prototype of such an orchestra must be the organ, the typically polyphonic instrument, projected back into David's time. Henceforth we find attested in Medieval Latin and in Romance an *organare, organizare*, "to sing polyphonically as to the accompaniment of an organ" or "to sing in a way resembling the music of an organ with its different stops"— though musicologists are quite right in insisting that really polyphonic singing or music is not attested in the Middle Ages.

In the ninth century we find the surprising definition of the *organum* (i.e., of polyphonic music, patterned on the many-voiced organ) with Johannes Scotus Erigena: "Ut enim organicum melos ex diversis vocum quantitatibus et qualitatibus conficitur, dum *viritim separatimque* sentiuntur longe *a se discrepantibus* intentionis et remissionis proportionibus *segregatae*, dum vero *sibi invicem coaptantur* secundum certas rationabilesque artis musicae regulas per singulos tropos, naturalem quamdam dulcedinem reddentibus" (Migne, 122, 638)—a definition which this original philosopher, who stands quite isolated in his period,[11] compares to the concept of "discord in concord" in the whole creation; this would seem to point to the actual existence of polyphony at this time. Erigena's theodicy is based on world harmony, that is, on the musical proportions which are rooted in man's inner sense, in his transcendental sensitivity (this concept is derived from the Augustinian "inner senses," senses which make us feel the sweetness of harmony). And the different tones of the organ stops, the strings of the lute, the holes of the flute, etc., considered as deep, high, and middle tones respectively (here we are back with the world lute simile of Athanasius who inserted the middle tones between the Heraclitean extremes), form, in their proportions, a certain consonance and a complete gamut of tones. In the moral scale there is a similar completeness and harmony: the wickedness of man is just one dissonance introduced into harmony in order to bring about the final triumph of goodness and harmony. For Erigena, in accordance with the idea of man's creation, fall, and redemption, and with the descendent-ascendent movement of Plotinus' Neoplatonic metaphysics, presents the discordant deviation present in man's history only as a sign of his ultimate return to his harmonious origin (the *finis* of the world being the return to the *principium*). Similarly, the seven liberal arts, in a circular movement, come from God and return to Him; this is true particularly of music, which starts from its Principle, its *tonus* (primordial mode?), moving through consonances (*symphoniae*) only to return to the *tonus*, in which music is virtually comprehended.[12] Whether we would be justified in interpreting this statement of Erigena as a clear indication of musical polyphony, as we did in the case of the Augustinian passage on the *organum* cited above, is not yet clear (cf. J. Handschin, *loc. cit.*); it is, however, unmistakably a beautiful manifestation of the musical conception of nature as a diversified universe. Erigena insists on the original independence of the different voices which "non confunduntur sed solummodo adunantur": they are like unto the candles of a chandelier which (according to the Pseudo-Dionysius) form one indivisible light; although any single candle can be removed, it will not take along with itself the light of the other candles. Since, in the *Musica enchiriadis* which Handschin considers contemporary with Erigena, there are similar allusions to polyphony, we may assume that at least theoretically the avenue to symphonic music was opened in the ninth century.

If we follow, in Dagobert Frey's synthetic history of all the arts, *Gotik und Renaissance* (Augsburg, 1929), the development of music from antiquity to the Renaissance (chap. 6), we may see how slow indeed was the progress of this art away from Greek monody: the Middle Ages persisted in appreciating music as a succession of tones and a succession on a horizontal line—we might call this the Augustinian approach. It is true that, in the tropes, where the *cantus firmus* was paraphrased by a second voice, we have the beginnings of polyphony—but only a parallelism of rhythm and of number of tones was permitted in these earliest attempts at *descant*, characterized by Frey as "akkordische Beziehungslosigkeit" and explained by him as connected with the lack of interrelation in Romanic art, with its purely enumerative, isolated formal symbols.

The Old French treatise on *deschant* insists on parallelism: "quiconques veut deschanter il doit premiers savoir qu'est quins et doubles" (i.e., follow the main voice in the fifth and in the octave, the fourth and, of course, the third are excluded). Guido of Arezzo[13] allows for a crossing of voices inasmuch as the *cantus* can descend below the "original voice"; in a *disjunctio vocum*, where the voices are relatively independent, the voices can proceed in different pitch so that "concorditer dissonant et dissonantes concordant" (here we recognize a "modern" [medieval] refinement logically derived from the ancient and Augustinian formula of the *concordia discors*). From now on the "original voice" becomes a more independent upper voice, and it is granted richer melismata: the polyphonic motets, in which every voice has its own rhythm, beat, and at times, even its own language, are the typically Gothic forms of thirteenth-century music—and yet here, too, the main principle is not the simultaneous, vertical consonance of the voices, but the melodious, horizontal succession. The *ars nova*, which flourished in Paris (and whose apex is Philippe de Vitry) favored three or four voices, equally important, an even flow of the melodious line, and the introduction of beats. The fourteenth century witnessed the invention of counterpoint, the essential of which is the possibility of distinguishing consonances and dissonances; e.g., the parallelism of fifths and octaves is prohibited because these represent complete consonances, in which the ear is unable to keep apart the two tones: the thirds (and sixths), on the contrary, are now tolerated because the consonance is not perfect—thus the independence of the voices has made considerable progress. The new *a cappella* singing of the fifteenth century is a development from the *rondeau* and canon: four voices enter one after the other, each imitating the preceding one. By now it is simultaneous, not successive, apperception which prevails; this is the very time of the Renaissance when perspective and space are introduced into painting, so that the beholder of the painting must take in simultaneously the depicted figure, and the space around it (which had been absent from medieval painting); now composer and painter alike compose vertically (not horizontally), two-dimensionally (not linearly). In medieval polyphony the development had always to be from individual to individual, never was there a supravocal principle: There could be unisons or parallelism, never the fusion of the particular (linear) voices in a totality.   It is interesting to see how the idea of concordances of voices, so consistent with that of Christian world harmony, could not, before the fifteenth century, lead to simultaneously apperceived polyphony; the Greek monodic trend dominated Western music for more than a thousand years; the shackles of a learned musical tradition checked what should have been the natural tendency of Christian music.   Any community gathered together in the name of God should, from the beginning, have celebrated by *discordia concors* the world music instituted by its Creator.

Let us now follow the reflections of medieval, of pre-Renaissance musicology, in medieval poetry.   With the concept (expressed by Boethius) of human music as a reflection of the *musica mundana* of the universe, all varieties of musical devices had to penetrate the other medieval arts.[14]   We mentioned the fact that, in the hymns of Ambrose with their conservative-revolutionary style, rhyme was not yet used.   With the exception of some traces in Ennius, rhyme was never to be found in ancient poetry.   To the Greek and Roman this massive phonetic device would have appeared to be a barbarism in poetry, a "drum beat," as Vossler says, in comparison with the fine "flute effects" of their quantitative prosody and musical accent. To the traditional interpretation of the new rhyme technique as due to the decay of ancient quantity and the rise of stress in the Romance languages, I should like to add a further explanation based on the different function of phonetic consonance in the ancient and modern languages respectively: The device of *homoioteleuton* was used in the ancient languages to express intellectual correspondences, e.g., in order to emphasize similarity of meaning in roots: *nect-*, *flect-*, *plect-*, or, especially, in the endings of the declension: *omnia praeclara rara*; *abiit, fugit, evasit*.   A language which has established the principle of rhyme as a basis of grammatical accord can draw from it little poetic effect (in French the scanty remainders of grammatical consonance -*é*, -*er*, -*ais* are never poetic).   Rhyme as a poetic device has originated in our modern languages because it is no longer used for grammatical concordance: it serves to link words which precisely are not easily connected, and therein lies its charm.

The Latin sentence quoted above appears in modern languages without grammatical rhyme (*toutes les belles choses sont rares*), and we may assume that the decay of the Latin nominal and verbal declension system must have contributed to the development of rhyme as a poetic device. While the inflectional system was still in full vigor, the poetic flavor of language could be enhanced only by quantitative prosody. That the disappearance of grammatical rhyme opened the way to poetic rhyme is also suggested by the fact that in late antiquity (and later, through the Middle Ages in the so-called *Reimprosa*) rhyme was used, in prose alone, as a device for underlining intellectual parallelism (*cola*).[15] It was employed by Tertullian (according to Vossler) because it belonged to the "sophistical and rhetorical apparatus of Greco-Latin artistic prose" —and Christian propaganda should not show a style inferior to that of the heathen. It is well known that Augustine, although in his discussion of metrics (*De musica*) he fails to mention rhyme as a "musical" phenomenon, was the first to use the rhyme form in a poem; it is to be found in a psalm, reminiscent of later Romance tirades, *Contra Donatianum*, which is somewhat in the middle between poetry and dogmatic propaganda. I would suggest that, in the rescue of rhyme from its prosaic commitments, nothing was more influential (in a Latin which had freed itself from the quantitative system and which—at least in the case of the spoken form, Vulgar Latin—was about to lose its declension system) than was the idea of (the musical) world harmony. With the Romans, the expression *consonantia vocum* (which, as we have already seen, was a by-product of their world harmony) was applied to grammatical accord, but now we find "consonance" used as the name for the rhyme ([*con*]*sonans, acordans* in the old Provençal *Leys d'Amors*, etc.), since this, likewise, is an echo of the world harmony (the German word for rhyme meant originally "order" and may render the idea of the *numeri*). Rhyme as a musical device is in line with Ambrose' addition of oriental music to the text of his hymns in praise of world harmony—oriental music that would have sounded as barbarous to the nice ear of the Greeks as the rhyme. The tremendous development of music is not thinkable without the Christian idea of world harmony: as Ambrose says in his *History of Music* (quoted by Vossler), music was "freed from the shackles of metrics": in the alleluias, or in the final lines of psalms, music went its own way, apart from the text. Now rhyme itself is perhaps of a parallel "barbaric," oriental origin (Lydian according to Vossler, but Syrian according to W. Meyer aus Speier); it is also a typically Christian device ("In the first six centuries there is hardly a single rhymed poem to be found in Latin that is not inspired by Christian sentiment"—Vossler). Is it, then, too bold to assume, along with the introduction of a music joined with words and expanding beyond the range of words, the introduction also of a second music *within the words* themselves, i.e., rhyme, used as a device in unison with the idea of world harmony and possessed of all the emotional, unintellectual impact of this idea?[16] The *Gesamtkunstwerk* technique implies generally synesthetic devices: the "musicalization" of poetry by the rhyme would be only another feature of the conception of art as musical art. The polyphony in which the manifoldness of the universe is brought to unity, is echoed within the poem by a device which holds together words that strive apart. Both polyphony and rhyme are Christian developments, patterned on world harmony; in the ambiguity of the word *consonantia* in the Middle Ages ("chord" or "rhyme") we may grasp the fundamental kinship of the two meanings. Rhyme is now redeemed from intellectualism, it is an acoustic and emotional phenomenon responding to the harmony of the world.[17]

There is another medieval art in which the concept of world harmony played a part: this was hermeneutics or exegesis, which was destined to become most important to the Bible-minded Middle Ages, in which the authority of the Scriptures was as strong as the variety of interpretations was overwhelming.[18] Agreement of the passages of Holy Writ with each other (involving a balancing of Old Testament and New Testament passages, or of the parts of the New Testament against each other) as well as agreement of the Bible with the documents of heathendom (Virgil, etc.)—this was most eagerly sought. And how could this "concordance" appear otherwise than as a musical harmony: already Greek and Roman philology had used in a similar reference, συμφωνεῖν, σύμφωνον εῖναι, *consonare, concordare,* etc. I suggest that the *concordance* of the Gospels (Ger. "Evangelien*harmonie*") was felt as a musical accord, reflecting godly peace, reflecting the order ruling in nature and man; surely this is suggested by the exegetical terms, *concordia, consensus, convenientia, consortium,* etc. (cf. Ambrose, "De *Concordia* Matthaei et Lucae in Genealogia Christi"; Augustine, "De *Consensu* Evangelistarum"). In the latter treatise (I, 35) we may read a simile in which the four Gospels are compared to the mystical (and, naturally, the harmoniously organized and unified—in spite of variety) body of Christ; our symphonic cluster, the *con-* words, are rampant in the passage:

> Omnibus autem discipulis suis per hominem, quem assumpsit [Christ], tamquam membris sui corporis caput est. Itaque cum illi scripserunt quae ille ostendit et dixit, nequaquam dicendum est, quod ipse non scripserit, quandoquidem membra eius id operata sunt, quod dictante capite cognoverunt. . . . Hoc *unitatis consortium* et in diversis officiis *concordium*[19] *membrorum* sub uno capite ministerium quisquis intellexerit, non aliter accipiet quod narrantibus discipulis Christi in evangelio legerit, quam si ipsam manum domini, quam in proprio corpore gestabat, scribentem conspexerit. Quamobrem illa potius iam videamus qualia sint quae putant evangelistas sibimet scripsisse contraria . . . , ut his quaestionibus dissolutis ex hoc quoque appareat illius capitis membra non solum idem sentiendo, verum etiam *convenientia* scribendo in corporis ipsius unitate germanam servasse *concordiam.*

Cf. Rufinus, *consona scripturis,* translating σύμφωνα ταῖς γραφαῖς, and the phrase in Venantius Fortunatus, *consono ore et concordi voto conclamare coeperunt* (ThLL, s.v. *consonus*), which, with its accumulation of *con-* compounds, renews such classical expressions as *concordi dixere sono;* as is usual, συμφωνία (> *consonantia*) and συμπάθεια (> *concordia*)—the acoustic and the psychological harmony—coalesce (cf. the translations of συμφωνοῦσιν, ἔστι σύμφωνα by *et huic concordant verba prophetarum* [Vulg.]; of βιβλίων ἀσύμφωνων καὶ μαχομένων by *volumina inter se . . . discordantia,* Rufinus). In San Marco at Venice there has been found an inscription which represents the four evangelists as singing watchmen (evidently like those vigilant Christians depicted in the watch song of Modena, of which we shall speak later): "Ecclesiae Christi vigiles sunt quattuor isti / Quorum *dulce melos* sonat et *movet undique caelos*"—the *Evangelienharmonie* is a harmony of voices. Finally, we find with Bonaventura, the thirteenth-century Church doctor (*In hexaëmeron collatio* XIX, §7, in *Opera omnia*, Quaracchi, 1891, V, 421), the following simile: "[Students of theology should study the text of Holy Writ in its spiritual (not its literal) meaning]: Tota Scriptura est quasi una cithara, et inferior chorda per se non facit harmoniam, sed cum aliis; similiter unus locus Scripturae dependet ab alio, immo unum locum respiciunt mille loca." Here, the Bible in its entirety forms a musical instrument.[20]

Not only in the preponderance of music among the arts, and not only in the musicalization of poetry, does the concept of world harmony make itself felt in the Middle Ages: it appears also in the treatment of music as a literary theme. Since the harmony of the cosmos, like that of music, is a gift of grace, so, wherever we find one of these four terms, it will have a close association with the other three; grace–nature–music–harmony is a kind of tetrachord formed within the *musicum carmen* of the world. Since harmony and music can be conceived as one, we may also find the triad, grace–nature–harmony. The same motif may be found with several variations, reminiscent of Ambrose, in the writings of Paulinus of Nola (cf. Curtius, ZRPh, LIX, 139 and 143): (XX, 32) "At nobis ars una fides et musica Christus; (43) "Ille igitur vero nobis est musicus auctor"; (59) " ... toto Christi chelys aurea mundi / Personat innumeris uno modulamine linguis, / Respondentque Deo paribus nova carmina nervis." The equation "music (harmony) = God's grace" is found with Clement of Alexandria (according to Eusebius, *H. E.*, 6, 14, 7 [3]), where the tongue of the Evangelist John is said to move μετὰ τῆς θείας χάριτος, while his voice is πάσης μουσικῆς ἁρμονίας ἡδίων.

In the fifth–sixth century acta of the martyr Cecilia there is a passage describing Cecilia, touched by grace, at her prayers: "Cantantibus organis Caecilia decantabat in corde suo" (cf. *Encicl. Ital.* s.v. *Cecilia*). This expression was responsible for the later conclusion that Cecilia had invented the organ. Since, however, *organum* has meant, ever since the time of Augustine, not only "organ" but "musical instrument" (cf. Du Cange; Gerold, *La musique au moyen âge*, p. 65), it seems evident to me that the correct interpretation would be "tuned to instrumental sounds"; in this way, the passage of the acta is seen as paralleling the inward musical prayer of the saint with an orchestration of the universe (in the Ambrosian manner).[21] The famous painting of Raphael—in which Cecilia, on hearing the angelic music of the beyond, is shown as dropping, enraptured, her earthly *organetto*, while vielle, tambourin and other earthly instruments lie on the floor about her—has returned to the inwardness of the text of the acta: she has "heard in her heart" heavenly music.[22] By now vocal music, that is, the music of the human heart, is superior to instrumental music (according to Frey, p. 240, this was a contemporary tendency); and, significantly enough, the equation "music = grace" is emphasized by the presence, in Raphael's painting, not only of Augustine (the author of *De musica*), but also of Paul ("Si linguis hominum loquar, et angelorum, charitatem autem non habeam . . ."), of John the Evangelist (the representative of the invasion by grace, cf. Benz, *Dtsch. Vierteljahrsschr.*, XII, 46), and, especially, of Mary Magdalen, a saint who has never been shown in any direct relationship with music, but only with that grace-which-is-music. Schopenhauer (*Welt als Wille* etc. I, 3, §52) has correctly defined this painting as marking the transition from the artist to the saint, from the playful beholder of beauty to the lover whom "der Ernst ergreift." This "being grasped" by the transcendental music of grace was described long before Raphael by the "father of English mysticism," the Franciscan of Yorkshire, Richard Rolle (fourteenth century) in his *Incendium amoris* (ed. Deanesly, p. 189); he describes the characteristic mystical transition from the state of "heat" (*calor*), which he felt with the same sensuous force that we know from Jacopone and Eckhardt, to that of song (*canor*):

> Dum enim in eadem capella sederem et in nocte ante cenam psalmos prout potui decantarem, quasi tinnitum psallencium uel pocius canencium supra me ascultaui. Cumque celestibus eciam orando toto desiderio intenderem, nescio quomodo mox in me *concentum canorum* sensi et delectabilissimam armoniam celicus excepi mecum manentem in mente. Nam cogitacio mea continuo in carmen canorum commutabatur et quasi odas habui meditando et eciam oracionibus ipsis et psalmodia eundem sonum edidi. Deinceps usque ad canendum que prius dixeram pre *affluencia suauitatis interne* prorupi, occulte quidem, quia tantummodo coram Conditore meo.

Again we have the inner experience of an individual being invaded by world music, just as was true of St. Cecilia; in Rolle's treatise the *decantare*, the more or less mechanical recitation, gives way to a song of the soul (a soul attuned to heaven) in which liturgical texts are recited with their full divine impact. Grace-endowed song has pervaded a formalized psalm text, imbuing it with deepest meaning: the words are those prescribed by the Scriptures, but they "break forth" spontaneously from the ecstatic mystic. Rolle knows that it is only an elect soul who is endowed with the gift of singing the songs of highest love inspired by Christ, and who thereby becomes a "flute of life" that forms a part of the great divine melody.

And, once it became possible to present a particular being as attuning his soul to the music of the world—his voice being considered as one instrument more in the world concert of praise to God—there was nothing to prevent the acceptance of caroling birds as fellow musicians; when Rolle, for example, compares his soul to the nightingale who sings the whole night through for the delight of its mate (his soul, too, should sing for its bridegroom in the night of his life), he is repeating a much older motif: Fortunatus (sixth century) had praised the nightingale ("Hinc philomela suis adtemperat organa cannis, / Fitque repercusso dulcior aura melo") which tunes its (vocal) "organs" or instruments to the music of man, awakening the response of the air (i.e., of nature). Compare also the medieval song mentioned by Gérold, *op. cit.*, p. 77: "Philomele, demus laudes in voce organica," in which the nightingale sings religious hymns.

The Christian connection between divine grace and music (song) is also illustrated by the legend which Chaucer has inserted in his *Canterbury Tales* and put into the mouth of the Prioress. Here, the emphasis is on the singing ("loude and cleare") of the Marian antiphon, *Alma redemptoris*, by the seven-year-old child, the "clergeon," on his martyrdom at the hands of the Jews, and on the miracle of his singing, after death, through the efficacy of the Virgin—that is, on the wonder-working power of religious song. Carlton Brown, *The Miracle of Our Lady* (1910), has pointed out Chaucer's close adherence to a particular group of previous versions of this legend, a legend also told by Caesarius of Heisterbach and

Gautier de Coincy, but I have not the feeling that he has seen the reason for the poet's own additions. The most substantial variation involves the age of the "little clergeon," which is changed from ten to seven years; Brown explains "that the pathos of the story would be heightened thereby," and points out that this change in turn made it necessary to have the clergeon study the primer (by which children were taught "to singen and to rede") instead of the anti-phoner, and to introduce an older "felaw" student, who teaches him to sing the anthem and explains to him vaguely, according to hearsay, the substance of the Latin song—which he himself has perhaps not quite understood. And Brown goes on to prove that Chaucer has portrayed the general grammar school life of that day—the purpose of which, as he shows, was to train all the pupils of a parish for participation in church services, particularly as regards the singing necessary therein.

It would seem that some of our most experienced scholars in English, so learned in *Kulturgeschichte*, are bereft of any organ for the medieval, Catholic atmosphere of miracle and grace which informs such literature; according to the demonstration offered us, Chaucer's desire was to portray contemporary school life for portrayal's sake, that is, in order to give the famous "realistic touch." But who could fail to see that we are here in the presence of one of the basic motifs of Christian teaching, which must empha-size grace as opposed to the law of the Old Dispensation, the spirit as against the letter—and the spirit of grace utters itself through music: There is a direct communion of the divine with that simple, childlike, unintellectual faith formulated in the Sermon on the Mount (and embodied in other legends such as that of the *Tumbeör Nostre Dame*, or of the monk whose exclusive knowledge of Latin was *Ave Maria*). This point has been seen by W. R. Hart in his article, "Some Old French Miracles of Our Lady and Chaucer's Prioresses Tale" (*Univ. of Calif. Publ. in Mod. Phil. XI*) 31–53, which proves that Chaucer had fully understood the demands of the literary genre of the *conte dévot*: "Like her French predecessors [in Gautier de Coincy, etc.], the Prioress wishes to enforce and illustrate the view that Our Lady will not forsake those who serve her, no matter how naïvely or humbly." Hart does not, however, mention the importance of the musical element, although it is similarly emphasized in Gautier's account of the parallel miracle ("the boy . . . was already a miracle of perfection: he went young to school, but was so aided by Our Lady that he learned more in six months than others in four years. He supported his mother by his singing. His voice was so piteous, pleasant and delicious that it seemed an angel's to the crowds who gathered in public places to listen to him . . . "); and although, in another Gautier legend, we have the musical miracle which befell the minstrel Peter de Siglar, in the church of Roc-Amadour, who, after playing the viol so excellently in honor of Our Lady, prayed that one of her tapers might descend upon his instrument—and who is granted this earthly expression of supernatural grace.   Music is the natural expression of innocent belief.

This motif is expressly stated in the prologue of the Prioress' Tale, who, herself, confesses her inadequacy for the task of conveying to her story the sense of the divine: "For noght oonly thy laude precious / Parfourned is by men of dignitee, / But by the mouth of children thy bountee / Parfourned is . . . " (1645-8).   It is echoed twice in the story itself: "O martir, sowded to virginitee, / Now maystow singen, folwynge evere in oon / The white Lamb celestial —quod she" (1769-71) [very important is this reminder by the poet that it is the Prioress who is speaking!], and "O grete God, that parfournest thy laude / By mouth of innocentz" (1797-8). Thus, the change in the age of the young martyr is due, not to any sentimental reason, but to a desire on the part of Chaucer to show a soul possessed by religious cravings at an age before he would be influenced by *book lernynge*: "Nought wiste he what this Latyn was to seye, / For he so yong and tendre was of age" (1713-14).   And the "felaw," too, is devoid of actual knowledge of Latin ("I lerne song, I can but smal grammere"): He is chosen by God only as an instrument through which the clergeon may receive the teaching which will become important in the hour of his death.   The details of contemporary school life only serve to stress that plenitude of faith in the souls of children.   It is exactly the technique of the *Tumbeör de Nostre Dame*; in the words of Professor Hart: "To contrast his ignorance and inexperience with monkish learning and skill, there is inserted a singularly complete picture of the devotional side of life in a medieval monastery."

Thus, with the song of the clergeon, the emphasis is on his *singing* in honor of Mary, rather than on the words themselves:

> And thanne he song it *wel and boldely*,
> Fro word to word, acordynge with the note,
> Twies a day *it passed* thurgh his throte,
> To scoleward and homward whan he wente;
> On Christes mooder set was his entente . . .
> This litel child, as he cam to and fro,
> Ful *murily* than wolde he *synge* and *crie*
> O alma redemptoris everemo.
> *The swetnesse hath his herte perced so*
> Of Christes mooder that, to hire to preye,
> He *kan nat stynte of synging* by the weye (1736–47).

And it is this heartfelt *necessity* in him for singing which ultimately brings about the tragedy in the ghetto (not any resentment of his gay song on the part of the Jews, as in some other versions of the legend). The acoustic display, so conspicuous in the poem, is the direct result of grace, a grace which works over the heads of men—and children. It is God who, through the agency of Satan, incites the "cursed folk of Herodes" to commit the murder, and to throw the corpse away into the "jakes," the spot from which later "th' onour of God shal sprede" (in the miraculous song of the martyr). The Jew of this time, like Shylock later, "hath no music in his heart"; and there is no reason for modern commentators to take exception to the Prioress' *conscience and tendre herte*, "unhappily [!] not incompatible with a bigoted hatred for the 'cursed Jewes' " (F. N. Robinson, *Complete Works of Geoffrey Chaucer* [Boston & New York, 1933], p. 12). Even Professor Hart, otherwise so understanding, speaks of the tender conception of Our Lady "curiously yet naturally enough" combined with "fanatic intolerance of the Jews," and of "ferocious invective" in Gautier. Such utterances show the fundamental misunderstanding of the inward form of medieval thinking on the part of the modern critic, who is shocked to find anti-Semitism in an epoch which knew hatred only on dogmatic, not on racial, grounds (the hatred against the state-of-no-grace in itself), which, that is to say, knew nothing of anti-Semitism as it is today.   It is not to be wondered at, then, that such historians, with their feeling of the cultural superiority of modern literature, when they turn by chance to medieval literature, find themselves disoriented; and their superior manner appears rather as naïveté, when they must confess, as did A. Schinz, when dealing with "L'art [!] dans les *Contes dévots* de Gautier de Coincy" (PMLA, XXII, 465–520, at 466): "au Moyen-âge il s'agit presque toujours de comprendre plutôt que d'admirer . . . "

One of the most interesting examples of the necessary relationship between grace, nature and music (harmony) is offered by the tenth-century poem (easily accessible in the *Primer of Medieval Latin* of Beeson, whose attribution of it to Bishop Fulbert is questionable) *De Luscinia*, describing the harmonious song of the nightingale:

> Hilarescit philomela, dulcis vocis conscia;
> Et extendens modulando gutturis spiramina,
> Reddit veris et aestivi temporis praeconia . . .
> Felix tempus cui resultat talis consonantia.

Oh, that the bird would sing the whole year through ("daret suae vocis organa": his "organs" are the instruments taking part in a polyphonic concert of nature)! But now the time has come for man's voice to share in the praise of the harmony of the world ("Tempus adest ut solvatur *nostra vox harmonica*"); his voice too is transformed into an instrument (he shall play upon the *plectra linguae*).[23] Then, after leading us from the grace-endowed bird to the song of man affirming God's gifts, the poem ends with the praise of Christian dogmas (Trinity, Resurrection).   There is no rift between dogma and the natural, springtime elation of bird and man: sincerely they partake of grace; it is possible for a poem to begin with the nightingale's spring song and end with the renewal of mankind by resurrection—the Christian theme parallel (and contradistinctive) to the pagan idea of the rebirth of sexual life in the spring.[24]   The most insignificant member of the world concert, the little bird, can stir up thoughts on the greatest mysteries revealed in Christianity.

A noncomprehending attitude toward such a "theme of themes" of Christianity has led a skeptical philologist of the last generation, F. M. Warren (PMLA, XXIV, xlviii–lxxii, at lxxi) to pronounce the following, all-too-mean judgment[25] on our poem: "Fulbert's ode to the nightingale . . . works over a popular theme which the good bishop endeavors [!] to turn into a means of edification." Warren seems to be thinking of a spurious addition of religious thoughts to the "real" popular theme of the nightingale in spring— only because his own desperately worldly organs of feeling are not tuned to world harmony! In reality, at the very beginning of the poem, the wording (*consonantia—vox harmonica—vocis organa*)[26] points already to that world harmony which is *the* subject matter of the poem as a whole, whose beauty rests in the gradual spreading of the praise of world harmony from bird to man. I see no reason why the modern philologist should find it necessary to adopt such a patronizing attitude toward the pious poet of the tenth century—as if deprecating an artistically unsuccessful religious treatment. In reality, given this religious theme, there could have been no better artistic treatment.[27]

Artistic music and the music of nature are one and the same for the Middle Ages: a bird sings like a learned organist (OF *orguener*, OSp *organar* mean "to sing," originally "to sing as to the accompaniment of an organ"); in Old French we also read: "cil oisel qui *estudient en lor latin*" (Meyer-Lübke, in such cases, translates, "Sprache, besonders eine fremde; *Wissen*"): The Middle Ages see no discrepancy in the combination "study," "Latin," and "birds."[28] And saints may sing like birds, for both alike are inspired by divine grace or world harmony. In the introduction to his *Milagros de nuestra Señora* ("Clasicos castellanos," *Berceo*, Vol. I [Madrid, 5th ed., 1958]), the thirteenth-century Spanish religious poet Gonzalo de Berceo tells us how, lying in the shadow of a paradisiac garden which was traversed by four rivers, he heard the sweet and varied (*modulados*) sounds of birds (st. 7–9):

> . . . Nunqua udieron omnes *organos* más *temprados* / Nin que formar pudiessen sones más *acordados* [*organum*, the word of Fulbert; *temprados*, *acordados* = "tuned," "harmonic"]. // Unas tenien *la quinta*, e las otras doblaban [the birds sang "chords," the quint and the octave, the *diapente* and

the *diapason*], / Otras tenien el punto [they held the tenor or counterpoint], errar no las dexavan [these master singers admitted of no error]; / Al posar, al mover todos se esperavan [every member of the band subordinates itself to the whole, there is a concert of "love and striving"], / Aves torpes nin roncas hi non se acostavan. // Non serie organista nin serie violero, / Nin giga, nin salterio, nin mano de rotero, / Nin estrument, nin lengua, nin tan claro vocero / Cuyo canto valiesse con esto un dinero [this heavenly song is compared with the performance of human instruments].

Who then are these birds, musicians paradisiac-sweet and learned at once, performing in the wondrous garden?[29] The following allegorical interpretation explains: the garden is the Virgin, the four rivers are the four evangelists whom the Virgin—become a schoolmistress in that didactic age—advised and corrected in their task of writing up the Gospels (st. 26–9):

Las aves que organan ["sing"] entre esos fructales, / Que an las dulzes vozes, dicen cantos leales ["loyal" to the Virgin, who appears like a beloved lady of the troubadours: the birds' song is morally perfect], / Estos son Augustint, Gregorio, otros tales [the saints who sang the praise of the Virgin, but who are also the promoters of Christian music—faith and music are identified], ... // El rosennor que canta por fina maestria ["Maestro Nightingale"], / Siquiere la calandria que faz grand melodia, / Mucho cantó mejor el varon Ysaya, / E los otros prophetas, onrrada conpania [Isaiah and the prophets surpass the birds in singing]. // Cantaron los apostolos muedo mui natural [the "modus" of the singing apostles is "natural" although they are artists and sing better than birds in nature!] ...

Gonzalo continues: and the confessors sing, too, and the martyrs, the eleven thousand virgins; in all the churches of the earth, and on every day, the praise of the Virgin is sung (st. 30): "Todos li façen cort a la Virgo Maria [everybody pays court to Our (courtly) Lady] / Estos son rossennoles de grand plaçenteria p. 9 [everyone who sings the praise of the Virgin is, *ipso facto*, a sweet nightingale]." The song of birds and of saints (the religious poets of long ago and the churchgoers of today), nature and civilization, natural gifts and schooling, poetry and music, manifoldness and order, the beautiful and the moral, art and ethics, are integrated into one musical καλοκαγαθία, into one paradisiac harmony of grace.

If now we turn to Augustine, we learn quite a different theory (I quote a passage from E. Chapman, *St. Augustine's Philosophy of Beauty* [1939], pp. 67–9):

If reason consists in observing harmonious proportions . . . , are not right proportions found in that which is made by irrational creatures . . . ? Birds and animals act with numbers in making. Man is superior to them, not in acting with numbers but in knowing numbers. . . . The nightingale whose springtime song is so harmoniously charming has no knowledge of art. Like the nightingales are the singers who instinctively sing with measure and charm yet have no knowledge of harmony. . . . Birds are intoxicated with their own songs which are rendered so well by the attraction of pleasure. Like the birds in this respect are the players of the flute, harp, or any other instrument who do not possess the knowledge of their art but accomplish their effects . . . through memory or clever imitation. . . . Art depends on reason and cannot be confounded with imitation. Neither animals which cannot proceed with reason yet are capable of imitation nor the virtuosi lacking knowledge possess art whose generative principle is reason.

Thus, what with Augustine was opposed—the natural musical gift of birds (together with the naïve imitation of art by human performers) and conscious artistry—is united in Berceo.[30] There is a reminiscence here of the dualism of Augustine (the birds sing artistically, the saints naturally), but with Berceo, as with Fulbert (to whom the nightingale was a "conscious" artist), it is bridged.

If we think that poets such as Fulbert and Berceo were clerics (the latter even boasts of his *clerecia*), we will realize how "integrated" the medieval artist was—he was indeed a *naïve savant* and he could conceive of the nightingale only as a "learned naïve"—so much of what falls into sections with us moderns (and with Augustine) is unified in the Middle Ages. The Augustinian tradition has here become a kind of *Vulgärantike* (to use E. Auerbach's coinage), which retains the distinction of Augustine, only to insist that it has been abolished by true faith. Thus the nightingales of Fulbert and Berceo have gone to school, they have *estudié en lor latin*; and, what is more (for this much would have been admitted by Augustine), they sing like Church Fathers; all this the Middle Ages could see in a bird's song—in which a modern poet such as Hebbel can see only the activity of singing, without the achievement of the song. If the reader should object that the birds of the medieval poets (or, at least, of Berceo) are, from the start, allegorical beings which stand for saints, I would answer that precisely the ease with which the allegorical relationship is established is significant: would *we* symbolize Church Fathers by sweet birds ? No,

this allegory is possible only within the frame of a belief in a world
harmony which encompasses both nature and art, of a Christian
tendency to hear music wherever there is love and faith.[31]   Since
religious worship is related to music, and music, in its turn, is
connected with order, discipline, and schooling, so, the idea of
birds in the guise of scholars (which is in line with the general
transformation imposed upon animals in allegorical treatment)
offers nothing incongruous to the medieval mind.   The song of
the bird can be only praise of God, and in this, man and bird may
easily concur.   Only in a world estranged from God is there a gulf
between the animal and the human kingdom.   Similarly there is
no conflict between the emotional and the intellectual: true love
must needs follow the right doctrine, true love is wise as well as
naïve.   There often appear in medieval texts animals endowed
with great wisdom—greater than that of their human masters (the
dog Husdent who recognizes Tristan before Isolt is able to do so;
the *bisclavret*—only half animal, it is true—who, in Marie de
France's *lai*, distinguishes the good from the wicked).   But more
wise and more learned than any other animal must be the bird,
since his "music" implies the *numeri*.

Similar to the old Spanish text is the episode in the Old French
Image du monde dealing with Brandan (ed. Hilka in *Sammlung
romanischer Übungstexte*, Vol. 13, pp. 15–16): here the learned
songsters are explained as angels fallen from heaven; since, however,
they had had no part in the revolt against heaven, they were permitted to fly between heaven and earth.   They offer responses
when the Psalms are sung; concerned always with God's praise,
they sing ("de bouche et d'eles") like canons at canonical hours:
"Au main et a tierce chantoient, / A midi, a none et a vespre /
Looient Dieu, le roi celestre, / A chascune eure sa chanson / Toute
propre et de mout dous son, / Et toutes leur chansons estoient / Dou
sautier dont les vers chantoient."   There is in such a passage the
sweet and strong inspiration, at the same time worldly and divine,
of Fra Angelico, himself a naïve cleric.[32]

The Gospel passages promising the joy of salvation to mankind,
such as the scene of Christ's birth and the adoration of the shepherds (Luke 2, 8–14, esp. 13) offered to the medieval poet an

invitation to shape a world harmony in whose music all animals (not only birds, but also fish and serpents!) participate. The Franco-Italian *Ystoire de la Passion* (B.N. Ms. fr. 821), which Dr. Edith A. Wright has published in the Hopkins Series, offers a description of the event of Christ's birth, in which it is the shepherds' horns, not the nightingale, which bid the animal orchestra chime in; and all the animals are well versed in the Christian doctrine of the "sweet," the "almighty" world Saviour:

> Et les pastors tuit *encornoie* / Por la grant leëce de Yhesu Christ. / . . . Tuit menoient joie et grant freor / Por la leëce dou creator / Meïsmement les *auselit* / Sus en les airs, grans et petit, / Cantoient vers mout doucemant / Por la grant douçor del omnipotant, / Et toutes les bestes petiz et grant[33] / Aloient toutes mout corrant, / Gietent lor voises en grant douçor, / Toutes a sa guise et por amor / Del aute Deu, seignors et roi. / Mes je vos dirai ancor por foi / Q'entre la mer ne fu peison / Petit ne grant qe a qest ton / Ne s'en joïst mout a sa guise / Por le douz roi et por sa franchise. / Et neïs sor la mer Noceant / I fu la joie demoustre grant, / Et droit en Inde Superior, / Et firent autre grant frebor / Cascuns serpent petit et grant, / Tot por amor del omnipotant. / Et tot le mondes fu en tiel joie / Qe mais dir ne le poroie, / Trosqe Herodes fist decoller / Les enfans petit a son berner (132–60).

Herod's murderous act brings the idyl of world harmony to an abrupt end, as with a violent blow (although it will be re-established with Christ's sacrifice).[34] Dr. Wright (p. 15) offers a parallel from Honorius of Autun, *Speculum ecclesiae*, who relates that "brute animals" are supposed to have spoken with a human voice at Christ's birth; she also cites such biblical passages as Daniel 3, 79–81 (cited earlier by me). I would add, in this connection, the verse from Revelations (5, 13): "Et omnem creaturam quae in caelo est, et super terram, et sub terra, et quae sunt in mari, et quae in eo, omnes audivi dicentes: Sedenti in throno, et Agno, benedictio . . . " It is not, however, in any particular passage, so much as in the general motif of world harmony, that the inspiration of such medieval treatments is to be sought.[35]

It is probably from religious Latin poetry, such as that of Fortunatus and Fulbert, with its theme of the world harmony of spring, that must be derived the so-called *Natureingang* of Provençal (and French and German) troubadour poetry: the procedure of opening a love poem with a stereotyped description of nature in

spring (birds singing, flowers blossoming, etc.), a background
from which the lover-poet is inspired to praise his love.[36] Thus
we would have a secular adaptation of the religious world harmony:
the unity of grace—love—nature—harmony—music is still present,
and, though secularized, something of the divine remains: the
beloved, although an earthly woman, spreads about her a heavenly
enchantment. The development of the *Natureingang* in Provençal
poetry has been treated by Scheludko, *Zeitschr. f. franz. Sprache*,
LX, 257-334, and by M. Casella, "Poesia e storia," *Arch. stor. ital.*,
1938, Vol. II, pp. 1-63, 155-99; the latter explicitly mentions the
theme of world harmony. I shall quote some sentences from him,
on Jaufré Rudel, in order to demonstrate to the reader how
excellently they fit into our scheme (p. 188-9):

> Così come è musica—Sant' Agostino qui direbbe *numerus*—la vita che si
> dà la propria perfezione, in virtù di un' attività che dall' interno si costruisce
> da se stessa. E questa attività è tanto l'azione immanente del vivente
> vegetativo che trascolora nel verde lucente o si schiude nel fiore, quanto
> l'azione transitiva dell' animale che cerca la sua compagna, mentre effonde
> il suo giubilo nel canto: "Quan lo rossinhols, el folhos / dona d'amor e·n
> quier e·n pren, / e mou son chan jauzent joyos / e remira sa par soven, / e·l
> riu con clar e·l prat son gen / pel novel deport que renha, / mi ven al cor
> grans joys jazer" (J. Rudel, I, 1-7). E questa musica è l'infinità della vita
> che il poeta vive nel proprio intimo, nel momento più vivo della sua interiore
> realtà, quand' essa è realmente vita, perchè agisce spontaneamente in lui
> come spirito creatore, come *ordo amoris*. È l'infinita realtà delle cose con le
> quali il poeta si sente indivisibilmente unito; e con le quali coopera con
> gioia, per un fine che è già suo, perchè immanente e comune a tutte le singole
> creature. "Quan lo rius de la fontana / s'esclarzis, si cum far sol, / e par la
> flors aiglentina, / e·l rossignoletz el ram / volf e refranh ez aplana / sous dous
> chantar et afina, / dreitz es qu'ieu lo mieu refranha: / —Amors de terra
> lonhdana . . ." . . . Il desiderio di una indicibile felicità lontana non è un'
> illusione. È una presenza invisibile. È una realtà operante. È l'occulta
> vita.

The "great delight" of the troubadour is the musical revelation
of divine grace (Presence) in spring, nature, and love; the revelation,
also, of order, of the *ordo amoris* ("Delectatio ordinat animam,
delectatio quasi est pondus animae"—Augustine). And "it is
right for him" to sing in unison with the birds, as an echo (*refranh*)[37]
to world harmony (cf. the *fragor resultat* of Ambrose), even though

his Beloved is far away (an *amors de terra lonhdana*), beyond the grasp of the senses—as is God to the Christian believer. At one point Casella, with his translation of a line of Jaufré Rudel, *ses ren que·y desconvenha*, "without anything that would not fit" suggests rightly, I think, that the Beloved, too, is a model of *harmony* (for whom we found the rendering *convenientia* in Cicero): "fiorente e fine è la sua persona, e *tutta una armonia*." I have discussed some of these problems in my article, "L'amour lointain de Jaufré Rudel et le sens de la poésie des troubadours" (Appendix to *Studies in Philology* [1944]), from which I shall quote only one passage: an aphorism (*metáfora moral*)[38] of the Catalonian religious poet Raymond Lull, who (in his *Llibre d' Amic e Amat*, inserted into the novel *Blanquerna*) admits a mixture of abstractions in inner life (closeness and remoteness of lovers) according to the pattern of mixture in climate, and of wine with water (*Els nostros classics*, Vol. 14 [Barcelona, 1927] p. 35, §49): "Eguals coses són propinqüitat e llunyedat, enfre l'amic e l'amat. Car enaixí con mesclament d'aigua e de vi, se mesclen les amors de l'amic e l'amat; e enaixí con calor e llugor, s'encadenen llurs amors; e enaixí con essència e ésser, se convénen e s'acosten."[39] Thus we are entitled to claim that (musical) harmony—grace—love—nature, a Christian tetrachord, subsists in secularized love poetry of the Middle Ages.[40]

With Petrarch it is the divine lady who has become the shrine of supernatural harmony; this theory (ancient, troubadour, etc.)[41] required the eyes to be the seat of love, but in that *Canzionere* which seeks ever anew to immortalize, in each of the hundreds of poems, *one* moment or aspect of Laura's existence, or of his love for Laura, thereby multiplying infinitely the immortal qualities of this *one* extraordinary being—in that poetry, it could not but be that every sound proceeding from the beloved (whose every utterance was aesthetic—and was considered aesthetically) should participate in the musical world harmony (ed. Mestica [Florence, 1896], Sonnet 123):

I' vidi in terra angelici costumi ... / E vidi lagrimar que' duo bei lumi, / Ch'àn fatto mille volte invidia al sole; / Ed udì, sospirando dir parole, / Che farian gire i monti e stare i fiumi. / Amor, senno, valor, pietate e doglia / Facean piangendo un piú dolce *concento* / D'ogni altro, che nel mondo udir si sogna: / Ed era il cielo a *l'armonía* sí intento, / Che non se vedea 'n ramo mover foglia: / Tanta dolcezza avea pien l'aere e'l vento.

In the *argomento*, which is put at the beginning of the Sonnet: "Il pianto di Laura fa invidia al sole, e rende attoniti gli elementi," the detail *fa invidia al sole* (which, in the poem, is not even ascribed to the moment of the weeping) is given undue preponderance.   It is clear that there is a shift in the poem from sight to hearing (with *udì*), and that the latter fills the second part of the poem.   In his aesthetic contemplation of the act of weeping, Petrarch has given equal weight to the seen and the heard; in both, Laura shows supernatural powers over nature (the eyes are a subject of envy to the sun, the music of her speech has the power of Orpheus).   The acoustic aspect of Laura's weeping is a "concert" (*concentus, harmonia*) given by moral abstractions, virtues (*amor, senno, valor*) which are *ipso facto* beautiful, and by grief which is beautiful with Laura.   The Pythagorean music of the spheres has been made accessible to the poet on this earth, and to heaven is left the part of silence and of amazed admiration of the earthly, and yet heavenly, harmony which fills the air; just as the whole person of Laura is atmospheric, her music is framed only by "air and wind."   It was Petrarch who, for the first time in occidental poetry, succeeded in weaving "air," an atmosphere, a kind of secular halo, round the person (cf. *Milieu and Ambiance* p. 21, on the use of *aria* by Petrarch); a human being is henceforth surrounded by a personal *ambiente* which emanates from her and also encompasses her.   Airy as is this environment, it is "full" (*pieno*) of substance, however imponderable.   This person-encompassing air may give new enjoyment to the inner senses, to sight and smell and hearing.   By this step we have attained a musical air (*musica òra* [= *aura*], as Tasso will say), or airy music—both of them achievements of the Christian mind, perhaps flavored by Tasso with a touch of revived pantheism, which tends to deify the individual being, even any moment or aspect of the life of the individual being.   Petrarch's Sonnet 134 is also built on the principle of the enjoyments of eye and ear combined: when Laura, before beginning to sing, lowers her eyes and sighs, the voice is "chiara, soave, angelica, divina," and the soul, though craving death, is made to rest in happiness by this sweetness.   It is one moment, filled with the contradictory feelings implied by this love which spells increased life and death at the time. "Cosí mi vivo, e cosí avolge e spiega / Lo stame de la vita, che m' è data, / Questa sola fra noi del ciel sirena"—the siren of Platonic origin is fused with the weird sister who weaves the fate of the lover, while an additional Christian touch is supplied by "del ciel," which, together with "angelica, divina voce," suggests an angel. In the six allegories illustrating Laura's death (Canzone 24), two are dedicated to musical phenomena; the one seems more Christian, the other more pagan: "In un boschetto novo i rami santi / Fiorian d'un lauro giovenette e schietto, / Ch'un delli arbor parea di paradiso, / E di sua ombra uscian sí dolci canti / Di vari augelli e tant' altro diletto, / Che dal mondo m'avean tutto diviso," (lines 25–30)—the supernatural music of birds of Eden on a tree which happens to be, not the Christian olive tree, but the laurel dear to Apollo, under whose protection Laura is.

> Chiara fontana in quel medesmo bosco / Sorgea d'un sasso, ed acque fresche e dolci / Spargea soavemente mormorando: / Al bel seggio riposto, ombroso e fosco / Né pastori appressavan né bifolci, / Ma ninfe e muse *a quel tenor cantando.* / Ivi m'assisi; e quando / Piú dolcezza prendea di *tal concento* / E di tal vista [sight and hearing are coupled as usual] . . . (lines 37–45)

—the harmony of a spring landscape and of the pagan demigods of music. In all these allegories the paradisiac or Elysian phenomena are described in all their beauty, only to be destroyed by shattering death (the laurel was eradicated; the spring itself engulfed in a landslide): supernatural beauty was, and is no more. World harmony is overshadowed by a feeling of the fleetingness of life, by a Christian melancholy.

CHAPTER III

IN DISCUSSING THE IDEA of musical world harmony we have had occasion to mention the tetrachord and the fourth (interval) in their symbolic or allegoric impact. The number four is a constitutive element in Pythagorean cosmology since the speculations on the "well-tempered" state—of the soul, of the body, or of the universe itself—rest on the harmonious combination of four elements. So let us return again to Greek primitive thought patterns, and examine the second skein of ideas mentioned above as influential in the shaping of "Stimmung"; we may avail ourselves of the guidance of H. Gomperz:

> In its efforts to reconstruct the development of the universe, speculation was guided by certain presuppositions or postulates. The most basic of these was the assumption that the development must have started with a state of things almost absolutely simple and homogeneous. "In the beginning" space was filled with one homogeneous mass. . . . This, with a term of Aristotle's, may be designated as the *principle* or the *beginning* [ἀρχή]. From this there must have arisen, in some way or other, a plurality of entities, conceived to be the essential constituents as now known to us: entities which we may style the *fundamentals*. These were of two kinds: either what was generated was a set of *qualities*, such as Hot and Cold, Moist or Dry, or else it was a set of *substances*, such as fire, air, water and earth. . . . From these fundamentals the world was then supposed to have grown by a series of steps described differently by different thinkers, but all conforming to the postulate that these developments must be intelligible by being analogous to events familiar to us from common experience [this is the same blend of the mythological and the rational as we have seen when dealing with world harmony]. It is not always easy to distinguish the qualities from the substances. The Hot, e.g., manifestly tends to be confused with fire, and the Moist with water. Nevertheless, the two kinds of fundamentals differ in one important respect.

The substances have definite location and are rather inert, whereas the qualities are all-pervading and possess a more dynamic character. The same duality, about a century later (fifth century), may be traced in Greek medicine: there was a more materialistic view according to which man consists of four humors: phlegm, blood, bile and black gall; but there was also a more dynamic theory conceiving the human body as a battleground on which the Hot strives to dominate the Cold, and the Moist the Dry.[1]

The Greek teaching about "temperaments" harks back to the Hippocratic and Galenian humoral pathology. The four basic humors were parallel, and often paralleled, to the four basic cosmic substances (which Empedocles was the first to establish according to the "sacred tetraktys" of the Pythagoreans): e.g., phlegm was parallel to water, etc. The four elements, and similarly the four humors, give a mixture which, in the "dynamic" theory of Empedocles, is the result of strife and love (νεῖκος καὶ φιλότης, ἔρις καὶ φιλία). Galen called the four humors by the same name as the four cosmic substances: "element" (στοιχεῖον), a term meaning literally "letters" since the letters (called *elements* in Latin), according to Democritus serve to build up the language, just as the atoms build up the things in the macrocosm, and the basic substances (our "elements"), the microcosm of our body. Moreover, the four basic qualities of Heraclitos, when mixed, constitute the climate; both mixtures, that of the basic humors which make up the body, and that of the basic qualities which make up the climate, were called by the Greeks κρᾶσις—a term which for us falls into "temperament" and "climate."[2] It is the preponderance of one of the four elements in either mixture which makes it possible to distinguish *different* temperaments (sanguine, phlegmatic, melancholic, choleric) and the varieties of climate (temperatures). It was in line with the Greek tendency (cf. Hans Diller, *Wanderarzt und Ätiologie,* [Leipzig, 1934]) of offering explanations based on psycho-physical analogies (ὅτι ταῖς τοῦ σώματος καὶ αἱ τῆς ψυχῆς δυνάμεις ἕπονται), that the predominance of a specific humor in the body was considered to determine, in the temperament of the soul, the predominance of a different "temper." The harmonious mixture of elements in the body (and the soul) entails health (εὐκρασία), the disharmonious, illness (δυσκρασία). Every unharmonious preponderance of an element in a mixture, in climates as well as in temperaments, was to the Greek mind not only an evil, but a guilt. H. Kelsen, *The Journal of Unified Science*, VIII, 78, points out how the Greek view of nature was laden with moral implications:[3] they saw natural laws in analogy with the laws of the state, with the laws of the well-ordered πόλις; their "natural laws" had to be "sociomorphic," and the idea of law in nature developed out of the principle of retaliation which is the basis for social law made by man and applied to man.   Thus Anaximander thinks of any violation of the harmonious mixture of basic qualities as of a guilt: heat is an evildoer in summer, cold in winter; in order to return to equilibrium, the two must turn back toward their ἀρχή.   He thinks of health as a phenomenon corresponding to justice: things punish each other or are punished by each other κατὰ τὴν τοῦ χρόνου τάξιν (according to the order imposed by time).   Empedocles would have criminal rioters punished by enforced wandering, far away from the Blessed, the four elements taking part in their punishment: "the violence of the air drives them to the sea, the sea vomits them to the land, the land to the rays of the shining sun, this in turn throws them into the whirlpool of the air."   And the commentary of Hippolytus remarks on this passage: "This is the punishment wrought by the Demiurgos who works like the blacksmith who transforms the iron and plunges it from fire into water."   Gomperz, too, states that some of the postulates underlying early Greek speculation on nature "amount to moral demands and judgments of value": "the order of nature is based on an equilibrium of rights and obligations (day, e.g., *has a right* to last a certain time, and night a corresponding time [Heraclitus], and should this order ever be violated, such violation would have to be avenged [Anaximander, Heraclitus]); the material for the building of a new world *must* never fail" (*id.*); whence a thing has arisen, thither it *must* return (Anaximander, Anaximenes), etc.   Such an anthropo-(socio-)morphic conception of the laws of nature enables us to understand how "temper" and "temperature" must be fraught with the moral connotation of "temperance" (our own modern terminology still bears faint witness to a relationship which the Greeks felt most deeply); and the remark of Hippolytus on the tempering of steel shows that all human balancing of antagonistic forces was considered as re-establishment of justice and health: temperature and temperaments are always threatened by intemperance, by disharmony.

If we turn again to Plato's *Timaeus* (31a, 32c), we find the Demiurgos, like a cup-bearer at a symposium, "harmoniously mixing" the body of the universe (τὸ γὰρ περιέχον πάντα ὁπόσα νοητὰ ζῷα) which he created the most akin to himself (i.e., in a spheric shape) out of the four elements, "fitting them together by means of proportion" (τὸ τοῦ κόσμου σῶμα ἐγεννήθη δι' ἀναλογίας ὁμολογῆσαν): each of the two middle terms, water and air, located between fire and earth, has the same relationship with each other, as the two together have with the first and fourth elements; the *tetraktys* is a kind of double balance. Thus it had necessarily to become, along with the sphere, a symbol of perfection and equilibrium. It is well known that in the Pythagorean oath, Pythagoras appears as the inventor of this *tetraktys* formula, which was associated by legend with the Apollonian oracle at Delphi. Inasmuch as it explained the laws of heavenly and earthly music, the *tetraktys* was the key to the laws of nature; inasmuch as it made possible the imitation of divine by human music, it permitted man to approach divine perfection, hence its moral, religious "cathartic" aspect (A. Delatte, *Études sur la littérature pythagoricienne*, p. 249). We understand now the pattern-making force of the number four: Philolaos (Diels, 44B, 13), for example, assumes four principles in man: the head represents the principle of reason, the heart that of soul and feeling, the navel that of the growth of the embryo, and the *partes naturales* that of procreation. Reinhardt (*loc. cit.*, p. 10) deals with the τετραφάρμακος, a remedy composed of four ingredients (wax, gum, tallow, pitch), the combination of which potentiates the virtues of the particular components which stand for the four basic qualities. We have seen the importance of the tetrachord in the Pythagorean harmony of spheres (the musical scale was but a double tetrachord; Rousseau, in his *Dict. de musique*, s.v. *tétracorde*, says rightly: "a tetrachord formed for the Greeks a whole as complete as is for us the octave"); the same term was applied by Varro to the four seasons. Boethius sees the harmony of the universe in the alternation of the four seasons (*De musica*, II): "that which contracts in winter expands in spring, dries up in summer and matures in autumn"; according to Claudianus Mamertus (Allers, p. 375), the four seasons "moderate et musice concinunt."[4] De Tolnay has pointed out a series of medieval and Renaissance works of art in which symbols of the musical harmony of the universe are allowed to accompany allegories of the four seasons (or of the four elements). The eight tones represented on the chapiters at Cluny (eleventh or twelfth century), based on the *numerus quaternarius*, are combined with the four seasons, the four cardinal virtues, the four rivers and four trees of Paradise, and the agricultural labors corresponding to the twelve months. It was only logical that Milton (1645) should call his "Expositions upon the foure chief places in Scripture, which treat of Marriage, or nullities in Marriage" a *Tetrachordon*; when treating a moral problem of Christianity, he remained in the medieval and humanistic tradition of the (musical) harmonizing of texts. Similarly, the name for the interval of the fourth, "diatesseron," was, as we have seen above, transferred to pharmacy and architecture. The τετρακτύς was also the ideal complex of moral virtues; just as health was secured by a good mixture of the four humors (κρᾶσις), so moral health is guaranteed by four virtues, justice, prudence, fortitude, and temperance—to which Augustine added the characteristically Christian (Pauline) virtues of faith, love, and hope, the sum of which would correspond to the seven strings of the Pythagorean lute (double tetrachord). The ideology of the Carolingian "Renaissance," which invested the modern ruler with ancient garb, revived the moral τετρακτύς; the poet Ingobert in his portrait of Charlemagne states: "Tetracty implevit virtutum quattuor alma" (Du Cange s.v. *tetracty*). One of the most familiar references of the *tetraktys* involved the four rivers of Paradise, which, as a symbol of perfection, could be variously applied: Rand (*loc. cit.*, p. 349) quotes from Johannes Monachus, *Liber de miraculis*, the sentence: "Ambrosius, Augustinus, Hieronimus atque Gregorius . . . fuerunt in eloquentia ueluti quatuor paradisi flumina" (i.e., they formed together the *ideal* of eloquence). Again, in n° 26 of the *Cambridge Songs* (about A.D. 1000) which is dedicated to St. Cecilia, we are told that the saint has chosen a galaxy (chorus) of four ladies (probably contemporary nuns of a Cologne convent) as her ladies in waiting, who represent four virtues or graces: "Hec sibi virgineas *quaterna virtute* choreas, fultas elegit quas hic sapientia componit" (Voda is distinguished by *luce clara*; Meginbergis, by *valetudine*; Merehilt, by *flore decoro*, Una, by *sophia*)—a clear reminiscence of the Pythagorean *numerus quaternarius*.

We have also seen that with Berceo the four rivers of Paradise could stand allegorically for the four Gospels; Augustine, in *De consensu evangeliorum*, explains that the four Gospels indicate the spread of the Christian doctrine to the four corners of the earth. The Jewish-Christian and the Greek number symbolism thus could coalesce, or, in other words, the Fathers could explain, in accord with their usual harmonizing of pagan and Christian documents, either that the heathen had had a foreshadowing of Christian thought, or that the Bible contains poetic devices similar to those of the much-admired ancient poetry. Finally, the Christians could use the number four to build up the number ten ($=1+2+3+4$), symbolical of divine perfection and self-containedness (cf. Curtius, *Roman. Forsch.*, LIV, 141–52).[5]

The symbolism of the four elements was seen everywhere in nature; according to the French dialogue, *Placides et Timeo* (written before 1303, and based on Chalcidius), which is Platonic only by virtue of the name of one of the interlocutors, the stratification in the egg is compared to that in the cosmos:

... la coque c'est le firmament; la peau blanche par dessous, c'est la terre; le blanc, c'est l'eau; le jaune c'est le feu.... Il y a tant de manières de "complexions" dans un œuf ... que les vertus de chacune s'équilibrent et se neutralisent; l'œuf est, en conséquence, un aliment qui, comme disent certains "naturiens," ne peut faire ni bien ni mal. D'autres philosophes ont dit que "la senefiance du monde est senefiée en l'arc en ciel, ou il apert grans cercles de couleur vermeil, de verd, de jaune et ynde" [variant: royes vermeilles, vers et bises, si comme les quatre elemens] (293) ... Les contrariétés [des éléments] sont tempérées par les affinités.... Ainsi explique le philosophe Naso, qui reçut le nom d'Ovide pour avoir assimilé le monde à un œuf (d'*ovum* et *divido*) (298) ... L'homme est un microcosme. Il est rond comme le monde (car il doit avoir autant de hauteur que d'envergure, en étendant les bras). On peut comparer sa tête au feu, sa poitrine à l'air, son ventre à la mer, et ses pieds, et ce "sur quoy il siet," à la terre (303) [cf. C.-V.

Langlois, *La connaissance de la nature et du monde*, p. 293 seq.; on the idea of the egg, cf. above.][6]

And here, perhaps, I may be permitted to offer the suggestion that the chimes of medieval belfries had originally to do with just such speculations on numbers: the French name (and the English name borrowed from French) *carillon* (OFr *quarreignon* = *quaternio*) indicates a group of four bells, just as the Prov *trinho* (< **trinio*)[7] indicates a group of three; Meyer-Lübke, *ZRPh*, XXIII, 476, states that a "complete" church bell ringing consists "in some areas" of four or three bells.[8]   May not the four bells represent a tetrachord, i.e., the four basic elements and, thus, the totality of the world (as the three represent the Trinity)? The Austrian poet Hofmannsthal writes in *Die Berührung der Sphären* (Berlin, 1931), p. 284: "wie in einem Glockenspiel klingt [in any work of Goethe's] die Harmonie aller irdischen Wesen und Himmelskräfte an"; while I do not know the exact source of this idea of the chimes indicating the harmony of the universe, it would seem evident that the poet derived it from a medieval or Renaissance source—which would concord with my suggestion.[9]   In support of this suggestion, I would refer to the history of the English word *chimes*, which first (anno 1300) meant "cymbals," "instrumental music"; later (1463) it was used to designate an apparatus for making bells sound; and in 1562 it is attested in the modern meaning (= *carillon*, Ger. *Glockenspiel*).   The derivation from *cymbalum* is obvious although the OED is not positive about the "how" of the semantic development.   It may suffice to copy from the *Distinctiones* of Alanus ab Insulis: "Cymbala proprie dicuntur parvae campanae quae acutum reddunt sonum. . . . Dicuntur etiam spirituales fidelium concordiae, unde David: *Laudate eum in cymbalis bene sonantibus*.   Dicuntur laudes ineffabiles quae ore plenarie exprimi non possunt, unde *Laudate eum in cymbalis iubilationis*" (Migne, 210, 759–60).   Just as *in cymbalis iubilationis* gave the Italian phrase *essere in cimbali* (*cimberli*), "to rejoice," so *chimes* is derived from an *in cymbalis bene sonantibus*, interpreted as a "consonance or chord in faith" (*spirituales fidelium concordiae*), i.e., as an expression of the musical harmony of the universe, and, at the same time, of the faith of the believers answering to it. With Milton's phrase *Nature's chimes* (cf. OED) there is the suggestion of nature responding harmoniously to God. It is possible that Schiller in his poem, *Die Glocke*, had in mind the *concordiae fidelium* of the Middle Ages, when he called his bell "Concordia" after the name of the medieval chimes.[10] If I am right in regard to *carillon*, we may see here the fusion of the idea of musical harmony with the idea of the "well-tempered mixture."[11]

It is interesting in this connection to follow Isidore of Seville who, in his explanation (*Etym.* 5, 30) of the pagan names of the days of the week by the activities of stars, arranges the seven days, not in their chronological sequence, but in an order that brings out a quartet of opposing temperaments, with harmony being followed by the corresponding disharmony by which it is threatened: " . . . a Sole spiritum, a Luna corpus, a Mercurio ingenium et linguam, a Venere voluptatem, a Marte sanguinem, a Jove temperantiam, a Saturno humorem (*humor* = melancholy which upsets the εὐκρασία, the harmony of the "jovial" temperament); again moral implications are present, just as in the time of the Greeks. We may remember also that, according to Cicero's *Somnium Scipionis* (the work which, through Macrobius, reached the Middle Ages), the world soul, identified with the Sun, and placed in a *media regio*, consisted in *temperatio* (= εὐκρασία): "deinde subter mediam fere regionem sol obtinet, dux et princeps, . . . mens mundi et *temperatio*" (*De republica* 6, 17).

If now we read the definition of peace, in the form of a decalogue, as given by Augustine in *De civitate Dei*, 18, 13, we see that, starting from the order and peace within the body ("pax itaque corporis est ordinata *temperatura* partium"), he goes over to the order and peace in the soul (here called *consensio*), and from there to the peace and order between body and soul; then we proceed to the peace of men among each other (called *concordia*): peace in the house and in the state, as well as the *ordinatissima et concordissima* peace of the souls enjoying God in the *civitas caelestis*. The whole table is summarized by the final statement "pax omnium rerum tranquillitas ordinis."[12] One sees that *temperatura* is on the lowest level, the bodily; *consensio*, a little higher in the scale, is used of man's *anima rationalis;* we find *concordia* in reference to the society of mankind, while *pax* and *ordo* (*ordinatus*) remain throughout as constituent elements. The state of bodily well-joinedness is alluded to elsewhere by words of the *temperare*-family: "carnis nostrae compago vel temperamentum" (*De trinitate*, 10, 14), "compositionem seu temperationem corporis . . . compaginem aut temperationem corporis" (*ib.* 15); there is also a *temperatio* of the soul which represents a *consensio* (*De musica*, 6, 10), a harmonious influence of the soul on the body: "Sed iste sensus, qui etiam dum nihil sentimus, inest tamen, instrumentum est corporis quod ea *temperatione* agitur ab anima, ut in eo sit ad passiones corporis cum attentione agendas paratior, *similia similibus ut adjungat repellatque quod noxium est*[= συμπάθεια] . . . agit haec anima cum quiete, si ea quae in unitate valetudinis *quasi familiari quadam consensione cesserunt* [var. *cohaeserint, concesserint*]."

Thus we may think that *pax* in the initial definition found in the "decalogue of peace" cited above may, at the lowest rung of the ladder, still be etymologically connected in Augustine's mind with *compages*, whereas later it becomes associated with *pacisci*, a pact, and with the otherworldly serenity of εἰρήνη; *temperatura, -atio*, similarly, is first mere "physical well-joinedness," gradually leading to *consensio* and *concordia* in a kind of Platonic ladder. And *ordo* sings its *basso ostinato* on all the rungs of the scale, while the God-willed *ordinatissima et concordissima pax* at the top of the pyramid is at the other extreme of intensity and range from the *ordinata temperatura partium*. With a comparatively small amount of word variation Augustine succeeds in building up a scale of gradations, denoting the ascension to the Infinite. We may infer that *temperatura* with him was drawn into this heavenward ascensional movement. (Anyone who is in the least sensitive to the personal style of Augustine must be aware of the impatient acceleration implied in *pax hominis mortalis et Dei* which replaces the last member of the progression: man – men – house – state – world.)

The concept "temperatio" (though not the word itself) is still present in a passage from Alanus de Insulis (cited by Allers, p. 345, who duly emphasizes the idea it contains of the "microcosm"); in

De planctu naturae, Nature is represented as saying, "Ego sum illa quae ad exemplarem mundanae machinae similitudinem hominis exemplavi naturam, ut in eo velut in speculo, ipsius mundi scripta natura appareat. Sicut enim *quatuor elementorum concors discordia, unica pluralitas, consonantia dissonans, consensus dissentiens,* mundialis regiae structuras *conciliat,* sic *quatuor complexionum compar disparitas, inaequalis aequalitas, deformis conformitas, diversa identitas,* aedificium corporis humani *compaginat.*" The symmetrical architecture of this sentence, with its two lists of (reconciled) opposing forces (the elements vs. human temperament) is in itself a splendid stylistic rendering of the beauty and balance of κρᾶσις or *temperatio.*

If we turn now to a much later document, to the *Summa theologiae* of Eustachius a St. Paulo—that codification of medieval Scholastic philosophy which a Descartes was still reading (cf. Gilson, *Index scholastico-cartésien* [Paris, 1912], s.v. *tempérament*), we find a definition of *temperamentum* in which our two skeins, musical harmony and the well-temperedness of climate and body, are interwoven: "*Crasis Graece, Latine temperamentum,* ex ipsa mixtione nascitur, estque concentus seu harmonia, seu naturae cujusque mixti apta primarum qualitatum dispositio, vel potius sunt ipsae primae qualitates certa quadam ratione in mixto temperatae." In the examples to follow it is clear that the author is thinking as well of physiologico-psychic as of climatic phenomena.[13]

We may remember the appearance, in the above-mentioned definition of *temperamentum,* of the *concentus seu harmonia*: again, in the earlier definition of beauty given by Thomas Aquinas we find: "Sicut accipi potest ex vestris Dionysiis, ad rationem pulchri sive decori concurrit et claritas et *debita proportio.* Dicit enim quod Deus dicitur pulcher sicut *universorum consonantiae* et claritatis causa. Unde pulchritudo corporis in hoc consistit quod homo habeat membra corporis *bene proportionata* cum quadam debita coloris claritate. Et similiter pulchritudo spiritualis in hoc consistit quod conversatio hominis sive actio eius sit bene *proportionata* secundum spiritualem rationis claritatem." This definition contains the Augustinian idea of *numeri* (proportion) along with that of world music: *universorum consonantiae*; although we must agree with

Handschin, *loc. cit.*, that Thomas Aquinas, who condemned Erigena *post mortem*, did not have the Augustinian ear for world harmony, ascribing to music a holy character only insofar as it was an element of the liturgy; as an Aristotelian he "reflects" the world as it is, rather than attempting to re-create it by forging it together into a unit.

Passages such as the aforementioned corroborate my belief that the concept of *concentus—consonantia*—ἁρμονία cannot be treated without that of *temperare* – κεράννυμι and vice versa. Two patterns, both of them ultimately originating in the same pattern of thought, must necessarily and continually have been intertwined. We are here faced with a remarkable phenomenon in semantics: for the modern German word *Stimmung* we must count, not with *one* etymon, as is usually the case (Lat *pater* > Fr *père*), but with a mixture, a fabric woven of different etymons which have lent each other parts of their respective semantic contents, so that the particular modern word *Stimmung* reflects semantically sometimes the one, sometimes the other etymon; other modern words, such as Fr *accord*, Eng *temper*, reveal the same texture as *Stimmung*, though they differ in details. The ancient word family, centered around a certain emotional nucleus, gives birth to several modern branches with particular emotional nuclei, so that there is no possibility of explaining *one* word strictly from *one* definite etymon. It is, so to speak, a system of railroad tracks radiating from one center, and branches out into new rail systems (using the same rail material) with new centers. The ancient picture:

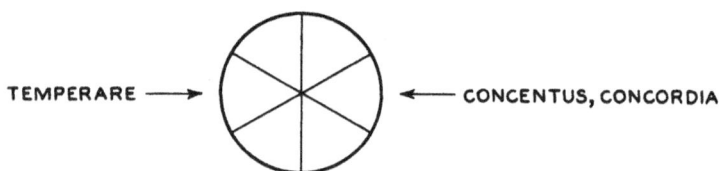

TEMPERARE ⟶   ⟵ CONCENTUS, CONCORDIA

changes into the following modern one, which includes (at least) three systems:

STIMMUNG
(TEMPERARE +
CONCENTUS)

ACCORD
(TEMPERARE +
CONCENTUS)

TEMPER-
TEMPERANCE-
TEMPERATURE
(+CONCENTUS)

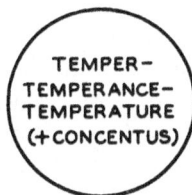

—while the last system could again be broken up into at least three others.

I doubt that the term *Feldforschung*, used by modern German linguists (Weisgerber, Trier), can be adequately applied to this linguistic situation (although, of course, our whole study finds its range within one enormous "field"). Those linguists are wont to speak of the changing distributions of the field (*Feld-Aufteilung*) such as *sapiens—prudens—cautus* etc. which are replaced by Germ *weise—listig—witzig—spahi* or Fr *sage—sen(s)é—engigneux—accort —cointe*, etc.; this means that some inherited terms share the field with newcomers, just as passengers share the seats of a railroad compartment (*sapiens > sage*, and even *sapiens – weise* may be said to be semantically the same word which has adapted its semantic range to that of a more recent word). In the case of *concentus – temperare*, words derived from the ancient word-cluster (e.g., *Stimmung, accord, temper*) have survived, but not as a texture; even the members of the word family constituting the word-cluster have sometimes become estranged from each other: the walls of the compartment which held them together have caved in, because the original emotional nucleus has vanished (for example, *temperance— temperature—temper[ament]*, reflecting an old unit, have developed in different directions). In truth, the *field* as such no longer exists, and consequently there can be no question of distributing it anew— there is rather *Felder-Umbau* than *Feld-Aufteilung*.[14]

The history of the disappearance of the one field (world harmony – well-temperedness) is simply the history of modern civilization, of the Weberian "Entzauberung der Welt," or dechristianization;

and we see, by our study, the necessity of a new periodization of occidental history. I shall point out how the destruction of the homogeneous "field" began in the seventeenth century and was completed in the eighteenth; the great caesura in occidental history is precisely this period, not the Renaissance; in fact, to the two periods, pagan antiquity and Christianity (the latter goes from the first century to the seventeenth, with the subdivisions: Middle Ages, Renaissance, Baroque), we should oppose the epoch of dechristianization (from the seventeenth century on), in which our field is radically destroyed. At the end of the eighteenth century *Stimmung* was crystallized, that is, it was robbed of its blossoming life. We cannot go wrong in ascribing this to the spirit of enlightenment whose deadening effect has been so masterfully described by Novalis in his treatise *Christenheit oder Europa* (1798); it is no chance that this historian of Europeanism (which he identified with Christianity), this advocate of a return to the *heiliger Sinn* (sense of the divine) of the Middle Ages, should, when describing the destruction of medieval godliness by the Reformation and the Age of Enlightenment (which last I would emphasize the more strongly), speak precisely in terms of the destruction of *musica mundana* by the modern mechanistic spirit:

> Der anfängliche Personalhass gegen den katholischen Glauben ging allmählich in Hass gegen die Bibel, gegen den christlichen Glauben und endlich gar gegen die Religion über. Noch mehr—der Religionshass dehnte sich sehr natürlich und folgerecht auf alle Gegenstände des Enthusiasmus aus, verketzerte Phantasie und Gefühl, Sittlichkeit und Kunstliebe, Zukunft und Vorzeit, setzte den Menschen in der Reihe der Naturwesen mit Not oben an, und machte *die unendliche schöpferische Musik des Weltalls* zum einförmigen Klappern einer ungeheuren Mühle, die vom Strom des Zufalls getrieben und auf ihm schwimmend, *eine Mühle an sich, ohne Baumeister und Müller,* und eigentlich ein echtes Perpetuum mobile, eine sich selbst mahlende Mühle sei (*Novalis Schriften,* ed. Kluckhohn and Samuel [Leipzig, 1929], p. 75).

In comparison with the musical metaphor, the metaphor "enlightenment" (which carries forward Petrarch's image of "darkness" as the attribute of the Middle Ages) has only a pejorative tinge for Novalis: "Das Licht war wegen seines mathematischen Gehorsams und seiner Frechheit [!] ihr Liebling geworden." Novalis thought that in his own time a renascence of religious values was in the offing—and, as he contemplates this, again the musical metaphor alone is called upon to convey to us the expression of the ineffable: the spirit of his time is weaving a veil for the Virgin, who under his pen becomes a medieval St. Cecilia: "Der Schleier ist für die Jungfrau, was der Geist für den Leib ist, ihr unentbehrliches Organ, dessen Falten die Buchstaben ihrer Verkündigung sind; das unendliche Faltenspiel ist *eine Chiffernmusik,* denn die Sprache ist der Jungfrau zu hölzern und zu frech, nur zum Gesang öffnen sich ihre Lippen. Mir ist er nichts als der feierliche Ruf zu einer neuen Urversammlung, der gewaltige Flügelschlag eines vorüberziehenden englischen Herolds [language is 'frech,' impudent, as was also the light of enlightenment described above, i.e., intellectual]" (p. 81).

A new world after the Revolution and the wars is conceivable only when men shall gather for Ambrosian choirs—in an Augustinian peace founded on religion:

> Es wird solange Blut über Europa strömen, bis die Nationen . . . , *von heiliger Musik getroffen und besänftigt* zu ehemaligen Altären in bunter Vermischung treten, *Werke des Friedens* vornehmen, und *ein grosses Liebesmahl als Friedensfest* auf den rauchenden Walstätten mit heissen Tränen gefeiert wird. Nur die Religion kann Europa wieder aufwecken und die Völker sichern, und die Christenheit mit neuer Herrlichkeit sichtbar auf Erden in ihr altes, friedenstiftendes Amt installieren. . . . Sollte es nicht in Europa bald eine Menge wahrhaft heiliger Gemüter wieder geben, sollten nicht alle wahrhafte Religionsverwandte voll Sehnsucht werden, den Himmel auf Erden zu erblicken? und gern zusammentreten und *heilige Chöre anstimmen?* (pp. 83–4).

For us it is important to see how Novalis identifies the Christian spirit with *musica mundana,* recognizing in the destruction of the latter that of the former. The disintegration of the semantic field *concentus—temperare* is the exact linguistic counterpart of our modern estrangement from the medieval teaching: "musica quasi ad omnia se extendit."

The building up in ancient times of the "musical" semantic field and its subsequent dislocation is an outstanding example for H. Sperber's general contention that "semantic change is due to cultural change" ("Bedeutungswandel ist Kulturwandel"), and that, since the emotional centers change in different periods, so a perpetual regrouping of the semantics of word families must take place; the predominant *Affektkomplex* of one period is not that of the next, and the particular "emotional cluster" dominant at one time leads to a semantic expansion of the word families which express it, and to the attraction of remoter word families into its orbit. And the next period will have other emotional clusters, so that the semantic groupings will obey other signals. In ancient Greece and in the Middle Ages, which were centered about music, musical terms expanded, attracting other words; from the period of Enlightenment on, European mankind came to lose the feeling of a central "musicality"; it is other *Affektkomplexe* which dominate our times (we watch today semantic expansions represented by the phrases "I agree with you 100 percent," "He tried to blitz something on us," which testify to influences from realms of life more peripheric, and to a more fragmentary world outlook than could be that of the synthetic and harmonizing Fathers).

The dislocation of a semantic field, whether we regret it or not, is a historical fact of greatest importance in the science of semantics. This conviction can evidently not be shared by the "antimentalistic" school of linguistics which, by banishing beyond its narrow pales any research dealing with the minds of the speaking communities, and by identifying language with mere "speech habits," brushes off the problem of the Why of semantic change; the possible reasons for the introduction and maintenance of a certain "speech habit" lack interest for this school, which has enormously exaggerated the pseudomathematical claim of the self-sufficiency of linguistics which was advanced by De Saussure: since, according to this school, there is supposedly no human mind at work in language, and the reaction of man to language is to be compared with mere "trigger effects," any history of language, which can be only a history of the civilized mind as embodying itself in language, collapses. The assumption of the "self-moving mill" is, as Novalis saw it, the consequence of the "Verketzerung" of "Phantasie und Gefühl, Sittlichkeit und Kunstliebe, Zukunft und Vorzeit." Antimentalism is really antihistoricism and anticivilizationism. This school, in effect if not in purpose, works against civilization, and fits excellently into—and helps perpetrate—our "God- and music-forsakenness" which dates from the eighteenth century; it is in fact a remnant of the eighteenth-century anti-Christian movement and has remained untouched by the thought of the founders of linguistic historical science, those Romanticists of the Novalis-Schlegels type.[15] We must hope that, just as Novalis predicted for his time of crisis, "Wahrhafte Anarchie ist das Zeugungselement der Religion," so our anarchic times will bring back linguistic science to a more "musical" understanding of change in language, in order that we may forget the dry and barren mill-rattling of their prescholarly activities: the young students to come will ask for "a miller" and an architect presiding over the doings of Language; they will demand bread for their souls, not pebbles.

CHAPTER IV

HITHERTO WE HAVE BEEN mainly concerned with the concepts of musical harmony and well-temperedness. We have witnessed, it is true, a recurrence of words suggestive of the fundamental unity or the harmonizing unification of certain concepts (*concordia, consonantia, temperare*). But we have not yet dealt with the linguistic facts per se. Now that we know of the concepts expressed by these terms we are ready to undertake the study of the history of these words, which will lead us gradually to that of *Stimmung*. There are mainly two word families we must follow: *temperare* and **accordare*.

As concerns Lat *temperare* we need do little more than copy the overwhelmingly rich article in Ernout-Meillet's *Dictionnaire étymologique de la langue latine,* which has done the spade work for us by its comparison of *temperare* with the Greek κεράννυμι, "to mix":

> 1. trans. correspond au grec κεράννυμι 'mélanger, mêler', en particulier 'mêler de l'eau au vin ou à un liquide pour l'adoucir, couper': *t. vīnum, pōcula* (cf. gr. οἶνον, νέκταρ, κρατῆρα), *t. acētum melle*; de là 'tremper' un métal, *t. ferrum*; 'mêler, combiner, allier' (souvent joint à *miscere*) et 'modérer, adoucir, tempérer' (cf. gr. ὧραι μάλιστα κεκραμέναι Hdt. 3. 106, à quoi correspond par ex.: *regiones caeli neque aestuosae neque frigidae sed temperatae,* Vitr. I. 4); *Etesiarum flatu nimii temperantur calores,* Cic. N. D. 2. 19. 49; *temperātus, -a, -um* 'tempéré, modéré' (d'où *intemperātus*), joint à *moderātus,* Cic. Fam. 12, 27, opposé à *meracus,* id., Rep. I. 43. 96: *non modice temperatam, sed nimis meracam libertatem sitiens haurire.* A ce sens remontent les formes romanes du type *tremper,* M. L. 8627.
> 2. abs.: 'se modérer' d'où 's'abstenir' (déjà dans Enn. Sc. 45), cf. *temperans* 'qui se modère, tempérant'. *Temperō* est également construit avec le datif: *t. linguae, t. sibi, animis*; l'abl.: *t. ā lacrimīs,* l'infinitif *t. dormīre*; avec *quīn*

(époq. impér.); à l'impersonnel *temperātum est* (T. Live). On trouve même à basse époque, sans doute d'après *sē abstinēre, sē temperāre ab* (St. Aug., Greg. M.). Dérivés et composés: *temperiēs, -ei* (poét. et postclass., auquel répond dans les l.romanes un n. **temperium*, v. fr. *tempier*, M. L. 8628) et son contraire *intemperiēs, -ei* f. attesté depuis Plaute et au pl. *intemperiae, -ārum* (Caton, Plaute); *temperātiō, -ōnis* (classique, spécialement fréquent dans Cic. qui le joint à *moderātiō*, Div. 2. 45. 94); pour le sens, cf. Cic., Tusc. 4. 13. 30, *ut enim corporis temperatio cum ea congruunt inter se, e quibus constamus, sanitas, sic animi dicitur, cum eius iudicia opinionesque concordant, eaque animi est virtus, quam alii ipsam temperantiam dicunt esse, alii obtemperantem sapientiae praeceptis*: 'juste mélange, équilibre' = κρᾶσις et 'température' *caeli temperātiō* Cic., Div. 2. 45. 94; *temperātor* (joint à *moderātor* par Cic.); *temperātivus* (Cael. Aur.); *temperāculum, -ī* (Apul.); *temperāmentum, -i* n. 'tempérament, combinaison' et 'modération'. D'abord de sens concret; cf. Cic., Leg. 3. 10. 24, *inventum est temperamentum quo tenuiores cum principibus aequari se putarunt*; puis à l'époq. impériale, employé pour *temperātiō*. De *temperāns: temperanter, temperantia, -ae*, cf. Cic., Tusc. 3. 8. 16, *temperāns, quem Graeci σώφρονα appellant, eamque virtutem σωφροσύνην vocant quam soleo equidem tum temperantiam, tum moderationem appellare, nonnumquam etiam modestiam*; et *distemperantia*, t. de la l. médicale traduisant gr. δυσκρασία... Rattaché souvent à *tempus*, mais le rapport de sens est obscur. A moins d'admettre que *tempus* signifie 'coupure', 'division (du temps)', ce qui cadre bien avec les emplois du mot, et que *temperō* présente le même usage que le fr. 'couper le vin'? En somme, rien de clair.

From these lines, which are inspired by the attempt to find the difference between the particularly Latin lexicological innovation *temperare* and that *miscere* which would seem the genuinely correspondent word to κεράννυμι, it appears evident that *temperare*— coupled as it so often is with *moderari* (*temperantia* can be varied by *moderatio, modestia*; *moderari* as well as *temperare, temperantia, -atio, -amentum, -atura*, refer to both moral harmony and to climate; Cicero: *temperatio lunae caelique moderatio*; Curtius: *temperantia et moderatio naturae tuae*; Cicero: *temperantia est moderatrix omnium commotionum*; cf. Cicero: *astrictus certa quadam numerorum moderatione et pedum*, which Georges [*Lat.-Deutsch Handwörterbuch, s.v. moderatio, moderatrix*) translates "harmonische Einrichtung, Messung, Modulation"]—suggested more strongly the idea of "order," both in nature (climate)[1] and in man (intellectual and moral health), than did *miscere* (Rom **misculare*), which indicates a "mixing" without moral or cosmic connotations. *Temperare* was the verb destined to denote the condition of εὐκρασία = "health, harmony, balance"; this is the ideal state well known to us by Horace's "Aequam memento rebus in arduis / Servare mentem, non secus in bonis / Ab insolenti temperatam ... laetitia" (*Carmina*, 2, 3, 1–4)—that sentence which, by its very syntactical structure (the contrasts are held in balance by imperious metrics and syntax), has become the classical linguistic embodiment of equipoise. With the *se temperare* of Augustine and Gregory, the verb descriptive of that classical equipoise is brought to a Christian revival: "to harmonize oneself," to imitate God in bringing about harmony in our own soul which is the image of the divine soul.

As for the etymology of the Latin verb, while not rejecting outright the explanation of Ernout-Meillet who refer us to the "mixing of drinks," I submit as the *ultimate* etymology a derivation from *tempus* (which originally must have designated a "segment" [of time], *loc. cit.*; s.v. *tempus*; cf. *templum* = τέμενος, litt. "a cut-off section"), on the same morphological level with *temperies, tempestivus* etc.—that is to say, from *tempus* in the meaning "the *right* time"; this is one of the meanings of Greek καιρός = "the right measure," "convenience," "the right time," and we may assume that *tempus* also took over the nontemporal meanings of καιρός. Accordingly *temperare* would mean an intervention at the right time and in the right measure, by a wise (σώφρων) "moderator" who adjusts, adapts, mixes, alternatively softens or hardens (wine, iron etc.). Any purposeful activity which proceeds with a view to correcting excesses was called *temperare*: for example *temperare calamum*, "to cut, sharpen a quill" (hence It *temperino*, "pocket knife");[2] the Greek idea of measure, order, σωφροσύνη, intervenes even in reference to the most menial everyday utensils. Again, in the description of the organ by Volstan (Du Cange, s.v. *organum*), the skillful organist is represented as moderating, "tempering" the stops of his instrument: "Sola quadrigentas quae sustinet ordine musas, / Quas manus organici *temperat* ingenii." There is one "moderating" activity associated with *temperare*, most important for the development of our *Stimmung*, which has been overlooked by

Ernout-Meillet: this verb may mean "to tune the strings to harmony"; Horace (*Carmina*, 4, 3, 18): "O testudinis aureae / dulcem quae strepitum, Pieri, *temperas*." We have seen above that the Pythagoreans spoke of mixing (into an ἁρμονία) the higher and lower sounds; accordingly Boethius, *De arithm.*, defines *temperamentum* as "modorum musicorum commixtio." Cassiodorus renders the Greek συμφωνία by "*temperamentum sonitus* gravis ad acutum, vel acuti ad gravem" (Forcellini-DeWit, s.v. *symphonia*). In an Old French passage from Heldric de Cornuaille (cf. Gelzer, *ZfFL*, 47, 73) we find: "Li uns [a *jongleur*] vijele uri lai berton [sic], / E li altres harpe Gueron; / Puis font une altre *atemprëure* / E font des estrumens mesture, / Si *font ensanble* un lai Mabon," which shows how what we would call a symphonic concert is conceived of as a "mixture," a "tuning together." With the Catalonian Auzias March (fourteenth century) we find a *temperament* used of the song of birds: it is a well-tuned "symphony." *Temperament* was used in the Middle Ages to refer to the art of tuning instruments, an art ascribed by Rousseau to the inventor of the pianoforte and the gamut, Guido of Arezzo. Later, in the seventeenth century, theories of the *temperament* were worked out by Mersenne, Rameau etc.; our modern "equal temperament" was first introduced in 1511 by Schlick (*Spiegel der Orgelmacher*); to the general public of today the use of *temperare* – "to tune" is known only from Bach's piano composition *Das wohltemperierte Klavier* (1722), which was intended to test the tuning of the keyboard with preludes and fugues in chromatic ascensions. All these developments have their source in the relationship between Latin *temperamentum* and the εὐκρασία.[3]

How *temperare* is associated with the expressions for order and musical harmony can be shown by a non-Christian late Latin text: Apuleius, *De mundo*, which, according to S. Müller, *Das Verhältnis von Apuleius' De mundo zu seiner Vorlage* (Leipzig, 1939), follows a Greek original. In this work *temperantia* is grouped, on the one hand, with *proportio* in chemical and medical reference, on the other, with *concordia* (and *figura*) where in the Greek we find such words as μῖξις, ἐγκεκρασμένη, διακόσμησις. Since we also find the musical terms *consensus*, *conventus*, *confusio* (corresponding to the Greek κρᾶσις, μίγνυμι, ἐγκεκρασμένος, ὁμόνοια, ὁμολογία, ἁρμονία) used in description of the cosmic order, we may assume that this reference, too, was possible for *temperantia*.

Since Greek ἁρμονία had developed from the general meaning of "order" to that of "order in music, harmony," while συμφωνία had followed the opposite development from "musical consonance" to "harmony, order," the Greeks had acquired two words each capable of both meanings. It was only to be expected that the Romans, so obsequious to Greek thought (and even to Greek wording), should attempt a literal rendering of these "two-way" words; we find in Latin such couples as *temperantia* (or *concordia*, *consensus*) and *consonantia* (*concentus*) ready to compete with ἁρμονία (συμπάθεια, ὁμόνοια) and συμφωνία. In late Latin which, as a living language, did not have to limit itself to Ciceronian terms, there were still new possibilities at hand: Vulgar Latin was able to coin one word, tributary to two word families. Due to a particular coincidence not extant in Greek, there was in Latin a radical *cord*-susceptible to two interpretations: it could be connected not only with *cor, cordis*, "heart" (which was the original meaning), but also with *chorda*, "string," the Latin loan word from χορδή; thus *concordia* could suggest either "an agreement of hearts, peace, order" (*concord-ia*) or "a harmony of strings, world harmony" (**con-chord-ia*). Thus psychological harmony and musical harmony (and disharmony: *disc(h)ordia*) were ensconced in one word of poetic ambivalence which allowed for a kind of metaphysical punning; the ThLL lists such passages as: Paulus Festus: "fides genus citharae dicta, quod tantum inter se *cordae* ejus, quantum inter homines fides con-*cordet*" [a double pun: on *chorda* and *fides*!]; Cassiodorus: "hinc etiam appellatam aestimamus *chordam quod facile corda moveat*"; Isidore: "*chordas* autem dictas a *corde*, quia sicut pulsus est cordis in pectore, ita pulsus chordae in cithara"; *Cypr.Gall.*: "Iobalus musica plectra repperit et vario *concordes* murmure *chordas*." Finally, cf. n° 30 of the *Cambridge Songs*: "Caute cane cantor care; clare conspirent cannule, / compte *corde* [=chordae] crepent concinnantiam. // . . . caput, calcem, *cor* coniunge / . . . *Cane corda, cane cordis* [=chordis], / cane cannulis creatorem.'' These are punning para-etymologies from the modern point of view, but for medieval as well as ancient linguistics, which sought the accord of things behind the accord of words, and saw the multivalence of creation reflected in that of the words, the phonetic assonance was a revelation of truth (ἔτυμον). We may remember the *concordare* found in the passages cited earlier (pp. 46–47) in reference to Biblical "concordance"; the verb is used to translate the Greek συμφωνεῖν, for which the literal translation would have been "consonant"; may it not be that "concordant" was chosen just because it could suggest both the agreement in spirit (*cor*), and the harmony of the well-ordered lute (**conchordare*)? And such a relationship, when perceived, could itself become an incentive to innovation, linguistically creative; a parallel case is the one I have studied in *Language*, XVII (1941), 50–53, where I pointed out that the para-etymological identification of *caritas* and χάρις by Christian writers made possible, not only the spelling *charitas*, but also the creation of a hybrid **caritosus* = χαριτ-δsus (whereas the adjective from *caritas* would have been **caritat-osus*); another case would be Eng *dismal* < OFr **dismal* = *decimalis* [*dies*], "a tithe of our time given to God," which was interpreted as *dies malus* and consequently received a new semantic, a "dismal" connotation (cf. MLN, XLVII [1942], p. 602–13).

Accordingly, should we not recognize in the new Vulgar Latin word family **acc(h)ordare*, **acc(h)ordantia*, a further semantic and morphological innovation, based on the same ambiguity of the *c(h)ord-* stem? This family is attested in all the Romance languages with the exception of Rumanian (the language that pays more allegiance to Eastern than to Western traditions, and which, by substituting *anima* [> *inimă*] for *cor*, "heart," has made impossible any punning with *chorda*): Fr *accorder*, Prov and Sp *acordar*, It *accordare*, etc. This verb **ad-c(h)ord-are* is based on *con-c(h)ord-are*, after the pattern of *consonare—assonare* (for the *ad-* innovation, cf. **adgratare* > *agréer*, *aggradare*, etc.), and means at the same time "to tune (be tuned) to" and "to be (put) in hearty agreement with." Here, indeed, is the breath of Christian spiritual life, and a new linguistic vitality, reviving an old word family.

The etymology of this Romance **accordare* family has been debated for centuries: R. Estienne proposed *cor* (= *ad unum cor*);

Ménage, *chorda* ("parce que leurs volontés [sc. of those who con-clude an agreement], devenant conformes, deviennent semblables à deux cordes accordées par unisson et consonance"; that the great French etymologist had a fine sensitivity to world harmony is shown by the very words which he has borrowed from a long tradition). Since that time etymological dictionaries have wavered between the two etymologies (REW and FEW side with Ménage), and, if we consider only morphological or intragrammatical alterna-tives, no decision can be reached. It does not seem to have occurred to anyone that **accordare,* formed after *concordare* had acquired its double meaning, could have both *cor* and *chorda* as etymons (just as **charitosus* or *dismal* have two etymons)—that, in other words, world harmony, perceptible to ear and heart alike (the Augustinian-trained ear does not hear without the soul), could have welded together, and wedded, two word families which, between them, express precisely the acoustic and the mental.

In a recent article published in *Language,* XVII, 119–26 ("Spanish *Acordar* and Related Words"), a pupil of Professor Castro, Mr. Mack Singleton, while admitting a double etymology, sees fit to cut the word family in two: the meaning "to tune" he separates from the meanings of the Old Spanish verb: "to agree," "to come to," "to awake," "to record," "to encourage, advise"; only in the first meaning, according to Singleton, should *acordar* be ascribed to *chorda;* the other meanings point to *cor* (just as is true of *discordari, recordari,* etc.). This is as drastic, but hardly as wise as a Solo-monic cut; Mr. Singleton himself proceeds to mitigate this by pointing out such Latin examples as *symphonia discors* or *concordi dixere sono* which suggest, even to him, the possibility of a *cor-*derivation, and indeed he concludes, by suggesting tentatively "that there is a mixture of two phonetically similar etyma; but that *acordar* and its derivatives may all eventually be derived from *cor, cordis.*" Here, Mr. Singleton is a victim of the current depart-mentalization of philology, and, more specifically, of the fallacies of translation into English; had he been a German, who uses *stimmen* as well as *übereinstimmen,* he would have sensed no division. Medieval word problems of such magnitude cannot be treated on the basis of two languages only, one of which (his native tongue) biases the student toward the other. Mr. Singleton proceeds rightly (pp. 119–20) when he puts together a "musical" quotation from the *Crónica general* ("assaco el despues por si temprar las cuerdas, las unas altas, e las otras baxas, e las otras en medio; e fizo las todas responder en los cantares cada unas en sus uozes e acordar ['to be in harmony'] con ellas, donde se fazen las dulcedumbres que plazen mucho a los omnes e los alegran") with those having a metrical or grammatical reference ("et assi sabie *acordar canto por canto* et *palaura por palaura* ['make correspond']" and "Los nomnes son revueltos e graves de *acordar*, Non los podemos todos *en rimas acoplar* ['make fit']"); we have already noted the ancient unity between music and grammar. But one may wonder why such examples are segregated from *acuerdan en una razon* (which Mr. Singleton translates "they agree in one idea," but which would be better interpreted " . . . in one discourse," which embraces both "thought" and "reason"), and even from "et plogol mucho por que *acordauan* [dos letras] *con* el so nombre ['corresponded']"; why should agreement in "letters" and "speech" be separated from agreement of sounds ? If *sabie acordar canto por canto et palaura por palaura* goes back to *acchordare, why not also *acordar palabras, razones* [*en una razon*] ? We may cite here a sentence from Santillana listed by Cuervo (s.v. *acordar*), in which is clearly reflected the ancient harmony of the spheres: "Los cuerpos superiores, que son las estrellas, se acuerdan con la naturaleza"; in another sentence also listed by Cuervo (Berceo) we find: "Nun qua udieron omnes organos mas temprados, / Nin que formar pudiesen sones mas *acordados*," where we are given a picture of men listening to cosmic, moral, *and* sensuous music: their ears hear well-tempered sounds while, at the same time, their hearts sense the well-tempered order of the world.   *Acordar* is coupled with *temprar*: the two constituents of the field of world harmony touch each other.   But Mr. Singleton could not "see" this order; he had not visualized the kinship of εἶδος and ἰδέα in the ancient world, as exemplified by our bicephalic *acc(h)ordare*.

But perhaps Mr. Singleton could have found in his native language a similar coalescence of the *cor-* and *chorda-* family, had he been aware of the theme of world harmony.   The Eng *chord* is the

equivalent of Ger *Akkord,* Fr *accord;* what the French Rameau
called *accords parfaits,* that is the pleasing combination of a tone
with the third, fifth, and octave, appears in the English translation
(1752) as *perfect chords.* This *chord* is explained by the OED as a
shortening of English *accord,* but this leaves unexplained the
spelling with -*h*-, which we would have to assume to be due to the
para-etymology, *chorda,* "string." It seems clear to me that *chord*
represents a fusion of *accord, concord* with *cord* [*chorda*], "string."
First we have to do with the development of meaning in the latter
word from "string" to "chord"; just as, in the *laudate eum in
cymbalis* of the Psalmist, the *cymbali* ["bells"] became *concordiae
fidelium* with Alanus de Insulis (see above), so the *chordae* ["strings"]
became the "harmony of chords" (achieved by strings of different
pitch).[4] Secondly, this "chord" is associated with *concord,* which
meant "pleasing combination of two tones"; Morley (1597) precisely
defines *concord* by *chord:* "What is a *concord?* ... It is a mixt
sound [=*temperamentum!*] ... entring with delight in the eare ... a
unison [the word of Boethius], a fifth, an eighth ... be *perfect
cordes*"; again, in the example, reminiscent of Plato (1592): "The
Syrens ... sound out heavenly melodie in such pleasing *cords,*"
the last two words could easily mean "harmony brought about by
a chord"="concord." As for Lat *concordia,* we may note the following passages (ThLL, s.v. *concordia*), where "(musical) harmony
shifts toward "(harmony brought about by) chords," Seneca:
"doces ... quomodo nervorum disparem reddentium sonum fiat
concordia" [*concordia* > Eng *concord; nervi* > Eng *chords*]; Columella:
"ex ... vocum *concordia* ... amicum quiddam et dulce resonat";
Martianus Capella: "tetrachordorum quippe est quattuor sonorum
in ordinem positorum congruens fidaque *concordia*" [*fida* pun with
fide]; Boethius: "est ... consonantia dissimilium inter se vocum *in
unum redacta concordia.*" In the *Speculum musice* (1340) we read
(cf. Frei, p. 345), in an invective against the contemporary musical
innovation called *ars nova,* "confundunt tales discantum *concordias*
nonnumquam nonne mutilant ... et hi propter ignorantiam dicte
artis si quandoque *ad concordiam venerint* cum tenore, nesciunt
concordia permanere, cito ad discordiam relabuntur. Heu pro
dolor!" (*concordia*="harmony, harmonious chord").

We find a broader meaning of our word in the passage from Dante's *Purgatorio*, XVI, 21: "Io sentía voci, e ciascuna pareva / Pregar per pace e per misericordia / L'Agnel di Dio che le peccata leva. / Pure 'Agnus Dei' eran le loro esordia; / Una parola in tutti era, ed un modo, / Si che parea tra esse *ogni concordia*." Here, the choir described by Dante is, not "monotonous," as Scartazzini would interpret, but rather "in unison"—or, perhaps, because of the *ogni*, "possessed of every harmony," a harmony achieved by the chord, which acts upon the listener as a unit (*in unum redacta, unisona*), as, according to Augustine, does all beauty which proceeds from the feeling for the unification of the diverse. Here we have illustrated one of the feelings which the Middle Ages has expressed the most convincingly: the feeling of the group, of being united in one *concordia* or world harmony, which extends from angel to star to man to bird. This is the same feeling which informs so many medieval pictures and sculptures: the union of hearts and minds, reflected in their relatively nonindividualistic attitudes which reveal only *one* direction of thought, a subordination to the meaning of the Whole. Thus we see a perfect identity between Eng *chords* (< Lat *cordae*, "harmonious [strings of a] lute") and *concord* (< Lat *concordia*, "harmony," "harmony of chords"); we can surmise that *chord* = "pleasing combination of tones" is the result of a telescoping similar to the one which we saw realized in **accordare*, a telescoping possible because of the phonetic and semantic closeness of the two word families. A spelling which would express the ambivalence and double parentage of *chord* (the συμπάθεια and συμφωνία at the same time) would be: *c(h)ord*.

The heart and ear are again in unison when a Provençal troubadour coins the word "descort" as the name of a lyric genre in which different languages, metric schemes, etc. are mixed: because his heart is "out of tune" (*verstimmt*) so, too, must be his lute. Jeanroy, *La poésie lyrique des troubadours*, II, 329–30, writes: "Tandis que le propre de la chanson est de faire 'accorder' entre eux tous les couplets, la loi du descort est de les 'désaccorder': l'auteur prétendait marquer ainsi, semble-t-il, le déséquilibre où le plongeait une passion malheureuse. Chaque couplet a donc, dans un descort régulier, sa structure et sa mélodie propres. . . . Ce qui faisait la valeur du descort, c'était évidemment la mélodie; les paroles, dès l'origine, avaient été l'accessoire, puisqu'elles étaient adaptées à une mélodie préexistante." The word *désaccorder* was borrowed by Jeanroy from the polyglot *Descort* of Raimbaut de Vaqueiras: " . . . vuelh un *descort* comensar / d'amor, per qu'ieu vauc aratges; / quar ma domna·m sol amar, / mas camiatz l'es sos coratges, / per qu'ieu vuelh *dezacordar* / *los motz, e·ls sos e·ls lenguatges*"—evidently *dezacordar los sos* [= *sonus*] is a fixed phrase to which the poet has added . . . *los motz* and, in bearing with the polyglot character of the poem, *los lenguatges*. We find the same wording in the *Leys d'Amors*: "las quals coblas [in the *descort*] devon esser singulars·*dezacordables·e variables·en accort* [= "rhyme"; the same text uses also *acordansa*]·*en so·et en lenguatges*." Appel, *ZRPh*, XI, 212–30, at 212, quotes the precept of the Old Provençal *Doctrina de compondre dictatz*: "Man solle im Descort von der Liebe sprechen als jemand der von ihr verlassen ist. . . . Im Gesange sei das Lied allen anderen entgegengesetzt; wo der Gesang ansteigen sollte, da senke er sich." (Appel uses also [p. 219] the medieval term *temperament* in this connection: "Das Temperament der Musik sind wir natürlich versucht als in Übereinstimmung mit dem Texte des Liedes stehend zu denken.") The "temperament" or "concord" or "harmony" of a piece of music or poetry was seen to depend on the "temper," "harmony," "*Stimmung*," of the musician or poet (and the same is true of "disharmony"). And it is no whim (as it would seem from the cautious wording: "prétendait . . . semble-t-il" of Jeanroy, who, unfortunately, does not understand the inward form of medieval thought) on the part of the author or composer if he chooses dissonances when his heart is in discord: medieval man saw his whole life, down to the smallest details, pervaded by symbolism. He acted within the frame of transcendental necessities; the artist did not willfully decide to conform to these, but rather felt his hand to be guided thereby; a Dante, too, chose *rime aspre e chiocce* when he felt his soul or his subject matter "out of tune". To be *dezacordat* means to be "individualistic" (cf. the *singulars coblas* above) in form; but individualism is permitted, for the sake of expressivity, only under certain conditions, and set up against a normative frame of nonindividualism, of measure and poise. The descort is thus no exception to the artistic rule which asked for "harmony"; it is significant that we find only rarely Old Provençal poems called *acort*: so much was the *acort* the regular mood of the artist, that the term is only created out of opposition to descort; the *acort* is, so to speak, a *des-descort*, born of an anti-disorder mood. And even in the seemingly disordered work of art there had to be harmony, that is, the disharmony willed by harmony and subservient to it; in addition, the correspondence of the outward features of a work of art with its source of inspiration was, in itself, "harmonious." We know that metrics and grammar are bound up with the "music" of a poem, since they are merely the reflections of the world harmony which any work of art imitates; in the phrase *dezacordar los motz e·ls sos e·ls lenguatges* we can as little disassociate *cor* and *chorda* as in the case of the Old Spanish couple discussed above, *acordar las cuerdas—las palabras*. The *cor—chorda* family is present with both.

It is time now to present to the reader a series of passages drawn from one medieval author in order to show the variety and consistency of the occurrence of members of the great *consonantia— concordia temperare—accordare* family.   I choose first the poem of the Catalonian Auzias March (fifteenth century) on the different forms of love (ed. Bohigas [Barcelona, 1955], n° 87):

> (19): Ladonchs ells [the different desires, *volers*] junts *mesclat* voler componen / que dura tant com d'aquell [with the body] se *conssonen* . . . (61): Tot amador delit no pot atènyer / fins que lo cors e l'arma *se acorden* . . . ; (74): D'abdós hunits [body and soul] se *compon* esta *mescla* [love] . . . ; (95): De tres *cordells* [strings] Amor deu fer sa corda [the bow of Amor] . . . si·l terç no·y es *la corda se descorda* . . . [here we are led from *corda*, "string," to concord, and *descordar*, "to come loose," becomes similar to *dezacordar*, "to get out of accord"]; (145): és feta gran seguons les parts s'acorden; / multiplican los béns don ella·s forma. / Del bé honest aquest· amor pren forma, / e los volers que·n surten *no discorden*; (117): junts, acordants [body and soul], en delit cascú puja; (314): d'aquests mesclats surt molt gran virtut una, / axí Amor suptil y enfinit *tempra* / la finitat de la del cors y aviva. / En cert cas mor nostr' amor sensitiva, / e l'esprit, junt ab ell, se *destempra*. / Amen ensemps e l'espirit sols ame, / perque tot l'om no·s trob qu'en res desame.

We find in poem n° 94:

> (12): en quantitat [my love] molt prop d'altres se jutja; / en qualitat ab les altres *discorda*; (17): Dins lo cors d'om les *humors se discorden*; . . . / en un

sols jorn regna malenconia, / n'aquell mateix còlera, sanch e fleuma. / Tol
enaxí las passions de l'arma / mudament han molt *divers o contrari*; (119):
Los grans *contrasts* de nostres parts *discordes | canten, forçats, acort,* et *de
grat, contra* [ἔρις καὶ φιλία: note the verb *cantar* which revives the musical
connotations of *discordes* and *acort*].

The same coupling of *accordare* and *temperare* occurs also in
Italian. Brunetto Latini's *Tesoretto*, VIII, 25–34 (the allegory of
Nature speaking of the four humors of the body): "E queste
quattro cose / Così contrariose, / E tanto disuguali / In tutti gli
animali / Mi convene *achordare* / E in lor *temperare* / E rinfrenar
ciascuno / Sì ch'io li *rechi a uno,* ['unison'], / Sì ch'ogni corpo nato /
Ne sia chonplessionato [on *complexio,* cf. note 3 to this chapter]."
Similarly in the *Canti carnascialeschi* (ed. C. S. Singleton, 149) a
"Trionfo delle quattro complessioni" has the following lines: "Per
quest si conserva nostra vita, / di qui deriva e vien la concordanza /
del corpo all' alma unita: / e se fra lor vien qualche discrepanza, /
ragion pronta ed ardita, / frenando il senso con su' giuste legge, / tal
consonanza defende e corregge"; the sanguine "Venus"-tempera-
ment makes the soul "quieta, *ridente, allegra, umana, e temperata,*
benigna e molto grata."[5]

And now let us follow the use of *tempra* associated with the idea
of world harmony in Dante. The literal meaning, "tuning of
strings," is obvious in *Par.,* XIV, 118: "E come giga ed arpa *in
tempra tesa* / Di *molte corde* fan *dolce* tintinno / A tal da cui la nota
non è intesa . . ."—but there is also a suggestion of the "sweet"
consonance, inaccessible to human ears, of heavenly music. In the
scene from *Purg.,* XXX, 91–8, Dante has been rebuked by Beatrice
and stiffens before the onslaught of her reproaches as the snow of
the mountains congeals before the blast of northern winds; later, as
the snow melts under the sun, so Dante, touched by the soft
consolation of the angels, melts into tears:

> Così fui senza lagrime e sospiri
> Anzi il cantar di que' che notan sempre
> Dietro alle note degli eterni giri;
> Ma poi che intesi nelle dolci *tempre*
> Lor compatire a me, più che se detto
> Avesser: "Donna, perchè sì lo *stempre*?",

Lo gel, che m'era intorno al cor ristretto,
Spirito ed acqua fèssi . . .

The verb *stempre* (line 96) itself is correctly translated by commentators as "mortifichi, avvilisci" [Scartazzini], "gli togli vigore" [Torraca], but its relationship with the word- and concept-family of *tempra*, "harmony" (in line 94 it is the "harmony of the spheres" that is involved) is ignored. Because of Beatrice, Dante has become "out of tune, out of harmony" (and the best translation would be the Ger *aus der Stimmung reissen*)—bereft of a harmony which, in accord with the ancient tradition, embraces the movements of the stars (*eterni giri*), the harmonious song (the *dolci tempre* which could be as well the *dolce consonanze*) of the angels which are identified in Christianity with the ancient harmony of the spheres, with the climate (the "congealing" snow indicating unharmonious excess), and with the human temper. And any translation which does not take into account the whole range of associations present to Dante's mind, is substituting unilinear poverty for the polyphonic richness of the text. The particular precision in Dante's use of words consists of their density, in the suggestiveness of their whole semantic field, of all the harmonic overtones. A real Dante vocabulary would place every word into its associational context or field; it would be rather a map extending in space than a series of columns.

How the harmonizing imagination of Dante succeeds in welding together, not only the spheres of the Beyond with those of this world, but also the techniques of modern humanity and the beliefs of antiquity,[6] how "modern" Dante really is while echoing ancient traditions (quite like his successor of today, Paul Claudel, who, in his *carmen seculare*, the first of the *Cinq grandes odes* [1910], sings the technical progress of mankind as a reconciliation of the purposes of God with human endeavors), we can see by *Par.* X, 139–48: "Indi come orologio, che ne chiami / Nell' ora che la sposa di Dio surge / A mattinar lo sposo perche l'ami, / Che l'una parte l'altra tira ed urge / *Tin tin* sonando con sì dolce nota, / Che il ben disposto spirto d'amor turge; / Così vid'io la gloriosa ruota [of the *Spiriti Magni*] / Muoversi e render *voce a voce in tempra / Ed in dolcezza*. ch'esser non

può nota / Se non colà dove gioir s'insempra." The Wheel of the
Blessed is compared to the morning clock which wakens folk from
their sleep. In ancient legends, morning was represented by the
rosy-fingered Eos who awakens her husband for amorous joys; the
Christian pendant to this sensuous picture must evidently center
around the "spouse of God," i.e., the God-loving soul "serenading,"
praising the Creator in a morning hymn which arouses the "be-
nevolent spirit of Love" (the Holy Ghost); but with Dante, modern
and "progress-minded" as he was, the morning hymn is sung not by
an Ambrosian congregation, but by the precisely and ingeniously
built technical device: the clock.[7] Thus the *numeri* of Augustine
have found their indicator in an engine which, with Dante, sym-
bolizes all the cosmic laws of interdependency, well-temperedness,
and beauty made of order ("l'una parte l'altra tira ed urge, / Tin tin
sonando con sì dolce nota"). The minimal sound, the childish
sound *tin tin* foreshadows the orchestra of the spheres which will
resound in the second part of the simile where the Wheel of the
eternally Blessed is presented as a dancing and music-making
whole which functions *in tempra ed in dolcezza*, producing what
Dante, in the same canto, calls "la dolce sinfonia dell' alto Paradiso"
(the familiar synonym). What is the meaning of *tempra* here?
The dictionary of Tommaseo-Bellini translates, "canto, consonanza,"
the old commentators explain, "proportionaliter conformare voces
eorum in cantu" or "in temperanza, rispondendo l'una voce all'
altra" (but the response is already expressed by *voce a voce*).
Without denying the presence of such meanings, I should think that
the clock and the *muoversi* should not be entirely forgotten, though
in tempra refers grammatically only to singing (*render voce a voce*);
tempra is, in fact, "well-temperedness, order," the order, the
numeri of music, of dancing, and of the technical device; the
exactitude which in our time Valéry points out (in *L'âme et la danse*)
in architecture, poetry, music, and dancing. The inaccessible music
of the spheres is subject to order and clarity, the *tempra* is the
Augustinian *temperatura partium*, and *pax* is *ordo amoris*; the whole
passage is penetrated by the "mystery of clarity" so dear to the
Latin poets, to Racine, Calderón, Péguy, Claudel, and Valéry. In
addition to the synesthetic devices of Dante, we find a mingling of

pagan myth with modern technics; the range in space and time of such a passage is immense. The comparison here offered between the dancing movements of the angels with the regular ticking of a clock is not isolated in Dante, nor is his use of *tempra* for "the harmonious structure and behavior of parts within a whole"; *Par.*, XXIV, 13: "E come cerchi *in tempra d'oriuoli* / Si giran sì, che il primo, a chi pon mente, / Quieto pare, e l'ultimo che voli, / Così quelle carole differente- / mente danzando, della sua richezza / Mi si facean stimar, veloci e lente" (again *tempra* is translated too narrowly by Tommaseo-Bellini as "congegno, struttura"). There is movement and peace, rich variety and unity (both are depicted in the adverb *differente-mente* which unites two lines while evoking variety) in the *tempra* of the clock and of the angelic dances.

Dante is no mystic. He emphasizes measure and order, not boundless enthusiasm. It was the mystic Bernard of Clairvaux who said of his love of God: "Confundis ordines, dissimulas usum, modum ignoras . . ." thus denying the *numeri*; in the mystic Jacopone da Todi excess and exultation, consequently disorder and "distemperedness" must predominate. Jacopone, however, was aware of the problem: How could excess in love for God be justified, since it goes beyond that order (*ordo amoris*) which is God's work? In the *Cantico dell' amor superardente*, when Christ speaks to the passionately loving mystic, the idea of *tempra* is implicit, though the word itself is not expressed (st. 21):

> Tutte le cose quali aggio create
> si so' fatte con numero e misura,
> ed a lor fine so' tutte *ordinate*,
> conservansi con *orden* in valura.
> E molto più ancora caritate
> è *ordinata* nella sua natura.
> Or come per calura,
> Alma, tu se' impazzita?
> *For d'orden* tu se' uscita,
> non t'e *freno* el fervore.

The fervor of the mystic has abandoned ἁρμονία καὶ ἀριθμός— this fervor is excessive heat, i.e., according to humoral pathology, madness; the harmony of the creation, of the human soul and body, is missing; the *x* which should unite all these is evidently *temperatura*.

And now, if we go back to the beginning of our poem, we shall find, in fact, a representative of our word family: Here the mystic is describing the boundlessness of his soul and its paradoxically powerless state, torn as it is between bliss and torture (st. 1):

> Amor di caritate,
> Perche m' hai sì ferito?
> Lo cor tutto partito
> Et che arde per amore?
> Arde et incende, e nullo trova loco;
> Non può fugir però ched è ligato;
> Sì si consuma come cera a foco,
> Vivendo mor, languisce *stemperato*:
> Dimanda di poter fugir un poco
> et in fornace trovasi locato
> Oimè, do' son menato
> A sì forte languire?
> Vivendo si è morire,
> Tanto monta l' ardore.

E. Auerbach, in his article "Passio als Leidenschaft" (*PMLA*, LVI, 1189), quotes this passage because of the new re-evaluation it offers of "passion" by the mystics ("passion" is no longer represented as a *perturbatio*, as in Stoicism and Epicureanism and earlier dogmatic Christianity, but as a positive, a good, thing), and compares the paradoxical expression *amore superardente of* Jacopone, anticipatory of Petrarchism, to the "inhitzige minne," inherent in the lover and imitator of Christ, of the German mystic Eckhart (cf. also Germ *Inbrunst*, "religious fervor," literally "inner conflagration," which originates in mysticism).   The superabundant heat of this mysticism is a *stemperatura*; the *super-* (which Jacopone may have derived from such expressions as the *supereminens* [used in Genesis in reference to God's spirit], commented upon by Augustine) is only a variant of the *dis-* of *stemperato*.

Petrarch in his metaphysical love poetry (*Sestina* VIII, ed. Mestica) imagines a Provençal setting of amorous springtime.

provocative of songs which should assuage the Alplike resistance of Laura; and as if to flatter her with sound the sweet air (*l' aura*) is made to allude to *Laura*: "Là vèr l' aurora, che sí dolce l' aura / Al tempo novo suol movere i fiori / E li augelletti incominciar lor versi. . . . " And thereupon the poet expresses a wish, "*Temprar* potess' io in sí soavi note / I miei sospiri, ch' addolcissen l' aura [= Laura], / Facendo a lei ragion, ch' a me fa forza!" This *temprar* is applied primarily to the tempering of the emotions, parallel to that of the climate (*addolcissen l'aura*) and to the placating of the beloved (*Laura*); but suddenly music is at hand (*soavi note*), music intended to gain her favor, this favor of the lady who is, as we have seen, a force of nature, and who, consequently, should be "tamed" by the *Orpheus redivivus*, Petrarch. The use of *temperare* is similar to that of *serenare*[8] (Petr. *Canzone* 23: "[Her voice has the power] Cantando d'acquetar li sdegni e l' ire, / Di *serenar* la tempestosa mente / E sgombrar d'ogni nebbia oscura e vile") which clearly alludes to the *Juppiter Serenator*, placator of nature, and is used here of Laura's voice. The classical moderation of Petrarch, in spite of the supernatural emotions of his love, is shown by his use of *temperare*, this time without musical connotation in a sonnet *post mortem Laurae*, in which he describes her "taming" influence on the strife in his heart: "Dolci durezze e placide repulse, . . . / Leggiadri sdegni, che le mie *infiammate* / *Voglie temparo*, (or me n'accorgo) *e'nsulse*." The "taming" is symbolized by the oxymoric expressions as well as by the hyperbaton (*infiammate voglie . . . e'nsulse*), which is, as it were, an echo of the resistance against the "tempering" (Sonnet 305).

Turning now to a quite different climate, to as late a text as Tasso's *Gerusalemme liberata* (Canto XVI, st. 12 and 16), we witness a revival of the troubadour atmosphere (which, as we have seen, was conditioned by the Augustinian identification of love, order, music), but with emphasis on the animal or sensuous instincts of love; still, however, the idea of world harmony, of response, of temperedness survives—and, along with it, the coupling of *temprare* and *concordia*: "Vezzosi augelli infra le verdi fronde / *Temprano* a prova lascivette note. / Mormora l'aura, e fa le foglie e l'onde / Garrir, che variamente ella percote. / Quando taccion gli augelli, alto risponde; / Quando cantan gli augei più lieve scuote: / Sia caso od arte, or accompagna ed ora / Alterna i versi lor *la music' òra* [=aura] . . . / . . . degli augelli il coro, / Quasi approvando, il canto indi ripiglia. / Raddoppian le colombe i baci loro; / Ogni animal d'amar si riconsiglia."

Birds, air, plants, brooklets give a concert of (lascivious) love, and the air of the enchanted garden through which Rinaldo and Armida walk, which sighs in response to the birds and plants is, itself, the musician who uses the *plectron* of leaves and of waves (*percote*). Although, in this all-too-earthly paradise, no religious note could resound ("is it chance or art?"—no divine motivation is invoked), and all things yield to luscious beauty, still the old patterns of thought work in a secularized form: the "musical air" breathes within the the "well-tempered" harmony of an (earthly but para-disiac) love which is but an image of the heavenly paradise; the heavenly climate on earth reminds us of how "human" the world has, by now, become with this poet of the Counter Reformation, who cannot refrain from depicting with paradisiac colors the sensuous which should be sacrificed to the celestial Jerusalem.[9]

Instead of piling up easily accessible evidence of the survival of the ancient texture *temperatura—consonantia—concordia* from the other Romance languages[10] (though we shall quote some Spanish texts when dealing with the word "concert"), let us turn instead to English Renaissance texts,[11] not only in order to show how un-broken the medieval tradition has survived—the words themselves (mainly of Latin or French origin, i.e., belonging to the international past of the English vocabulary) being identical to those of a Dante or an Augustine—but also because of the great poetic beauty of the English texts. It is perhaps not inappropriate to place them in a Latin-Romance frame, since the predominant trend with commen-tators has been to explain a Shakespeare passage by adducing English parallels, or perhaps those from ancient literature (preferably from the classic, rather than Late Latin and Christian tradition), thereby destroying the continuity of the patristic, medieval, and Renaissance tradition, and the real parallelism offered by contem-porary Romance poetry.[12] Indeed, to me *Hamlet* and some of the Shakespeare sonnets read like a Spanish *comedia* or the poetry of

Lope—and this, not only because of the themes, but also because of the wording in detail. In Shakespeare's *Merchant of Venice* (V, 1) Lorenzo, after giving a definition of the harmony of the spheres (in a passage which we shall quote later), thus makes answer to Jessica's remark that sweet music fails to rally her spirits: "The reason is your spirits are attentive" (an obvious reference to the opinion of Diocles, v. *supra*); he then goes on to compare her state of mind to the wildness of colts "which is the hot condition of their blood," but is susceptible to being tamed by music:

> You shall perceive them make *a mutual stand*,
> Their savage eyes turn'd to a *modest* gaze . . .
> Since naught so stockish, hard and full of rage,
> But music for the time doth change his nature.
> The man that hath no music in himself,
> Nor is not mov'd with *concord of sweet sounds*,
> Is fit for treasons, stratagems and spoils;
> The motions of his spirit are dull as night,
> And his affections dark as Erebus:
> Let no such man be trusted. . . .

To be brief: underlying here are the ancient equations: music = *concordia* = *temperamentum* (neither "hot," "raging," nor "dull as night") = *temperantia*, *moderatio* ("modest") = response, concert ("mutual stand"). To "have music in oneself" is to be in harmony with the world, tempered and temperate (this line is generally but erroneously quoted as if it were only a banal equivalent, for example, to the German proverb: "Böse Menschen haben keine Lieder"). Gundolf, in his *Shakespeare*, distinguishes in the *Merchant of Venice* two central motifs: music and grace: "Gnade, der göttliche Strahl von oben, und Musik, der heimliche Zauber der Welt. Porzia, das Lieblingskind und der Anwalt der Gnade, singt deren Preislied. Lorenzo, einer aus der klangfreudigen Schar, das der Musik." Thus Shylock is the "gnaden- und musiklose Mensch."[13] It is interesting to see how Gundolf, concerned though he was with a static analysis of the inward organization of the play, has come to discern in it our historical theme of world harmony; and he blames the modern public for misinterpreting the figure of Shylock according to juridical, moral, ecclesiastical, or racial considerations, on the grounds that such interpretation shows no understanding of the "Weltfeier" feeling of Shakespeare—I would say, in my terminology, his feeling of Christian world harmony.[14] A man devoid of grace and music, somewhat like Shylock, is also lean Cassius (*Julius Caesar*, I, 2), who neither sleeps nor plays nor smiles, but (and such men are "dangerous") thinks, reads, observes: he is evidently a melancholic, of untempered body and soul, a man unredeemed by music ("he hears no Musicke"). In *Richard II*, V, 5:

> . . . how sour sweet music is,
> When time is broke and no *proportion* kept!
> So is it in the *music* of men's lives.
> And here have I the daintiness of ear
> To check *time broke* in a disorder'd string;
> But for the *concord of my state and time*
> Had not an ear to hear my true time broke.
> I wasted time, and now doth time waste me;
> For now hath time made me his numbering clock,

we find the equation, "music = proportion, harmony, order, concord"; as with Archytas and Cicero, political and musical order are interwoven; and, as with Augustine and Dante, the *numeri* of time must be kept in harmony. The "true time" as opposed to the "time of the clock" anticipates again Bergson's opposition of *durée réelle* and *heure de la montre*.

Another, equally ancient turn is given to the idea of world harmony in *Troilus and Cressida*, I, 3: "Take but degree away, *untune that string*, / And, hark! what *discord* follows: each thing meets / In mere *oppugnancy*." The equation here is *distemperamentum = discordia rerum* of which *repugnantia rerum* (Cicero) and *repugnantia naturae* (Pliny) are variants. Commentators remark on this passage that Shakespeare has used an ancient maxim (by Publius Syrus): "If the first rank is not preserved the place is secure for nobody"; but more interesting is the fact that the derangement of hierarchy implies anarchy, political disorder, the untuning of musical harmony.

Finally, we may consider Sonnet VIII, of which every line, as well as the fundamental idea, is pervaded by Pythagorean-Platonic thought:

> Music to hear, why hear'st thou music sadly?
> Sweets with sweets war not, joy delights in joy.
> Why lovest thou that which thou receivest not gladly,
> Or else receivest with pleasure thine annoy?

> If the true concord of well tuned sounds,
> By unions married, do offend thine ear,
> They do but sweetly chide thee, who confounds
> In singleness the parts that thou shouldst bear.

> Mark how one string, sweet husband to another,
> Strikes each in each by mutual ordering;
> Resembling sire and child and happy mother,

> Who, *all in one, one* pleasing note do sing:
> Whose speechless song, being *many* seeming *one*,
> Sings this to thee: '*Thou single wilt prove none!*'

The poet starts from two empirical observations about the beloved youth: the latter does not listen gladly to music, and he will not indulge in marital love, though being fit for marriage (for he is "sweet" and a "joy"); of these two grievances, the second is of more concern to the poet. Familiar as he was with ancient philosophy, Shakespeare must needs connect these two traits, as being both indicative of disharmony ("war")—and of the same disharmony: for are music and love not one? The sonnet is conceived as a pleading admonition to the youth that he should not counteract the laws of harmony; the poem is itself a "sweet chiding," achieved by the formulation of the dialectic oppositions underlying the young man's disharmonious attitude (such oppositions being characteristic of the sonnet). The art of the poet consists in limiting his remarks, until the last line, to the youth's reluctant attitude toward *music*—while so adroitly choosing his terms from the ancient metaphorical sphere of love and marriage ("why lovest thou"; "by unions married"; "sweet husband"; "resembling sire and child and happy mother"), that the reproach of remaining unmarried ("singleness"; "single") becomes evident long before it is outspokenly framed. According to the poet it is music itself, that "concord of well tuned sounds," which chides the youth, first "sweetly," by its nature, as a model of perfection must challenge the imperfect (thou "who confounds in singleness the parts"), then, outspokenly and harshly, by the message it speaks in the last line: this is the dagger plucked from the velvety sheath of music, to give the vital wound. This stroke of annulment (the last word of the poem is "none") has been intellectually prepared by the musical simile, with its philosophical implications; music is union, a family of sounds: "each in each," "all in one," "many seeming one," and a single note is no music, a single man, no man. The protest against disharmony, which had been latent during the whole poem ("war," "annoy," "offend," "confounds"), though overlaid by the sweetness of musicality and order, comes out finally in the open, as a threat of destruction against the being without music, whom the poet so musically loved.

In the poet's plea for wedlock, I cannot see, as Gundolf does, the "inbrünstige Verlangen . . . , der sinnliche Widerstand gegen das Schwinden der im Augenblick ewig gefühlten und ewig begehrten Schönheit"; for, if the poet were moved by the egoistic desire to prolong the beauty of his friend for his own sake, he would surely not urge him to found a family, nor allude to the happy mother and child. Rather, I find here the dialectical play underlying any love: love asks for perfection in the beloved; the beloved who is self-sufficient in his beauty and refuses to yield to the universal laws of reproduction, is imperfect, undeserving of the love of the Platonistic poet, and inviting the annihilating judgment which must wound the poet's own heart. The sweet music of his profession of love is finally shattered by the intellectual condemnation of "disharmony" which he must pronounce.

If we turn now to Milton we will see that the linguistic tradition is still unbroken in this militant Protestant;[15] in *On the Morning of Christ's Nativity* (IX–XIV), the ancient idea of world harmony is "harmonized" with Christ's birth, and in a manner not essentially different from that characteristic of the Middle Ages—except,

perhaps, acoustically: the colossal world-organ voice of Milton
resounds in ninefold harmony:

> When such musick sweet / Their [the shepherds'] hearts and ears did
> greet, / As never was by mortal finger strook, / Divinely-warbled voice /
> Answering the stringed noise,[16] / As all their souls in blissful rapture took . . . /
> She [Nature] knew such *harmony* alone / Could hold all Heav'n and Earth in
> happier *union.* . . . / Ring out, ye crystal spheres, / Once bless our human
> ears, / (If ye have power to touch our senses so) / And let your silver *chime* /
> Move in *melodious* time; / And let the Bass of Heav'ns deep *Organ* blow,[17] /
> And with your ninefold *harmony* / Make up full *consort* to th' Angelick
> symphony [*consort* = *consonantia*].

The poem *At a Solemn Music* is a true Christian hymn with Jewish
and Platonic accents; its music is "solemn" because it has the
primordial and primeval aim of all Christian music: religious
elation; the poem itself is simply a translation into words of this
music celebrating the music of the world:

> Blest pair of Sirens, pledges of heav'n's joy,
> Sphere-born harmonious sisters, Voice and Verse,
> Wed your divine sounds, and mix'd pow'r employ
> Dead things with inbreath'd sense able to pierce;
> And to our high-rais'd phantasy present
> That undisturbed song of pure concent,
> Aye sung before the sapphire-colour'd throne
> To him that sits thereon
>
> With saintly shout, and solemn jubilee,
> Where the bright Seraphim in burning row
> Their loud up-lifted angel trumpets blow,
> And the cherubic host in thousand quires
> Touch their immortal harps of golden wires,
> With those just Spirits that wear victorious palms,
> Hymns devout and holy psalms
> Singing everlastingly:
>
> That we on earth with undiscording voice
> May rightly answer that melodious noise;
> As once we did, til disproportion'd sin
> Jarr'd against nature's chime, and with harsh din

Broke the fair music that all creatures made
To their great Lord, whose love their motion sway'd
In perfect diapason, whilst they stood
In first obedience and their state of good.
O may we soon again renew that song,
And keep in tune with Heav'n, till God ere long
To his celestial consort us unite,
To live with him, and sing in endless morn of light!

The poem opens with a proemium invoking the blessing of "solemn music" (poetry and music combined), which, coming to us from above, may lift our hearts toward heaven; in the second stanza, with heart and gaze uplifted, we drink in the beauty of the heavenly court resounding with the songs of the cherubim, the seraphim and the souls of the just; in the third, it is our own response to that music which is invoked, the response which once, in time, we gave, ere lost through sin; the final stanza looks forward to that eternal reunion with God—which once again, in time, we shall know.

If we now consult the variant material given by one of the commentaries we see that, with the exception of the last line, which was written seven times without involving any ideological change, the hesitations in phrasing occur mostly when it is a question of words or concepts traditional with the world harmony complex.   Three passages were finally omitted:

(after line 4) And whilst your equal raptures, temper'd sweet,
                In high mysterious spousal meet,
                Snatch us from earth a while . . .

(after line 16) While all the starry rounds and arches blue
                Resound and echo Hallelu

(after line 18) By leaving out those harsh ill-sounding [later var.: chromatic] jars
                Of clamorous sin that all music mars

In the first, the "mysterious spousal" of Voice and Verse, descended from the *saints accords* of French Renaissance poets, would detract the attention from the main problem; " . . . a while" would emphasize the temporal aspect, which, in the final phrasing, would come in only later. In the second, "Hallelu" is an Old Testament expression which would be in place only in stanza two; "starry rounds" would hardly be appropriate as a beginning of the third stanza, which turns from heavenly music to that on earth; "blue" was already contained in "sapphire-colour'd." In the last, "chromatic" is too learnedly Greek, alluding as it does to an ancient theory no longer valid in Milton's time; "clamorous" would really mar the solemn music of the poem, without suggesting the norm itself, while "disproportion'd" reminds us of the proportion (of "nature's chime"). Finally, instead of line 11 ("Their loud uplifted angel-trumpets blow"), Milton had put earlier: "Loud *symphony* of silver trumpets blow," where *symphony* would be too Grecian in a "Hebrew" stanza. One sees how traditional was Milton's vocabulary for world harmony: even in the rejected lines we find "temper'd sweet," and "resound and echo" (*resultare*— συνηχεῖν); he worked within the given by choosing the "locally" more fitting words. His imagination is guided by a doctrine with its own fixed expressions. His poem, a poem of immortal beauty, is "beautiful within a tradition" as is all great poetry, and is an epitome of this tradition; it welds together the voices of all the civilizations (Greco-Roman, Jewish, medieval Christian) whose religious cult involved music and which are component parts of our civilization. It constitutes in itself, to use the terminology of Novalis, a "Christian or European" cultural feat.[18]

Of both Shakespeare and Milton it is undeniably true that their texts are tinged with a new, a Renaissance richness and enthusiasm, due to the humanistic revival of ancient traditions; nonetheless we must insist on the lexicological stability of the terms since the Middle Ages; but they are still links in the great chain. We are lifted, as is done by sublime music, from the oppression of time into timelessness, from the burden of sin toward communion with God; and our battle with time (once we lost paradise, once again we shall regain it) results in everlasting triumph. What, in the beginning, is a conscious effort on our part (hence the imperatives: "wed," "present") is achieved, in the end, as a supernatural reality ("to live with God"). In Warton's commentary we find the remark: "Plato's abstracted spherical harmony is ingrafted into the

Song in the Revelations" (5: 11: "Et vidi, et audivi, vocem angelorum multorum in circuitu throni . . . / Et erat numerus eorum millia millium / Dicentium voce magna . . . "); I should rather formulate: "the ancient spherical harmony is ingrafted into the Christian history of man: paradise, sin, and hope for redemption." There is an Ambrosian hymn of world harmony ("the fair music that all creatures made") offering up the responses of mankind to the angelic song, coupled with an Augustinian history of mankind: though the Pythagorean world music is now inaccessible to human ears, it had been so once and may again be so for the Christian. The distribution of tenses in the poem (presents in the first, perfects in the second, futures in the last two stanzas) corresponds to the rhythm of Christian thought. It is no accident that the syntactical division shows one long sentence, coming to a close at the third stanza (in the first two stanzas the "divine sounds" and the human "high-rais'd phantasy" are made to meet above the earth, while the third stanza suggests a "respond" of man to primeval goodness), and that the metrical division, somewhat parallel, shows the scheme a-b-b-a when we are in suspense before the vision of God in His heaven, but rhymed couplets from the moment that the human voices answer with their undiscordant "respond." Nor is it an accident that the ancient reminiscences occur mainly in the first stanza (the "sirens" of Plato—though two, not seven; "mix'd pow'r" = temperatio; "inbreath'd sense" = animization of the universe by sympathy; "pure concent" = concentus), the Jewish (Old Testament) allusions mainly in the second ("jubilee," "Seraphim," "cherubic," "psalms"), the medieval Christian concepts ("undiscording," "disproportion'd," "nature's chime," "love their motion sway'd," "perfect diapason," "keep in tune," "celestial consort") in the last part: first there is presented world harmony, in its Greek form; then the Jewish monotheistic God appears; and the poem closes with a picture of the Christian life of the soul, in the well-known musicological terms of Boethius. The Christian God, as a simple reality, appears only at the end: He is first mentioned allusively (line 8) "to him that sits thereon," then as "their great Lord," and finally, in the simplest and most touching part of the poem, as "God." There is also evident a circular movement: a return to the beginning, to the harmony whence music comes ("heav'n's joy," "sphereborn," "divine sounds," "Heav'n," "celestial consort," "sing in endless morn of light"). Colors are blended with tones from beginning to end: "sapphire-colour'd throne," "the bright Seraphim in burning row," "harps of golden wires," "in endless morn of light," with an infinite prolongation of light beyond the end of this poem which is devoted to the paradise regained of world music.[19]

CHAPTER V

One of the trumpets asked Bodanzky in despair: "I'd just like to know what's beautiful about blowing away at a trumpet stopped up at high C!" This gave me an insight at once into the lot of man, who likewise cannot understand why he must endure being stopped to the piercing agony of his own existence, cannot see what it is for, and how his screech is to be attuned to the great harmony of the universal symphony of all creation. Bodanzky answered the unhappy man very logically: "Wait a bit! You can't expect to understand it yet. . . . When all the rest come in, you'll soon see what you're there for!"—Letter of Gustav Mahler.

IN THE PRECEDING chapters we have had occasion several times to use the modern word "concert" in order to render *symphonia, concentus,* etc. What of the history of this modern word itself? Has it to do with world harmony?

The Latin verb *concertare,* "to fight with someone," "to emulate" contains, as we have seen, the two elements ἔρις and φιλία; it translates such Greek words as συναγωνίζομαι, προσφιλονεικεῖν, συναθλεῖν, συνερείδεσις (even a loom, as we see from a poem of the Greek anthology, can be called συνέριθος "co-operative," for it vies with the spinning woman), which likewise express that "agreement in disagreement," that "harmony within strife" of *concertare.* An application of this concept to cosmic order is found with the Latin verb in Hydatius Lemicus: "In sole signum in ortu quasi altero secum *concertante* monstratur" and in Martianus Capella (ThLL): "Saturnus nimia cum mundo celeritate *concertans.*" Again, the idea of *militia Christi,* developed by the Fathers (Tertullian, etc.), soon led to a *concertare,* "to be a *commilito,* a fellow soldier in the continuous warfare against evil and disbelief incumbent upon the Christian"; the Itala has one passage "quae in evangelio collaboraverunt vel concertaverunt mihi vel mecum"—an expansion, in Ciceronian style, of the single Greek verb συνήθλησάν μοι (the Vulgate has simply *mecum laboraverunt*, cf. ThLL); another: "*concertantes* cum fide evangelii" (Gr συναθλοῦντες; Vulgate, *collaborantes*). The idea of militant collaboration expressed by the verb is also found in such examples as (in a sermon: ThLL): "si vero *festinans concertetur* unusquisque in omni virtute animae vel corporis"; Augustine: "*concertatores* tuos et in huius vitae stadio [*stadium* suggesting the ἀγών of the Christian] *tecum laborantes atque currentes* [= "commilitones]"; Cassiodorus: "*unanimes atque concertatores* nobiscum contra eorum estote praesumptionem." In a scholion on Virgil we find the transfer to friendly "rivalry in singing": "pignus futurae *concertationis*" (*Schol. Verg. Sermon. ecl.* 3, 37, cf. ThLL), which means that the idea of the "musical concert" was already latent as early as the fifth–sixth centuries (the simple *certare* itself had already had the musical connotation, since it rendered the idea of an ἀγών; Cicero: "antequam legitimum certamen inchoent [citharoedi]." (Schiller sensed the analogy between the athletic and the musical when, in one of his famous ballads, he wrote "Zum *Streit* der Wagen und Gesänge"; the ancient ἀγών or *certamen*, athletics in the service of world music.) And finally we may remember the *certare* in the Ambrosian passage mentioned above: "ut *cum* undarum leniter alludentium *sono certent cantus psallentium*,"[1] where the chants of the devout vie with the music of the elements. Thus we may assume that the idea of world harmony, to which one must strive to adjust oneself, is ever present in the word family (*con)certare*.

A slightly different meaning is to be found in one example from the fifth/sixth-century Latin translation of the *Hippocratic Prognosticon* (ed. Kühlewein. *Hermes*, XXV, 123), where the deponent *certor* could be translated, "to cope with": "[some patients die] priusquam medicus arte ad unumquemque morbum *concertetur*" (this text is mentioned by F. Arnaldi in his medieval Italian glossary, *Bull. Ducange*, X, 122), the doctor fights the disease in order to control it, to "come to terms with it." It is this meaning which must have led in Italian and Spanish to "to come to an agreement," "to devise, contrive something"; Boccaccio, *Teseida*, 7, 95: "Ed i fatti futuri tutti quanti / Del giorno *tra di loro concertaro*"; *Calila e Dimna*, R. 51, 542 (thirteenth century): "E todos los ximios concertaron que era buen consejo"; *Siete Partidas*, 3, 19, 12 (2, 642): "... concertándola [la carta] con el registro" (= "compare for verification": somewhat akin to LL *contropare*, "compare" > Fr *controuver*, Eng *contrive*).[2] This Sp *concertar*, "to devise something (together)," came to have many specific technical applications: In the language of hunting, it referred to the tracking down of an animal by concerted efforts of the hunters ("... tenían una garza *concertada*": *Crónica de Alvaro de Luna*, 11, 35; fifteenth century); again we find it in the language of business in the meaning "to arrange a contract." One special application of the meaning "to devise, contrive" (and which was not extant in Latin) was "to arrange a musical performance"; A. Caro (first half of the sixteenth century), has the sentence (Tomm.-Bell.): "Fileta *concertò una musica* di sampogna"[3] (though still in Lope's *Peribáñez* [1614], Act II, we may find *concertar* not yet restricted to a musical reference; Bartolo: "Cantar algo se concierta"—Chaparro: "*Y aun contar algo* por Dios"). The It *concertare una musica*, "to contrive a piece of music," must have led inevitably to a **concerto di musica*, which, though unattested in older Italian, is probably reflected in the entry of Cotgrave's French and English Dictionary (1611): *concert de musique*, "consort of musicke" (where *consort* is no erroneous representation of *concert*, as the OED would have it, but the organic development, or reborrowing, of a Lat *consortium* which we have seen coupled with *concordium* and other synonyms of harmony in Augustine). It is the It *concerto di musica*, which, though by chance unattested before the seventeenth century, must have led to the use of *concerto* alone, which, itself, is listed for the first time in Florio's dictionary (1598). The fact that this *concerto* is only to be found in a cross reference to *concento* might lead us to believe that it is the general, not specifically musical concept of world harmony which is alone involved; on the other hand it is quite possible that Florio may have listed a technical (musicological) term, a **concerto di musica* (echoed by Cotgrave), derived from *concertare una musica*, "to contrive a musical composition." And indeed there is a possibility of a second argument in favor of a technical interpretation: Florio may be echoing Luigi di Viadana's use (the first in modern musical history) of *concerti ecclesiastici* in reference to musical compositions: though these were not published before 1602, they were performed five or six years earlier (i.e., a year or so before Florio's dictionary). In either case we would have to do with the original idea of *concertare*, "to strive harmoniously together (by making music)."

So much for Florio (who may have been influenced by Viadana): what of Viadana himself? His term was indisputably technical; on what did he base himself? Again, it may be said that, just as Florio *may* have been influenced by a *concerto di musica (and not by Viadana directly), so Viadana *may* have been influenced by the same. But let us leave behind this unattested expression, and see what *is* attested for *concertare*, before Viadana's time, which would explain this use—the first unquestionably technical use we have.

In order to establish the pre-Viadana usage in connection with our word, I propose to consult Renaissance texts of Spanish, not Italian, since none of the latter, besides those previously mentioned, are available to me. One is safe, however, in using contemporary (or even later) Spanish texts in support of an hypothesis concerning Italian usage, since Spain, in its literature and its art, was slower than Italy (or France) to dissolve its ties with the Middle Ages. Though the Renaissance was fully known and appreciated in Spain, it did not bring about a complete abandonment of medieval other-worldliness; rather, this was fused with the new attitude toward the world, to form a third entity which scholars of art and literature have agreed to call the "Spanish baroque" (of the seventeenth century). Thus, though the term "concert" had reached its new meaning in Italy[4] by the beginning of the seventeenth century with Viadana, it will be possible to show, by Spanish texts which extend to the end of that century, why such a shift was imminent. The extraordinary procedure of consulting the texts of one country for the vocabulary of another may be justified on the grounds that (as I believe) what exists in Spain in the seventeenth century, must have existed in the sixteenth in Italy.

We may begin by considering a passage previous to the sixteenth

century (fifteenth century: *Cancionero de Baena*, ed. 1851, p. 107),
which will help us to connect the term *desconcierto* with the Provençal use of *descort* referred to above: the poet Villasandino
expresses his criticism of a fellow poet for his "syllabas menguadas,
laydas y *desconcertadas*," declaring himself to be "disconcerted,"
i.e., out of tune, in disharmonious mood: "Quien eres, non *me
concierto* ["I cannot agree with myself, decide . . . "] / . . . Bestia
pecora en dissyerto, / Tus palabras avyltadas / Fazen las mias
erradas / Tanto que *me desconcierto*." Here, *desconcertar* is clearly
a variant of the *destemprar—descordar* family, used both of metrics
and of psychological states ("temper"),[5] which we have met with in
the poetry of the Provençal troubadours.[6]

   Again, we find a reference to the *concierto*, to the order, peace,
and harmony of the starry night sky (in the tradition of the *Somnium
Scipionis* and of Augustine) with Luis de León (1591), who has
absorbed the Pythagorean harmony of the spheres, revived by
humanism, and fused it with Christian mysticism. In his "Noche
serena" we find *concierto* associated with *proporción, concordia,
armonía, paz, templar*:

> Cuando contemplo el cielo / De innumerables luces adornado, . . . // Quien
> mira el gran *concierto* / De aquestos resplandores eternales, / Su movimiento
> *cierto*, / Sus pasos desiguales [= *consors discordia*], / Y en *proporcion concorde*
> tan iguales: . . . // Y cómo otro camino / Prosigue el sanguinoso Marte
> ayrado / . . . el Júpiter benino / De bienes mil cercado / Serena [= *temperat*]
> el cielo con su rayo amado: // Rodéase en la cumbre / Saturno, padre de
> los siglos de oro, / Tras él la muchedumbre / Del *reluciente coro* [of the
> spheres] / Su luz va repartiendo y su tesoro: / ¿Quién es el que esto mira / Y
> precia la bajeza de la tierra . . . ? // Aquí vive el contento, /Aquí reyna la paz
> . . . [the last sentence is reminiscent of the cadenza of Du Bellay's Platonistic
> sonnet on the "idea"].

We could vary the words of the poet, applying them to his own poem:
"Who could contemplate . . . the peaceful vision seen by this mystic,
whose eyes are calmly fixed on the tranquil sky, and not desire to
shun the turmoil of earthly life in order to immerse himself within
this vision?" Never has nostalgia for the Beyond assumed so
dispassionate, so classic a form. In his ode to the musician
Salinas (stanzas 2–6), the harmony of the skies is no longer an
object of nostalgia; this harmony has been realized in the harmony

of soul of the musician, while the harmony of the spheres is blended with the music of the Golden Age (that blest stage of mankind before Original Sin)—a music sounding clear through the ages to the ear of the primitivistic poet:

[Salinas] a cuyo son divino / el alma que en olvido está sumida, / torna a cobrar el tino, y memoria perdida / de su origen esclarecida. . . . // Traspasa el ayre todo / hasta llegar a la más alta esfera / y oye allí otro modo / de no perecedera / Música, que es la fuente y la primera. // Ve cómo el gran maestro / a aquesta inmensa cítara aplicado, / con movimiento diestro / produce el son sagrado, / con que este eterno templo es sustentado. // Y como está compuesta / de números concordes, luego envía / *consonante* respuesta, / y entre ambas a porfía / se mezcla una dulcísima armonía.

It is precisely this last stanza, with its note of grandeur, which, according to modern criticism (cf. Vossler, *Poesie der Einsamkeit in Spanien*, 172–3), would seem to be of dubious attribution; but if this is not authentic Luis de León, it is, at least, in the authentic spirit of the *musicum carmen*, the *numeri*, and the world lute of God the musician. Here, it must be noticed, it is not *concierto* but *armonía* which is used of the heavenly concert; but one of the ideas underlying any concert, the amicable rivalry of the performers— their *concors discordia*—is implied by *porfía*. In his "Ode on Christ's Ascension," the word *concertó*, "order, moderation," appears in reference to Christ appeasing the elements: "¿Aqueste mar turbado / quién le pondrá ya freno ? ¿quién *concertó* / al viento fiero, ayrado ?" (stanza 4).

The *concierto* and peace of the starry skies invades the heart of man, who contemplates it. This *concierto* is also represented by the untranslatable Spanish term *sosiego*, which includes bodily and mental rest, the subsiding of pain and the philosophical poise that follows. It is remarkable how the prose of the following passage (from Luis de León's treatise *Los nombres de Cristo*, chapter "Príncipe de la Paz," opening paragraph), with its wide-sweeping waves closing in upon us slowly, succeeds in lulling the reader ("como adormeciendose") until his heart becomes a quiet mirror of the quiet skies; the identity of these "two peaces" is underlined by the binomial phrases *concierto y orden, subjección y concierto*, and by the recurrence of *sosiego*:

Que si la paz es, como sant Augustín ... concluye, una orden sosiegada [= *ordinata temperatura partium*] o un ténero sossiego y firmeza en lo que pide el buen orden, esso es lo que nos descubre agora esta imagen [of the starry night sky]. Adonde el exército de las estrellas, puesto como en ordenança y como *concertado* por sus hileras, luze hermosísimo, y adonde cada una dellas inviolablement guarda su puesto ... antes, como hermanadas todas, ... todas juntas, *templan* a veces sus rayos y sus virtudes, reduciéndolas a una pacífica unidad de virtud, de partes y aspectos differentes compuesta, universal y poderosa de toda manera ... (§3): si estamos attentos a lo secreto que en nosotros passa, veremos que este *concierto y orden de las estrellas,* mirándolo, pone en nuestras almas sossiego, y veremos que con sólo tener los ojos enclavados en él con atención, sin sentir en qué manera, los desseos nuestros y las afecciones turbadas, que confusamente movían ruydo en nuestros pechos de día, se van quietando poco a poco, y como adormeciéndose, se reposan, tomando cada uno su assiento, y reduciéndose en su lugar propio [*delectatio = pondus,* which brings everything to its "natural" locus], se ponen sin sentir en *subjeccion y concierto.* Y veremos que ... la razón se levanta y recobra su derecho y su fuerça y ... se recuerda de su primer origen. ...

Surely the pious Platonist has succeeded in his purpose as outlined in the Prologue of *Los nombres de Cristo*: to depict the harmony of the world ("el pío de las cosas").

The transition to the musical concert is imminent in a passage of Luis de León's commentary on Job (quoted, in reference to our passage, in *Clásicos Castellanos,* XXXIII, ed. Onís): " ... se dice de Dios que da *cantares en la noche* [Job 35:10] porque siembra entonces el cielo con las estrellas, las cuales con su claridad, hermosura y muchedumbre, convidan a los hombres a que alaben a Dios. ... y llama *música de cielos,* a las noches puras, porque con el callar en ellas los bullicios del dia y con la pausa que entonces todas las cosas hacen, se echa claramente de ver y en una cierta manera se oye su *concierto y armonía* admirable, y no sé en qué modo suena en lo secreto del corazón su *concierto,* que le compone y sosiega." Heavenly music is not connected here with the harmony of the spheres or with choirs of the angels; it is a mysterious emanation from the ordered sky itself; the classical, Latin mysticism of this poetry rests on the basis of clarity: the emotion never verges on passion. The underlying idea is the same as that expressed in the *Símbolo de la Fé* of Luis de Granada:—"En el día reparte Dios sus misericordias y en la noche pide sus loores." The mysterious emanation comes about by the extension of visual perception to the other senses (a synesthesia)—*"se echa* claramente *de ver* y en una cierta manera *se oye"*—and to the soul: "y no sé en qué modo suena *en el secreto del corazón."* The passage of Luis de León has the technique of synesthesia of Ambrose plus the unification and inwardness of Augustine; in this classic Spanish mystic of the sixteenth century, Ambrose, Augustine, and the new humanism with its regained sense of world-wideness, converge. And, in the quiet contemplation of the "night music of the sky" we may even hear an echo of the Pythagorean truth that, though "sounds are produced by moving bodies, and their pitch is in proportion to the velocity of these bodies," nonetheless "a sound may be heard only against a background of silence" (*Anonymous Pythagoreans*, p. 35, quoted by Gomperz, p. 173). With the Renaissance, the cosmos has been widened and the landscape of humanity broadened, but the infinite roof of the sky that encompasses the *gran teatro del mundo* has not lost its connection with the microcosmic soul of man: the greater sky is still but an image of the greatness of the human heart possessed of God. The greater the expanse of the world scene has become, the better the creative pause in the stillness of the night can be sensed. Again, in the *Guía de pecadores* of Fray Luis we find an allusion to the music of the night that awakens the soul: "pues con el dulce y blando ruido de la noche sosegada, con la dulce música y harmonía de las criaturas, arróllase dentro de sí el anima, e comienza a dormir aquel sueño velador . . . " Here, Mme M. R. Lida (*RFH*, V, 394) would point out that the Platonistic theology of Fray Luis required the cosmological proof of God's existence and suggested to him an "anthology" drawn from the Book of Nature, which is God's creation.

If now we read the much later text (1651–57) of Gracián's *Criticón* (ed. Romera-Navarro, I, 124: *Crisi* II), we recognize the atmosphere of didacticism of the *Somnium Scipionis*: the *concierto =armonía* is the principle of the skies, of nature, and of man, but the musical silence of Luis de León is missing, instead there is playful baroque "conceptismo" (*artesonada bóbeda . . . florón y estrella*):

Porque ya que el soberano Artífice hermoseó tanto esta artesonada bóbeda del mundo con tanto florón y estrella, ¿por qué no las *dispuso . . . con orden y concierto* . . . ? . . . advierte que la divina Sabiduría que las formó y las repartió desta suerte atendió a otra más importante *correspondencia*, qual lo es la de sus movimientos y aquel *templarse* las influencias. Porque has de saber que no ay astro alguno en el cielo que no tenga su diferente propiedad, assí como las yervas y las plantas de la tierra: unas de las estrellas causan el calor, otras el frío, unas secan, otras humedecen, y desta suerte alternan otras muchas influencias, y con essa essencial *correspondencia* unas a otras *se corrigen y se templan*. . . . De este modo, se nos haze cada noche nueva el cielo y nunca enfada el mirarlo, cada uno *proporciona* [= "dispone con proporción o correspondencia"] las estrellas como quiere.

And similarly I, 137 (*Crisi*: III):

(Andrenio:) . . . me estava contemplando esta armonía tan *plausible* de todo el universo, *compuesta* de una tan estraña contrariedad que, según es grande, no parece avía de poder mantenerse el mundo un solo día. Esto me tenía suspenso, porque ¿a quién no pasma ver un *concierto* tan estraño, *compuesto de oposiciones?* (Critilo:) . . . que todo este universo se compone de contrarios y *se concierta de desconciertos*: uno contra otro, exclama el filósofo. No ay cosa que no tenga su contrario con quien pelee, ya con vitoria, ya con rendimiento; todo es hazer y padecer; si ay acción, hay repasión [the philosopher can be Seneca: "Tota huius mundi concordia ex discordibus constat," as the editor suggests, but as well any of the Greek philosophers quoted above].

Finally in the anonymous *Epistula moral a Fabio*, there is a fusion of order (*concierto*) and measure (*templanza*) with the Horatian ideal of the *aurea mediocritas*: "Una *mediana* vida yo posea, / Un estilo común y moderado, / Que no le note nadie que lo vea . . . / Sin la *templanza* ¿viste tu perfecta / Alguna cosa ? . . . Así, Fabio, me muestra descubierta / Su essencia la verdad, y mi albedrío / Con ella se *compone y se concierta*." As Luis de León had said, *compone y sosiega*.

I should like to point out here how this ensemble of quiet and starry night sky, of the idea of order and love and of music (the Pythagorean night concert, so to speak), represents also a current motif in Spanish dramatic,[7] lyric,[8] and novelistic art of the Golden Age. In the *Don Quixote*, the connection of night sky, music, quiet, and order is apparent, as has been pointed out in the excellent article of J. Casalduero, *Rev. de fil. hispánica*, II, 329: after one of his "victories" the hero speaks of the Golden Age with melancholy. It is not that Cervantes insists expressly on the religious character of world harmony in itself; such values are concealed, withheld, from the reader; rather, it is the loss of the Golden Age[9] of Horace and Ovid which his Quixote laments; the comments of Casalduero at this point, as he describes the scene, fit admirably into our theme: "... empieza a sonar, en la oscuridad primeriza de la noche, con el núcleo ardiente de los cabreros, la música de un rabel. El resplendor de la victoria, la serenidad del diálogo, el cielo dilatado y luminosamente oscuro, el silencio de la noche, el crepitar del fuego, la sencillez de los cabreros, la naturaleza elemental de Sancho, la frugalidad de la cena..., el discurso sereno, melancólico y con lejanas perspectivas nostálgicas, crean el ambiente al mundo idealizado." In Chapter 43 (the tavern of Palomeque), there appears an ensemble of love, moonlight, and music, of which Casalduero writes (p. 334): "La venta rodeada de noche y de luna, tanta belleza junta, una canción, una historia de amor"; in this *tanta belleza junta* of Cervantes there is, however faint, a remembrance of the world harmony.

In this detour of the historical development of the idea of the "concert of the stars" it has surely become evident that this idea was but a consequence of the topos of world harmony. And underlying this cosmic "concert" are the associations of order, *consensus*, harmony, peace, "numbers," the reflection of world harmony, of its Institutor and Ruler, and of love inspiring His praise: "Brudersphären-Wettgesang," in the words of Goethe. And now only may we fully understand the spiritual connotations of the term *concerto* which Viadana chose in his expression *concerti ecclesiastici* (or *di chiesa*) for polyphonic (vocal and instrumental, i.e., organ) compositions. These compositions reflected world harmony; his *concerto* was a *concento*. To recapitulate: perhaps a **concerto di musica* (like the *concert de musique*,[10] *consort of musicke* of Cotgrave) was already at hand in the meaning, "an arrangement of music," but this more rational expression benefited by the emotion evoked by the world concert.[11]

Viadana, in the preface of his *Cento concerti ecclesiastici* tells us that when one, two, or even three singers wished to sing with the organ, they were sometimes forced by the lack of suitable compositions to take one, two, or three parts from motets in five, six, seven, or even eight parts, and that he has, therefore, composed his concerts in order to make such mutilation unnecessary. Musicologists such as Grove consider that it is not the *basso continuo* itself, but an application of it that he has, and claims to have, invented: that he built up his compositions from the bass instead of from a *cantus firmus*, and succeeded in creating self-contained melodies, that, in a word, he created more according to the melodic than to the contrapuntal principle. "The wording of his title, 'A New invention, suitable for all kinds of Singers, and for Organists' alone makes it clear that the novelty of the invention resided, not in the continued bass only, but in the character of the vocal compositions as well." The *bassus continuus* or *bassus generalis*, whether it was invented by Viadana or not, is characterized by a supra-individual treatment of the voices, concerned as it is with all the parts together; there is no break in the bass from the beginning of a piece to the end, and whenever rests occur in the bass, whichever, at the moment, happens to be the lowest sounding part (tenor, alto, treble), is incorporated in it. It is this interweaving of the voices, possible only by a close collaboration, a "loving and vying fusion" of the singers, suggesting as it does all the religious connotations of world harmony, which must have prompted the name *concerto*,[12] as well as the synonym *concento* given by Florio (see above) and by Praetorius. This was the same Praetorius who, in admiration of Viadana's invention, wrote, in 1619 (the year in which Kepler's *De Harmonice mundi* appeared): "Cantio, Concentus, seu Symphonia est diversarum vocum modulatio, Italis vocatur *Concetto* vel *Concerto*. . . . Usurpatur autem hoc Vocabulum *Concert* 1. in genere, quo [*read*: pro] quavis Cantione Harmonicae" (quoted by Schulz-Basler, *Deutsches Fremdwörterbuch* s.v. *Konzert*; but here the meaning is not only [unilinearly] that of "Wettstreit der Stimmen," but also of "peace, agreement, etc."). The religious connotation of the word appears still in the *concerts spirituels* (about which Rousseau, in his *Dictionnaire de musique*, made a slighting remark), those concerts given in Paris at the Tuileries during the period of fasting when all other public performances were forbidden. Here, obviously, we have a French derivation from Viadana's *concerti ecclesiastici*.[13]

But the musicological conception of the "concert" was secularized in the eighteenth century:[14] it was not yet (as it is today) the performance of a virtuoso accompanied by an orchestra, but was indistinguishable from the *sinfonia* (which, in turn, had become an orchestral part before and after a sung part)—a fact which is clear from the *concerti grossi* of Handel, for example. Rousseau, in the *Encyclopédie* (1751), uses *concert* for any musical composition in which there is a concurrence of different instruments, including the human voice; cf. s.v. *harmonie*: "[the Greeks] donnoient . . . le nom d'harmonie . . . aux *concerts de voix et d'instrumens* qui s'exécutoient à l'octave . . . " Again, s.v. *symphonie*, he says of this word: ". . . signifie dans la musique ancienne, cette *union de voix ou de sons* qui forme un concert . . . Ainsi leur symphonie . . . résultoit du *concours de plusieurs voix ou instrumens* . . . ; ou tout concertoit [=agreed, performed harmoniously] à l'unisson . . . : ou la moitié des parties étoit à l'octave . . . de l'autre . . . "

The Italian form *concerto* (used by Desbrosses in 1713, and still found in Voltaire's *Candide*), which means either the same as the It *sinfonia* ("où tout se joue en rippieno") or else an orchestral piece with one soloist (our notion of the musicological term "concert")—this, Desbrosses distinguishes from the French form *concert*, used for an orchestra with at least seven or eight performers. I infer from all this that the original genuine meaning of Fr *concert* must have been that of a "concerted effort by musicians,"[15] and only later was specialized under Italian influence to the meanings "orchestral work" and "solo performance with orchestral accompaniment"—the technical meaning of today for Fr *concert*, and It and Eng *concerto*.[16] In loose usage, however, Fr and Eng *concert*, and It *concerto*, can be used for any musical performance.

When, today, we attend a "concert," whether symphonic or otherwise,[17] and listen to the wide variety of music offered, in comfortable and worldly surroundings to a fashionably dressed audience, it may be difficult to remember the religious origin of this genre, a genre intended to reflect a performance of music not made by human hands. The original concert was no performance on a narrow stage, to be witnessed by an audience of neutral observers. It was a song in praise of God, uttered by nightly-ordered nature, and by the human community serving as echo.

Today the expression "concert of the stars"[18] gives an impression contrary to the original impact of our word: it seems to represent a metaphor taken from the concert-hall and applied to the starry night,[19] whereas, originally, it was the night itself that gave the concert in praise of God. The monogram of Christ in the starry night has disappeared.[20]

As we have said, Viadana's *concerti ecclesiastici* are of 1602. It will be remembered that the first modern grand opera, the *Euridice*, of Rinuccini, Peri, and Caccini, was performed in Paris in 1600. Both the modern "concert" and the modern "opera" are creations of the Baroque Age, whose particular cosmic feeling is reflected in these two parallel expressions of world harmony. As for the history of the opera, the article in Grove's *Dictionary* is highly informative, though it should be completed by the essay of Vossler, "Die Antike und die Bühnendichtung der Romanen" in *Vorträge der Bibliothek Warburg*, VII; whereas Grove emphasizes only the revival of the Greek drama (which was indeed a *Musikdrama* or "opera") in the sixteenth-century *opera (favola) in musica, dramma per la musica*, or *commedia armonica* of the Italians, Vossler, while not denying some Greek influence on the *recitativo*, stresses the renovation, in the melodrama or opera, of the medieval drama (which was also, and necessarily, a *Musikdrama*, given the medieval conception of *musica mundana*) and, more especially, of the Italian mystery (*sacra rappresentazione* or *lauda*), which came to be fused with ancient pastoral poetry, as revived by the humanists at the court of the Medici in the fifteenth century. The *Favola di Orfeo* (1471) of Poliziano (whose poetry was to be continued by Tasso and Guarino) leads to the *Euridice* of 1600, to Gluck's *Orpheus*, to Mozart's *Magic Flute*, to Beethoven's *Fidelio* and, finally, to Metastasio. Vossler defines the melodrama and the opera of the baroque and rococo periods both as "ein ins Sinnliche, Heidnische und Arkadische umgekleidetes Mirakelspiel" and as a "spiritualistisch ausgehöhlte, christlich durchsüsste und überzierte antike Tragödie."

What I would point out particularly in this connection is the fact that, in the opera, we have to do with a theatrical and musical genre essentially devoted to the glorification of *music*—indeed, the self-glorification of music—on the stage of the theater: Witness the numerous treatments of the Orpheus theme in the earliest operas (to those mentioned above may be added the *Orfeo*'s of Monteverdi [1607] and of Rossi, the latter performed at Paris in 1647—at the very time when Cardinal Mazarin was taking steps to establish the Italian opera in Paris: it is no chance that *opéra* is first attested in French in 1646). In other words, the Greek musician-god was brought back to life to prove in person on the stage the magic power of music, which, when put to the service of love, can master nature and conquer hell (in the modern "optimistic" versions, nothing is said of the tragic end of Orpheus at the hands of the maenads).[21]   In Rinuccini's *Euridice*, the chorus formulates the main problem of the opera in the following words (lines 735-42):

> Vidi a' tuoi dolci accenti
> E 'l corso rallentar fiumi e torrenti
> E per udir vicini
> Scender da gli alti monti abeti e pini;
> Ma vie più degno vanto oggi s' ammira
> De la famosa lira,
> Vanto di pregio eterno,
> Mover gli Dei del ciel, piegar l' Inferno.

As for the *Orpheus* of Gluck, we have, conveniently for our purpose, the testimony of Mathilde Wesendonk who, in a letter to Wagner (June 24, 1868) emphasized the importance of the passage in which the Spirits of Hell thunder their "No! No!" against Orpheus, who has asked permission to enter, while the soft sounds of the harp help us to have faith in the final victory of music (of "the beautiful," as Mathilde puts it).   The fact that the first opera (as well as several later ones) owes its birth to the gala occasion of a royal wedding (which was to be graced, as it were, with an enacted epithalamium) must have conveyed the flattering implication that the love of the rulers was as deep and powerful as that of the mythological figures Orpheus and Eurydice.

Again, in the *Magic Flute,* Tamino and Pamina are revivals of Orpheus and Eurydice, the "magic flute" itself being a replica of the Orphic lute; and if, in *Fidelio,* the protagonist Leonore-Fidelio is no musician, she is given the power of Orpheus to conquer, by love, the Tartarus of a Spanish prison ("Ja, die Liebe wird's erreichen"). Even in *Tannhäuser* and in Walther Stolzing we can see a reflection of Orpheus; Walther, in winning Eva, feels he has attained the rewards of two heavens, the Christian and the pagan ("durch Sieges Sang gewonnen / Parnass und Paradies").

Now, in Rinuccini's opera, it was the love of a royal couple that was celebrated by the presentation, on the stage, of the trials of the wedded pair Orpheus and Eurydice: the love that was glorified by music was doubly marital. And in the *Euridice* it was to reconquer married bliss that Orpheus, the musician, brought into play every accent of human emotion. This range of "passion become music," once won for opera, was not to be always confined to marital love, but was allowed to include all shades of passion, chaste or unchaste—expressed in music chaste or unchaste (for with Wagner, music learned to become unchaste): Now it may be the invigorating, articulate clarity of "Celeste Aïda," which is maintained throughout the opera, even in the face of death; now the languorous, formless, disquieting music of *Tristan und Isolde,* constantly sinking and dying before the final death; but, always, it is love that has been the main theme of the occidental opera, that love of which the tenor sings in *Traviata:* "Amor è palpito dell '*universo intero,* misterioso altero, croce e delizia al cuor."

Again, while in the first operas, it was, alone, the ensemble of human voices that, in their polyphonic concurrence, formed the architecture of world harmony, in later works, the human voice was joined by *sinfonia;* and, indeed, all the other arts, subordinated to the triumphant music of love, came to be fused, to give us the baroque *Gesamtkunstwerk.* The glorification of music by music became a glorification of music by all the arts.

In many of the operas we will find definitions of music offered in the libretto itself: in Rinuccini's *Euridice,* the chorus says of Orpheus (761–66): "Del bel coro [of the Muses] al suon *concorde* / L'auree *corde* / Sì soave indi percuote, / Che tra' boschi Filomena /

nè Sirena / Tempra in mar sì care note"; in the prologue of Striggio's
Favola d'Orfeo, Music appears on the stage to tell us:

> Io su cetera d'or cantando soglio
> Mortal orecchia lusingar talora
> E in guisa tal de l'*armonia sonora*
> De le *rote del ciel* più l' alme invoglio.

Obviously, such comments consist only of traditional motifs, and
describe nothing of the development peculiar to baroque art: that
invitation to sensuous rapture which is produced by the dense
accumulation and combination of the arts.

Now, this very accumulation of effects tended to give emphasis
to the sensual as such; and, long before Nietzsche had objected to
the ambiguity of Wagner's music, a simpler critic arose to question
the sensuous appeal of operatic art. In Grimmelshausen's pica-
resque novel, the hero Simplicissimus, a German peasant, joins the
opera and finally wins the stellar role of Orpheus(!) at the Royal
Opera in Paris, where, as the "Beau Aleman," he becomes a seducer
of beautiful ladies. Soon, however, he comes to realize the danger
for his soul, inherent in the aesthetic illusions (which he himself was
so well able to foster) produced by that feast of the senses which
the opera offered (for, as Burkard says, in his essay on Grimmelshausen [Frankfurt, 1929]: "was der Mensch spielt, dessen Opfer
wird er leicht"). With the opera, particularly, the subordination
of sensuous means to ethereal ends tended to be reversed; so that,
in the nineteenth century, Stendhal, the constant attendant at La
Scala, could enjoy the operas he witnessed, precisely as stimulants
to passion. And Orpheus himself has suffered in this sensuous
development of the opera (as may already have been suggested by
the emphasis given to this figure in Grimmelshausen's critique):
in Offenbach's parody, in which the additional element of satire is
introduced in order to offset the amoral tone of relativity, spirit and
reason are undermined by the appeal to voluptuous pleasures:
Orphée aux enfers offers a veritable cancan of the senses.

But it is not alone the sensuous nature of the opera that has
called forth criticism. In the eighteenth century, this genre was
attacked in the name of *vraisemblance.* Addison and Steele, for

example, protested against the peculiar convention that required human beings to communicate with each other by singing songs. The nonpoetic approach of these two English critics (so characteristic of the Age of Enlightenment, which was no longer able to hear the "world concert") may today be widely current among the masses of most countries, who can no longer easily imagine (as, however, the Italian peasant still can do, who, when he sings, sings always an aria)[22] a level of existence on which man spends his life in song. In most countries, at Bayreuth or at the Met, opera has become the privilege of the rich, who, themselves, perhaps, can pay only lip service to the glorification of world harmony by music.

A further reason for the relative unpopularity of the opera (relative in comparison with the symphony concert, for example) today, may, indeed, lie in its suggestion of an aristocratic pattern, once a feature of actual life (the fabulous baroque courts, which furnished the background of the early opera, were once very real), but no longer at hand, even for the very rich, to offer a pretext of reality.

Perhaps, if the opera could abandon the outworn baroque and courtly tradition, while still preserving its essential motif of love and music, we would find that the theme of world harmony, musically and dramatically portrayed, has not entirely lost its appeal. There exists, for example, in America, the reality of a simple and devout community that is given to express itself in song and mimicry; when this community came to life on the stage in the opera *Porgy and Bess*, with its black, crippled Orpheus as a central figure, and the Negro community as chorus, perhaps a new start was made. Another attempt to revive the opera, this time with a national inspiration, may be found in Moussorgsky's *Boris Godunov*, in which we hear the voice of all religious Russia: its various classes, rulers, priests, and people, its choirs and its church bells, fused into one tone of primitive Christian humility (to Jacques Rivière, it is the tone of the simplest of all prayers, "Give us this day our daily bread"). Here, the theme is no longer that of personal love, but love of country; and the musical polyphony tends toward a liturgical simplicity and monotony: the art of this opera is pre-baroque— operatic only on the surface, in the tableau it offers of vast Russia under God.

Finally, we may find, in a comparatively new genre, and one which is accessible to the masses to a degree never before achieved, a combination of drama and music, "in praise of music," which in its way serves to continue the spirit of the opera: a cinema representing the life of Chopin, or Liszt, or Handel (or Toscanini, not to mention Gershwin and others) is able, thanks to the modern developments of technicolor and sound recording, to offer the masses a fusion of the dramatic, the pictorial, and the musical in which praise of music consists in re-enacting the genesis of given musical compositions or performances, with a historical Orpheus as hero of the photoplay. Perhaps the opera (operetta) itself helped make this transition possible: such an opera as Pfitzner's *Palestrina*, or such a banal operetta as the Viennese *Dreimäderlhaus*, featuring the composer Schubert.

With the concert of the stars in Shakespeare and Milton, Luis de León and Cervantes, and with the development of "music in praise of music" in operatic form, we have gone far ahead of our story and must now retrace our steps in order to follow the history of world harmony in the Renaissance and baroque periods. The Thomistic definition of beauty, true to Aristotle, had insisted on *proportio, consonantia*, and *claritas*. The Renaissance (cf. L. Olschki, *Deutsche Vierteljahrsschrift*, VIII, 516) insisted particularly on *proportio*, and "Massästhetik," the aesthetics of measurement, was accordingly preferred: ἁρμονία καὶ ἀριθμός, the correctness of harmonious proportions, was taken seriously—and literally. A kind of normative grammar of the arts was founded, which placed the arts on the same level with natural sciences, by applying the Roman canons (Vitruvius, *De architectura*, 3, 1, 2: *proportio* = "ratae partis, membrorum in omni opere totoque commodulatio"), and by seeking to combine observation and proportions (set a priori in the anatomy of man), the beautiful and the exact—an ideal which ultimately led to that of the French classical *clarté*. In such an approach, music had to represent primarily the measurable as determined by *numeri*. Julius Schlosser, *Ein Künstlerproblem der Renaissance: L. B. Alberti* (1929), reports that this Italian artist of the fifteenth century refers to the proportions of an architecture as "tutta quella musica"[23]—though here it is a question rather of the medieval *ars liberalis* than of musicality—which was lacking in the cupolas built by Alberti.   He defines the harmony of an architecture as "finitio, concinnitas, consensus et conspiratio"; here we have the words of Cicero, inspired by the spirit of Vitruvius.   It is interesting in this connection to note the use of *Stimmung* precisely in a German translation of Vitruvius, in Rivius' *Bawkunst*, Nuremburg, 1547 (to which Professor Kurrelmeyer called my attention); here, in Book II, Chap. 2, "Von der Sculptur . . . ," we find the word used in the following simile:

> Dann gleicher gestalt wie ein Lauten / oder ander Instrument / hoch oder nider gestelt werden mag / das er doch gleichen / *Concent der Stimmung* unnd lieblicheit behalte / also mag auch die rechte eigentliche Simmetria / in *gleicher Harmoni* / in kleinen unnd grossern Corpern / gefunden werden (p. 24).

Concent der Stimmung is evidently the "temperament" of music which is brought about by tuning, and is identified with the "harmony of symmetry."   We see that the musical possibilities of Vitruvius' term *commodulatio* are exploited, as in the case of the "tutta quella musica" of Alberti: music is subservient to proportion. Though the word *Stimmung* shows itself capable of absorbing all the glorious fullness of "harmony," it is as yet far from the expansion it will enjoy later (in another passage, Rivius uses *Stimmung* only in the meaning "laut, sprachlicher ausdruck"; *DWb*, s.v. *Stimmung* [1]).

But the Renaissance brought with it the revival, not only of the ancient "Massästhetik," but also of the more mystical Neoplatonism which condemned this aesthetics.   Thus, for example, we find Marsilio Ficino and Leo Hebraeus objecting to the concept of beauty based on proportion, arguing that in the theory of their adversaries simple things (e.g., the light so dear to Neoplatonists, color, simple geometrical forms, the circle, etc.) could not be beautiful.   "Bei Leone nimmt man wahr," says C. Gebhardt (Introduction to the edition of the *Dialoghi d'amore*, 1929), "wie die Kunst des Quattrocento, statische Kunst der Linien in der Frühzeit der Pollajuolo, Botticelli und Mantegna, deren Tendenz Alberti formuliert hat, nunmehr im beginnenden Cinquecento dem

Dynamismus des Lichtes und der Farbe mit der Sehnsucht Lionardos und Giorgiones zustrebt" (p. 65). The beauty graspable by the senses is an image of that intellectual beauty which God has achieved in nature and which the human artist achieves in his art. The most intellectual senses are those of seeing and hearing, the former communicating to us light, the reflection of intellectual beauty, the latter, the musical beauty of the world soul, "l' ordinationi de le voci in harmonico canto, in sententiosa oratione, o in verso, si comprende dal nostro audito, et mediante quelle [sic] diletta la nostra anima per l' harmonia e concordia di che lei è figurata da l'anima del mondo (III, 108)." Light and music thus become the truly divine in art, or, to use the modern German term: *Stimmung*, that is, pictorial and musical variations thereof, predominates in art.

With Neoplatonism there is still another element which leads to the "musicalization," to the "Stimmung," of the soul. Reviving the speculations of the ancients concerning the astrological influence of the stars upon the human temperament, the Neoplatonists taught that man had, consequently, to "attune" his soul to the universe. Marsilio Ficino, *De concordia mundi et de natura hominis secundum stellas*, says: "Quoniam vero coelum est harmonica ratione compositum, movetur harmonice et harmonicis motibus atque sonis efficitur, ... merito per harmoniam solam non solum homines, sed inferiora haec omnia pro viribus ad capienda coelestia praeparantur.... Neque vero diffidere debet quisquam, hos atque omnia quae circa nos sunt praeparamentis quibusdam posse sibi vindicare coelestia." In order to establish a state of harmony with the universe, man must expose himself to the particular heavenly body which is "consonant" with him; and the best means of re-establishing an uninterrupted unity between man and the cosmos is that of music: "Mercurius, Pythagoras, Plato jubent dissonantem animam vel moerentem cithara cantuque tam constanti quam concinno componere." And, in *De vita*, Ficino (as D. C. Allen shows, in his *The Star-Crossed Renaissance* [1943], p. 9) uses the simile of the harp whose strings, when plucked, make vibrate along with them the strings still untouched—a simile which depicts the influence of the stars on stones, plants, human characters, and talents.   Here we have to do with a theory of the Arabian Averroes, viz., that the vibrations of the world soul are communicated to the individual souls by the rays of the stars: a vision of a vibrating universe whose infimous parts share the sensitivity of the whole.   Thanks to his *anima intellectualis,* which is in an intermediate position between the angels and the earthly forms (this is the Neoplatonic scale!), man can free himself from the base and earthly, and lift himself toward heaven; as Allen remarks, somewhat cynically, "the good influence of the stars becomes then a form of ethical gymnastics."   In other words, man can "attune" himself to the vibrating world harp; his "Stimmung" depends upon the "Stimmung" of world harmony, which has its own (musical) laws.   Already we find in Nicholas of Cusa, *Idiota de Mente,* cap. 6, p. 69 (ed. Baur, Leipzig 1937): "Agit enim *mens eterna quasi ut musicus,* qui suum conceptum vult sensibilem facere, recipit enim pluralitatem vocum et illas redigit in *proportionem congruentem harmonie, ut in illa proportione harmonia* dulciter et perfecte resplendeat."   Thus the individual human soul, though a minimal thing in this infinite space, can attune itself to the whole world.   The heterodox pantheism of Giordano Bruno (compare his *Eroici furori,* 1585) therefore insists on that spaciousness of space which makes possible the fusion of individual beings with the whole: this "furioso ['demoniac' in the Platonic sense] quasi inebriato di bevanda de' dei" sees deity as ἕν καὶ πᾶν, as a One in the All. The apple of Paris to which he refers is the symbol of the all-dimensional infinite:

> . . . nella semplicità della divina essenza è tutto totalmente, e non secondo misura . . . [this is contrary to the Augustinian teaching of the *numeri*]; ma tutti gli attributi sono non solamente uguali, ma ancora medesimi et una istessa cosa.   Come nella sfera tutte le dimensioni sono non solamente uguali (essendo tanta la lunghezza, quanta è la profondità et larghezza) ma ancora medesime. . . . Cossì è nell' altezza de la sapienza divina, la quale è medesima che la profondità de la potenza et latitudine de la bontade.   Tutte queste perfezioni sono uguali, perchè sono infinite (1, 5, 11; ed. Lagarde [Göttingen, 1888], p. 683).

Where there is infinite wisdom there must be also infinite power and infinite beauty.   Already within the sphere of the divine there is a fusion of the different qualities into one: Bruno, taking the orbit of the sun as a symbol, draws up a diagram with two circles, one within, one outside, the orbit. We are meant to visualize that when the heavenly body is in movement, it is at the same time moving (inner circle) and moved (outer circle), and, at any one moment of its movement, lies on *all* points of the two circles, since motion and rest, temporal and eternal, coincide. Indeed it is not true that the sun revolves, as is generally believed, around the earth in twenty-four hours; nor does it pass through the zodiac in one year, causing the four seasons: "ma è tale, che, per essere la eternità istessa e conseguentemente una possessione insieme tutta e compita, insieme insieme comprende l'inverno, la primavera, l'estade, l'autumno, insieme insieme il giorno et la notte, perchè è *tutto per tutti* et in tutti gli punti et luoghi" (1, 5, 7; p. 675). The Cusanian idea of *coincidentia oppositorum* is emphasized by Bruno's stylistic insistence on the key word *insieme*, "together," but it has taken on another meaning with the heterodox philosopher: nothing stands alone, individual, and separate; everything is fitted into the Whole—in fact, represents the Whole; no *one* aspect is ever valid. We have a law of continuous metamorphosis figured by the wheel whose antipodes are man and beasts, but whose motion (*rivoluzione*) is effected by "necessità, fato, natura, consiglio, volontà" (a variant of the ancient Wheel of Fortune), so that man can become animal, the animal man: even the different species in nature can change one into another. In the realm of the divine *prima intelligenza* Bruno sees revealed the following picture:

> Quá è conseguente il canto e suono, dove son nove intelligenze, nove muse, secondo l'ordine de nove sfere; dove prima si contempla *l'armonia di ciascuna, che è continuata con l'armonia dell' altra*; perchè il fine et ultimo della superiore è principio e capo dell' inferiore, *perchè non sia mezzo et vacuo tra l' una et altra*: et l' ultimo de l' ultima *per via di circolazione* concorre con il principio della prima. . . . Appresso si contempla *l' armonia et consonanza de tutte le sfere, intelligenze, muse et instrumenti insieme*: dove il cielo, il moto de mondi, l' opre della natura, il discorso degl' intelletti, la contemplazione della mente, il decreto della divina providenza, tutti d'accordo [Calderonian résumé!] celebrano l'alta e magnifica vicissitudine [the metamorphosis], che aguaglia l'acqui inferiori alle superiori, cangia la notte col giorno, et il giorno con la notte, *a fin che la divinità sia in tutto,* nel modo con

cui *tutto è capace di tutto*, e l'infinita bontà infinitamente si communiche secondo tutta la capacità de le cose (Argomento; pp. 620-1).

In the previously quoted passage, the stylistic key word was *insieme*; here it is *tutto*: the continuous metamorphosis, as the law of the universe, makes it possible that "all be in one," and God in all.   For Bruno, infinity is coupled with the idea of participation on the part of every creature in the divine.   In the infinite space of the love-permeated universe, all things are fused; in contrast to the medieval landscape where heavenly bodies, mankind, beasts, plants, stones were neatly divided, and subjected all together to a hierarchically superior divinity, the pantheistic landscape and the "world-scape" of Bruno offer fusion, representing the divine as susceptible of becoming the human, and vice versa.   Bruno does not discard the Christian idea of divine providence, but he submerges it in the *magnifica vicissitudine* of the law of metamorphosis.   His pantheistic landscape is infused with "Stimmung."   We may find, in Renaissance painting, the pictorial analogy to this philosophic landscape; here, however, we shall consider only the impact of world harmony upon the art of music proper.

The main impression which we gain from the *a cappella* church music of Palestrina (music approved by such popes of the Counter Reformation as Marcellus II and Pius IV) is that of infinite space and harmony.   The following is the description of this music given by Palestrina's modern biographer, Z. K. Pyne (London, 1922), pp. 173-4:

> . . . a certain quality of indefiniteness . . . was as the very breath of the unaccompanied polyphonic school. . . . Paradoxical as it may seem, modern music, while gaining in subtlety, coloring and weight, has lost in *size*.   An unaccompanied six-part mass [such as the *Missa papae Marcelli*, 1555] (obviously there is no restriction in the multiplication of voices) is practically immeasurable, for it is confined in no limit of rhythmic beat, thematic structure, or chromatic formula. . . . The uniformity of timbre through the sole employment of the human voice, the absence of percussion, or of violent changes of any sort, create a certain atmosphere [Stimmung!] on which the spirit floats.   To borrow a simile from architecture—it is unlikely that any one could enter the Pantheon in Rome without a sudden and startling sense of the vast space.   Reflection alone reveals the art hidden in the cunning gradations of the enormous dome. . . . In other words, there is no apparent

standard by which to gauge the proportions of the whole. In Pierluigi's music there is the same absence of a definite point of comparison by which to measure. . . . There is something inexpressibly quietening in these "exquisite rhythms" [these are words used by Palestrina himself about his music], for time and space fall away, and with them, the contemplation of earthly things.

And on p. 226, Pyne writes, " . . . and no doubt the large open spaces with lofty roofs in which these works are usually performed are for something in the sense of delight aroused in the hearer." Thus the contemporary funerary inscription defining Palestrina's fame (p. 185) could as well apply to heavenly music: "Ut re mi fal so la ascendunt, sic pervia coelos / Transcendit volitans nomen ad astra tuum (o Prenestine)." Here the Renaissance feeling of space has become tributary to a reformed Christianity and a new otherworldliness[24]—it is rather the Renaissance feeling of the infinite subjected to Christianity than Bruno's solution of Christian providence subjected to metamorphosis.   Or, as E. T. A. Hoffmann has expressed it, in words inspired by the patristic equation *chord* = *concordia fidelium* (in the article "Alte und neue Kirchenmusik" [1814], to be found in *Deutsche Selbstzeugnisse*, ser. 17, vol. XII: "Romantik," edited by Kluckhohn, pp. 261–70):

> Ohne allen Schmuck, ohne melodischen Schwung folgen meistens vollkommene, konsonierende Akkorde aufeinander, von deren Stärke und Kühnheit das Gemüt mit unnennbarer Gewalt ergriffen und zum Höchsten erhoben wird.—Die Liebe, der Einklang alles Geistigen in der Natur, wie er dem Christen verheissen, spricht sich aus im Akkord, der daher auch erst im Christentum zum Leben erwachte; und so wird der Akkord, die Harmonie Bild und Ausdruck der Geistergemeinschaft, der Vereinigung mit dem Ewigen, dem Idealen, das über uns thront und doch uns einschliesst.   Am reinsten, heiligsten, kirchlichsten muss daher die Musik sein, welche nur als Ausdruck jener Liebe aus dem Innern aufgeht, alles Weltliche nicht beachtend und verschmähend.   So sind aber Palestrinas einfache, würdevolle Werke in der höchsten Kraft der Frömmigkeit und Liebe empfangen und verkünden das Göttliche mit Macht und Herrlichkeit.   . . . es ist wahrhaftige Musik aus der andern Welt (musica del' altro mondo) . . . sein Komponieren war Religionsübung (pp. 265–6).

Bearing in mind that the Palestrina choirs performed in the vastness of St. Peter's, on the one hand, and the speculations of Giordano Bruno about infinity, on the other, we may now turn to

Kepler's *Harmonices mundi*,[25] the Renaissance synthesis of art and sciences (mathematics). For Kepler, we may best consult the article of A. Wellek, "Renaissance- und Barocksynästhesie," *Dtsch. Vierteljahrsschr.* IX, 534 ff.; synesthesia, the "Doppelempfinden," is indeed only another manifestation of world harmony,[26] and the history of synesthesia is, to a great extent, the history of the Renaissance spirit, or, in other words, of "pantheism":

Der Anbruch der Neuzeit: die 'Wiedergeburt' des antiken Geistes, schafft für die kosmische Sinnensymbolik, deren Verfall den Ausgang des Mittelalters begleitet, unmittelbar frischen Boden; in ihr erlebt die klassische Lehre vom Sphärenklang nicht nur ihre Miterneuerung, sondern sogar eine letzte Vollendung und Hochblüte....

Das synoptische Vorstellen und Denken, das dieser Lehre von altersher zugrunde liegt, verleugnet sich auch hier nirgends und nie; selbst dann nicht, wenn, wie dies etwa bei Kepler der Fall ist, das "Denken" darin aufs äusserste betont wird. Für die von ihm in den heliozentrischen Winkelgeschwindigkeiten der Planetenläufe errechnete Planetenharmonie stellt Kepler in seinem Meisterwerk, der *Harmonice Mundi* (1619), eine ganze Reihe fortschreitend komplizierterer musikalischer Symbole auf: bis zur sechsstimmigen Darstellung in Quart-Sext-Akkorden, denen der Saturn zum Bass dient, während Merkur den bewegteren Sopran "singt". Sinnes-psychologisch gelten alle diese Zusammenklänge für Kepler als Gegenstand der Vorstellung; er vergleicht sie dem Zusammenklang, den "ein Tonkünstler beim Schaffen eines mehrstimmigen Tonstücks im Geiste überdenkt," ohne ihn doch "von aussen zu empfangen": es sei dies gleichwohl "den wesentlich sinnlichen Wirkungen" zuzuzählen. Schon in seinem Erstlingswerk, dem '*Mysterium Cosmographicum*', führt Kepler weitgehende musikalisch-geometrische Spekulationen durch, im Sinne der Pythagoräer und des Platon: Vergleichungen der Konsonanzen mit den geometrischen Grundgebilden; dann aber auch musikalisch-astrologische Entsprechungen, indem er die Wohlklänge den Aspekten zuteilt. Diese Spekulationen werden ein Vierteljahrhundert später in der *Harmonice Mundi* aus dem Frühwerk übernommen, anderwärts aber durch das Axiom erhellt: "Die Wurzeln der Harmonielehre liegen nicht in den Zahlen, sondern in den Gesetzen der räumlichen Anschauung." Erreger des "sinnlichen Zusammenklangs" kann für Kepler so gut ein Ton sein "wie der Strahl eines Gestirns,"...

Wenn also die kosmische Musiklehre Keplers von seinem Übersetzer dahinaus formuliert wird: "Was dem äusseren Sinn als geordnetes Gefüge, als wirkendes Ebenmass gegenübertritt, das beantwortet das innere als Klang", so ist dies zugleich ein Ausdruck des synoptischen Weltgefühls der Renaissance überhaupt. Das scheinbare Paradoxon, dass hier aus dem Weltgefühl, nicht, wie später im Barock, aus dem Sinneserlebnis, Synästhesie entspringt, erklärt sich aus der ursprünglich-naiven Anschauungshaftigkeit dieser Welt-Anschauung der Renaissance. Für Kepler ist der Weltenbau nicht bloss im Sinne eines Akkords, sondern ebensowohl "vollkommen getreu nach dem Bilde eines belebten Leibes" geschaffen. Eben dies aber ist zugleich die theoretische Grundidee der Malerei und Plastik der Renaissance, die Ausfluss des gleichen synästhetischen Weltgefühls ist. Lionardo da Vinci legte die Gesetze der malerischen Komposition, der perspektivischen Verkürzung und der idealen Proportion des menschlichen Körpers nach den musikalischen Intervallen fest; und es ist bezeichnend, dass er "als erster unter den Neueren", will sagen nach Aristoteles, dem theoretischen Vergleich zwischen Farben und Tönen Interesse widmet. Nach dem *Trattato della Pittura* beruht das Augenschöne auf *"una armonia delle bellezze"* oder *"un dolce concento"*; "der schöne Anblick ist süssem Einklange *(concento)* gleich"; und mehr als das: "Das Massgefühl des Auges wird von gleichen Gesetzen beherrscht wie das Taktgefühl des Ohres" (pp. 538–42).

To this Renaissance synesthesia of the classicists, who explain the sensuous by reference to a Pythagorean theoretical speculation on number-harmony, Wellek opposes the baroque synesthesia in which the individual sensations and sensuousness itself dominate. Examples of baroque synesthesia are, according to Wellek, to be found in Robert Fludd, who sees in light the flute of the spheres, of God, and also, in Athanasius Kircher; here Wellek comments:

Einem Kepler gegenüber stellt Kircher nach alledem sowohl als Forscher als auch als Sinnenmensch—charakterologisch und als "Charakter"—den genauen Gegenpol vor; er reiht sich sinnesverwandt zu Fludd. . . . Das Wesentliche hiebei ist aber die sinnliche Besonderung dieser Synästhesien, das Überwiegen der farbigen und klanglichen Synopsie über die allgemeine Sinnensymbolik der Sphärenharmoniker, welch letztere hier nunmehr in verblasster und verwirrter Form ein spätes Leben fristet; während zweifellos das Ton- und Klangfarbenhören in der ganzen Geschichte der Synästhesie bis auf Kircher nirgends so hoch und mannigfaltig entwickelt anzutreffen war. Hiezu kommt noch seine synoptische Theorie, welche Licht und Klang ausdrücklich und allgemein, nicht erst indirekt und in einem Dritten, untereinander gleich oder wenigstens in engste Beziehung setzt. In diesem Sinne ist Kircher tatsächlich der vollendetste Typ des Barock-Synästhetikers, wie ja des Barock-Menschen überhaut (p. 559).[27]

While a literary example of a classic synesthesia is the passage from Shakespeare's *Merchant of Venice*, V, 1:

> How sweet the moonlight sleeps upon this bank! / Here will we sit, and
> let the sounds of music / Creep in our ears: soft stillness and the night /
> Become the touches of sweet harmony. / Sit, Jessica. Look, how the
> floor of heaven / Is thick inlaid with patines of bright gold [cf. the *artesonada
> bóveda* of Gracián]: / There's not the smallest orb which thou behold'st / But
> in his motion like an angel sings, / Still quiring to the young-ey'd cherubins,—
> / Such harmony is in immortal souls; / But whilst this muddy vesture of
> decay / Doth grossly close it in, we cannot hear it.

we find a programmatic passage of the baroque synesthesia in the
verses of Crashaw: "Eyes are vocal, tears have tongues, / And
there are words not made with lungs." For our problem of *Stimmung*, synesthesia is most important: it is thanks to this practice
that the musical term could be freely used, not only in the other
arts, but also in the realm of the human psyche. Consequently,
we will find in Renaissance poetry many passages in which the poet
(conceived of as a musician) is represented as "attuning his instrument" to accord with the song he is to sing; mindful of the *Pieri . . .
tempera* of Horace, these poets thought of consonance of form
together with contents. Régnier, in his satire on the *Repas
ridicule* (X, 135–8), calls upon his (satiric, and consequently, more
pedestrian) Muse to choose a natural tuning: "Laisse-moi là
Phébus chercher son aventure, / Laisse-moi son B mol, prends *la
clef de nature* [evidently this is the major key, the key of health free
from melancholy]. / Et viens, simple, sans fard, nue et sans ornement,
/ Pour *accorder ma flûte avec ton instrument.*" In Satire IX (line
45), a slur directed at Malherbe and his school consists of the
remark that they believe "Que Phoebus à leur *ton accorde sa vielle*"
[i.e., that true poetry, Apollonian poetry, must choose their form].
Even the little dog Peloton in Du Bellay's *Epitaphe d'un petit chien*
has, in his way, a concern with artistic performance; when he is
catching flies he creates musical harmony: "Faisant accorder ses
dents / Au tintin de sa sonnette / Comme un clavier d'épinette."
D'Aubigné, when looking back (*Tragiques*, I, 73) to his own
juvenilia in the style of Ronsard, remarks: "Le luth que *j'accordois*
avec mes chansonnettes / Est ores estouffé de l'esclat des trompettes"
(the tuning, the *Stimmung* of the *Tragiques* will be different from
that of his love poem, *Le Printemps*); *ibid.* 1347, the Protestant
church music is "tuned to Him" with delight: "Tu aimes de ses

mains la parfaicte harmonie: / Notre luth chantera le principe de vie, / Nos doigts ne sont plus doigts que pour trouver tes sons, / Nos voix ne sont plus voix qu'à tes sainctes chansons"; VI, 68: "Que le haut ciel s'accorde en douces unissons / A la saincte fureur de mes vives chansons"; VII, 1049: "Où *l'accord très parfaict des doulces unissons* / A l'univers entier *accorde ses chansons*" [the astonishing feminine testifies to a feeling on the part of the poet that *unisson* is *un-isson*, an abstraction, *unitio*, "union"].   In these examples we witness no longer the tuning of a musical (or, in the metaphor, poetic) instrument to the exigencies of a musical-poetic genre, but the tuning of man and nature to the mood of God the *Archimusicus*; with this use of the simile we are in the midst of *Stimmung* as a religious tuning of the soul—an idea which must have been dear to the fervent adherents of the new Protestantism.   In the following passage from Milton, the poet, as he attunes his instrument, still obeys the laws of the poetic genre, but the genre itself is prescribed by God: *The Passion* (I) prescribes a particular tuning of the poet's song and soul to the divine: "Ere-while of Musick, and Ethereal mirth, / Wherewith the stage of Air and Earth did ring, / And joyous news of heav'nly Infant's birth, / My Muse with angels did divide to sing [this Milton had done in *On the morning of Christ's nativity*, see above] / . . . / For now to sorrow must I tune my song / And set my Harp to notes of saddest woe."

Already in Bunyan's *The Shepherd Boy's Song* we find the figure of the instrument of the souls mystically attuned to God: "The first string that the musician usually touches is the bass, when he intends to put all in tune.   God also plays on this string first, when he sets the soul in tune for himself."   It is with Donne (*Sermons*, ed. Potter and Simpson [Berkeley, 1955], vol. II, no. 7, p. 170) that we can best observe the process by which the religious idea of the "tuning of the heart" in its Protestant version developed out of that of the world lute:

> God made this whole world in such an uniformity, such a *correspondency*, such a *concinnity* of parts that it was an *Instrument, perfectly in tune*: we may say, the trebles, the highest strings were disordered first [cf. above, Shakespeare's "disordered strings"; "the highest strings" = the ὑπάτη of Plato]; the best understandings [= *intelligentiae*], angels and men, put this instrument

out of tune [= *Verstimmung*]. God rectified all again, by putting in *a new string, semen mulieris,* the seed of the woman, the Messias: And onely by sounding that string in your ears, become we *musicum carmen,* true *musick,* true *harmony,* true peace [=*concordia*] to you. [The world harmony, destroyed by original sin and the fall of the angels, was restored by Christ, the "new string," to the world lute.]

And again (X): "Heaven and earth are as a musical instrument; if you touch a string below, the motion goes to the top. Any good done to Christ's poor members upon earth affects him in heaven." Here the idea of a world harmony of the Ficinian variety is combined with that of the *corpus mysticus* (the *tertium comparationis* is the sensitive reaction of a Whole when its parts are touched)—a development of the idea of the completeness of the instrument of the well-tempered body. M. A. Rugoff, *Donne's Imagery* (1939), p. 104, quotes the passage: "God is a God of harmony and consent [= Lat *consensus*], and in a musical instrument, if some strings be *out of tune,* we do not presently break all the strings, but *reduce and tune* those which are out of tune." This moral maxim opens up a vast perspective of the possible "tunings" of the soul to the pitch of world harmony—and anticipates *Stimmung.* In the following passage (furnished me by Wolfgang Spitzer) from Donne's *Hymn to God, my God in my sickness,* we see the faithful believer, in the throes of death, endeavoring to "tune" his soul, on this earth, before entering into the sanctum of God's harmony in the beyond:

> Since I am coming to that holy room
> Where, with their choir of saints for evermore,
> I shall be made thy music, as I come
> I tune the instrument here at the door,
> And what I must do then, think here before.

A human soul vibrating to the tune of God must be a most delicate instrument, easily put "out of tune."

The Catholic mystics will dwell on the care that man should take to prevent his soul from being too easily diverted, by minor disturbances, from "attunedness to God." A warning against such distraction (the *divertissement* so vehemently excoriated by Pascal) may be found with the Spanish mystic, Antonio de Rojas (I quote from the French translation of 1663, mentioned by Bremond, *Prière et Poésie*, p. 119):

> Ne soyez pas semblables à ceux qui entendent l'aubade d'un *agréable concert de musique*, et qui, pour jouir de cette douceur, se lèvent promptement du lit, et à demi habillés se mettent à la fenêtre. . . . Mais lorsque les musiciens . . . servent la meilleure pièce de leur sac, un petit vent leur venant à souffler au nez, aussitôt ils se retirent et ferment la fenêtre et s'en retournent au lit. . . . Non, non, n'imitez pas ces délicats ou ces inconstants. Dieu vous donne une musique céleste, non dans la rue, mais dans le Palais Royal de votre âme; vous l'entendez avec contentement, et vous dites qu'il vous est bon de vous approcher de ce souverain et incomparable musicien. . . . Mais qu'arrive-t-il ? Un petit souffle d'une pensée importune, ou de plusieurs, qui vous combattent dans la jouissance de *cette douce harmonie*, et aussitôt vous laissez-là *toute la musique*, vous vous retirez au quartier des sens, où vous vous gelez davantage et vous laissez ce qui vous profite plus . . .

There are other mystics for whom the divine influx into the human soul is so immediate and irresistible, so far above any diversion of the moment, that the need for tuning to celestial music is never mentioned. According to the *Traité inédit* (1696) of the Jesuit Surin (as quoted by Bremond, *Histoire du sentiment religieux en France*, V, 306) the religious tranquility of the soul is comparable to the flow of a gigantic river or ocean, which no earthly incident is permitted to ruffle:

> Cette mer vient en majesté et en magnificence. Ainsi vient la paix dans l'âme, quand la grandeur de la paix la vient visiter après les souffrances, sans qu'il y ait un seul souffle de vent qui puisse faire sur elle une ride. Cette divine paix, qui porte avec soi les biens de Dieu et les richesses de son royaume, a aussi ses avant-coureurs, qui sont les alcyons et les oiseaux qui marquent sa venue: ce sont les visites des anges qui la précèdent. Elle vient *comme un élément de l'autre vie, avec un son de l'harmonie céleste*, et avec une telle raideur que l'âme même en est toute renversée, non par aucune opposition à son bien, mais par abondance. Cette abondance ne fait aucune violence, sinon contre les obstacles de son bien, et tous les animaux qui ne sont pas pacifiques fuient les abords de cette paix . . .

Bremond points out in this Jesuit mysticism the presence of a classicism based on reason ("trop de sublime lui fait peur") as opposed, for example, to the mood of Mme de Guyon's *Torrents spirituels*; for the purpose of our discussion, we may point to the subdued quality of this mystical treatment of musical world harmony ("an element of the beyond," "a sound of the celestial harmony").

In the preceding pages we have quoted texts from Protestant as well as from Catholic sources, as evidence that the idea of world harmony was not shelved by Protestantism: with D'Aubigné, Milton, Donne, we find an awareness of the musical unity of the world and, sometimes, a welding of Renaissance (Neoplatonic) thoughts into a Christian teaching—that is, attitudes not unlike those revealed by the Catholic poets. Thus the death of this concept cannot be attributed to Protestantism as such—as one might be tempted to assume from Novalis' *Christenheit oder Europa*—but only to the destructive process of "demusicalization" and secularization, in the sixteenth and seventeenth centuries, to which we have several times referred in the previous chapters. How this process is connected, in turn, with Calvinism and Cartesianism, with the growth of analytical rationalism and the segmentary, fragmentary, materialistic, and positivistic view of the world—all this would have to be shown in another study. An inquiry into this era of disintegration would put into relief once more the ancient and Christian tradition of world harmony, that is, the spiritual and intellectual background on which alone a future linguistic and semantic interpretation of the word *Stimmung* itself can be built.

NOTES TO INTRODUCTION

1. Along with this essay the volumes of G. Reese, *Music in the Middle Ages* (New York, 1940) and T. Gérold, *Les pères de l'église et la Musique* (Paris, 1931), as well as Rudolf Allers' learned article "Microcosmus" should be read.

NOTES TO CHAPTER I

1. Cf. for example Léon Vallas, *Claude Debussy* (English translation, 1933, p. 104): "To use a phrase which has become stereotyped because of its exactness and truth—they [the new expressive mediums] enable Debussy to *create an atmosphere* unprecedented in its fluidity and vibration."

2. Romain Rolland, in his *Musiciens d'aujourd'hui* (1908), p. 188, uses the German word wrongly, since for him it is only the German equivalent (used because he is dealing with things German) of *état d'âme*, this expression of such precise connotations: " . . . il n'est pas douteux qu'elle [the music of G. Mahler] ne soit toujours l'expression d'une *Stimmung* . . . qui fait l'intérêt de sa musique." Conversely, when Stendhal lists, as he does so often, the possible *états d'âme* of man, he is always thinking of the more permanent states of mind (hatred, envy), not of the *Stimmungen* of the moment.

3. How the lack of an equivalent to the German *Stimmung* forces the French writer to wordy explanations and improvisations, may be seen in the following passage from Claudel's *Positions et Propositions* (I, 43): "Dans l'œuvre d'un écrivain, sous les moyens et les procédés, . . . il y a une espèce de tonalité essentielle, *une note* éclatante ou sourde, mais sensible et obsédante partout, *une espèce de patrie intérieure* et de *climat vital* où la pensée trouve refuge et réfection. Eh bien, cette vue directe sur l'âme de Victor Hugo, . . . le *premier paysage* qui nous attendrait si nous pouvions passer de l'autre côté de ces yeux sans espérance, ce sont les tragiques dessins que nous avons tous regardés . . . *le sentiment le plus habituel* à Victor Hugo, . . . sa chambre intérieure de torture et de création, c'est l'épouvante." It is interesting to note that the musical element is represented in this passage (*tonalité, note*), but that no crystallized expression was at the disposal of the writer; he admits this lack implicitly by using, twice, "une espèce de . . . "

And we find this admitted explicitly in the delightful passage from *La Suède* of André Bellessort (1910; p. 13 ff.), in which he attempts to define the Swedish word *stämning*, which is obviously the equivalent of *Stimmung* and a loanword from German:

Le mot dont aucun Suédois n'a pu me préciser le sens, doit signifier la sensation que toutes les autres concordent à créer une harmonie. Il s'établit parfois une entente sympathique entre les choses et nous. Sur les lignes monotones de la vie, des notes se rencontrent qui spontanément s'organisent et forment une musique charmante. Le crépuscule tombe; le paysage se voile comme un visage attristé. Ni le jour qui s'en va, ni la nuit qui vient, ni la nature qui se décolore ne sont mes amis. Mais tout à coup le chant d'un inconnu s'élève, et voici que le ciel mourant, l'agonie du paysage et la cendre de ma rêverie, nous entrons dans le cercle fraternel de cette onde sonore. Tant que durera ce chant, j'aurai l'impression que je fais partie d'un tout, et, si j'ai l'instinct religieux d'être un des éléments indispensables du concert que, sur un point du monde, Dieu voulait se donner ce soir. Évanoui, j'en retiendrai l'écho pour endormir en moi la fièvre de l'isolement et pour y prolonger le délicieux *stämning*. Plus délicieux encore lorsqu'il m'unit à d'autres cœurs ! Ces individualistes scandinaves ne communiquent entre eux que par le chant, la poésie ou les sombres tunnels de l'inexprimable. Ils ne cherchent pas à penser, mais à sentir ensemble. Le *stämning* ne naîtra pas d'un échange d'idées ni même d'une causerie familière. Il éclot au bruit d'une chanson qui passe, à la clarté d'une lampe, sous l'haleine d'un parfum, devant des verres servis où l'on savourera le même apaisement; et il ne s'épanouit que sur les étages du silence. Il est fait de coïncidences heureuses, mais qu'on sait provoquer. Nous aimons, au déclin d'une fête, à nous regarder dans les yeux et à nous en envoyer les dernières étincelles ou les derniers éclairs. Ils préfèrent éteindre les flambeaux, ne plus se voir, rentrer en eux-mêmes et partager, à la faveur de l'ombre, le charme vaguement senti d'un accord éphémère. Les cloches du dimanche et des jours carillonnés répandent du *stämning*. Autour des héros et des morts chéris le *stämning* entretient un air de fête religieuse.

The Swedish philologist Karl Michaëlsson who, in his article on *ambiance*, quotes this passage, corrects the description of *stämning* offered by Bellessort by stating that the Swedish word has a wider range: it expresses anything from the " 'cafard' d'un solitaire jusqu'à l'entrain d'une tablée à la fin d'un bon dîner." Michaëlsson considers *ambiance* to be the best French equivalent of *stämning*, though he states that *ambiance* has a more objective connotation than the latter (and, we would add, than Ger *Stimmung*). I would say, more exactly, that the Romance word has a different *reference*: a landscape etc. may constitute an "ambiance," it cannot *have* "ambiance," whereas the Germanic words refer to a quality possessed by a landscape (as well as to the feelings induced in man). (Léon Daudet, *apud* Michaëlsson [p. 105], expresses something of this distinction when he says: "L'ambiance ne se confond pas avec la pensée, . . . elle sert de véhicule à la pensée"—though I would replace *pensée* by *émotion*.)

The difficulties which faced Albertine Necker de Saussure, the excellent French translator of Schlegel's *Vorlesungen über dramatische Kunst und Literatur* (1808), in her attempts to translate the word-family of *Stimmung*, can be easily seen from the tables appended by Josef Körner to his book, *Die Botschaft der deutschen Romantik an Europa* (Augsburg, 1929). Thus, for example (p. 136), Mme Necker translates "das Wesen der musikalischen Stimmung" as "l'essence de ce qu'on peut appeler en nous [!] la disposition harmonieuse"—and still feels the need to put part of the original German phrase (though, interestingly enough, not the crucial word *Stimmung*) in a note: "Musikalische (Note du Trad.)." Compare also (pp. 120–1):

dies ist die tragische Stimmung . . . wenn jene Stimmung die auffallendsten Beispiele von gewaltsamen Umwälzungen menschlicher Schicksale . . . in der Darstellung durchdringt und beseelt: dann entsteht tragische Poesie.	telle est cette disposition . . . qu'on peut appeler la disposition tragique. Et lorsque . . . l'âme, ainsi modifiée . . . s'empare des . . . exemples les plus frappans des vicissitudes . . .

Here, *Stimmung* is rendered now by *disposition*, now by *âme modifiée*. P. 119:

das ganze Spiel lebendiger Bewegung beruht auf *Einstimmung* und Gegensatz.	les mouvement des êtres animés s'expliquent par le jeu des organes, tour à tour excités et détendus; partout on ne voit que dissonances et consonances, contraste et accord.

Both these French passages are listed by Körner as "Verwässerungen, Amplifikationen, Paraphrasen"; but, in the second one at least, Mme Necker cannot be accused of "watering down"; she has simply recognized the Latin and Romance prototypes of *Einstimmung* and *Gegensatz*. P. 140:

[die Musik wird vom Theater zu Hilfe gerufen], um die Gemüter zu stimmen, oder die schon ergriffenen durch ihre Anklänge noch mächtiger zu treffen.	la musique y seconde la poésie de toute la puissance de ses accords.

Here, *stimmen* is not accounted for at all in the French translation.

At one point, the translator feels the need to explain *Stimmung* in a note, where she arrives at the interpretation "teinte": "Lors donc que de certains rôles ont une teinte d'exaltation très–prononcée, l'on y introduit d'autres rôles, appelés ironiques, qui font ressortir de diverses manières l'exagération des premiers et produisent eux-mêmes une *impression* toute opposée. . . . [Le poète a] désiré nous introduire dans un monde créé par lui, où toutes les *couleurs*, beaucoup plus tranchées et plus éclatantes qu'on ne les voit dans la nature, ne sont cependant pas sans harmonie. (p. 97)"

In Russian, the semantic range of *Stimmung* is divided between расположение духа or настроение (literally = "state of mind," "constitution") referring to the mood of a person, and впечатление ("impression"), referring to the unity of atmosphere adhering to a situation.

It is in Sanskrit, perhaps, that we come the closest to finding an equivalent (or rather, two equivalents) of *Stimmung*, embracing a reference both to mood and to atmosphere. In his article "Indirect Suggestion in Poetry" (*Proceedings of the Am. Phil. Soc.*, LXXVI, 687) Franklin Edgerton discusses the two terms *dhvani* and *rasa*. The first, meaning literally "tone, resonance, reverberation," is used in the Hindu *ars poetica* to refer to the "unsaid or suggested meaning of poetry" (only the "suggested" meaning being truly poetic); it is the "soul" (the "breath of life") of poetry as opposed to its "body," just as the charm of a lovely woman is something distinct from the physical beauty, more or less analyzable, of her anatomy. Though Edgerton does not attempt to find a European equivalent for the Sanskrit term, one sees easily the similarity with our *Stimmung*. The second term *rasa*, literally "flavor, taste," constitutes an important subdivision of the general literary term *dhvani*, being applied particularly to drama; in dramatic art eight different types of *rasa* are distinguished: the erotic, heroic, etc. It is the latter term alone that Jacobi (apud Edgerton) had rendered by *Stimmung* (Edgerton, for his part [p. 701], proposing the Eng *flavor*); I should say that both terms are parallel to *Stimmung* in that they are metaphors derived from sense perception ("tone," "taste") and are intended as technical terms in poetics; because of the limitation, however, of their metaphorical use, the range of connotations is much narrower.

4. When Guido Errante, *Sulla lirica romanza delle origini* (New York, 1943), quotes this sentence, he renders the phrase in question by "la 'Stimmung' fuggitiva del momento," retaining this word throughout the book—where occasionally it alternates with *tonalità*—when he wishes to emphasize the general tone of a poem. We find, for example (p. 387): "Si tratta di tendenza, di 'tonalità,' di 'Stimmung,' non certo di imitazione precisa e circoscritta . . . : è impulso che eccita a creare. Il temperamento del nostro poeta lo porta ad attingere di preferenza nelle acque irruenti e tempestose." Similarly, *Stimmung* is rendered in Spanish today by *umor, temple, tonalidad*: three words instead of one.

5. The (*innere*) *Stimmung* = *Gestimmtheit* (already extant in the first edition of 1819) is evidently the older meaning. It is significant that the passage on lyric poetry is still missing in the 1819 edition, and appears only in that of 1844. In the former we find only the phrase *lyrische Stimmung*: "Darum geht im Liede und der *lyrischen Stimmung* das Wollen . . . und das reine Anschauen . . . wundersam gemischt durch einander . . . von diesem ganzen so gemischten und getheilten *Gemüthszustande* ist das echte Lied der Ausdruck" (*Die Welt*, I, 3, 38). It is clear that the *lyrische Stimmung* is something between a passing mood and a *Gestimmtsein*.

6. As concerns the actual historical development, Boyancé, in his work, *Le culte des muses chez les philosophes grecs* (Paris, 1937), points out that the myth which presents Pythagoras as imitating the heavenly concert with his lyre, is farther from the truth than the one which describes his discovery of the principles of musical harmony after listening to a blacksmith hammering on his anvil. And, just as the Pythagorean theory of harmony arose from the empirical observation of sounds, so, from human music, as it existed at the time (and as it was applied, in the religious practice of the Pythagoreans, for the purification of the soul), was derived the concept of the harmony of the spheres.

7. It is well known that the Greeks did not utterly condemn Eris: Hesiod in his theogony distinguishes between a good and an evil Eris. Jakob Burckhardt always insisted on the importance of the agonic idea for the Greeks; in this connection, Hermann J. Weigand, "*Wandrers Sturmlied*—'Neidgetroffen,'" *Germanic Review*, XXI, 170, quotes from Nietzsche's treatise, *Homer's Wettkampf*

"Um sie [die griechische Geschichte] zu verstehn, müssen wir davon ausgehn, dass der griechische Genius den einmal so furchtbar vorhandenen Trieb gelten liess und als berechtigt erachtete. . . . Der Kampf und die Lust des Sieges wurden anerkannt: und nichts scheidet die griechische Welt so sehr von der unseren, als die hieraus abzuleitende *Färbung* einzelner ethischer Begriffe, zum Beispiel der *Eris* und des *Neides*."

8. As professor A. Rüstow has pointed out to me, the Greek words ἁρμονία and ἁρμόττειν stem originally from the tactile and visual (tactile > visual) sphere: they are terms of the carpenter (the "joiner") who "fits together" (cf. also Lat *pango—compages—pax*), and have been secondarily applied to the acoustic sphere.

The reapplication of the visual is also characteristic of Heraclitus' speculations; for example, the analogy of the bow and lyre, stressed in Fragment 51, rests only on the visual aspect of the two objects (the bow, obviously, does not produce music); and the same visual tendency informs also his diagrammatic visualization (Fragment 31) of the development: water 1) producing fire 3) [via either "lightning" or "earth" 2)], and, conversely, of fire 3) producing water 1) [again, via "earth" or "lightning" 2)]. Professor Rüstow has designed for me three diagrams which show, alike, the visual symmetry on which the corresponding cosmic speculations rest:

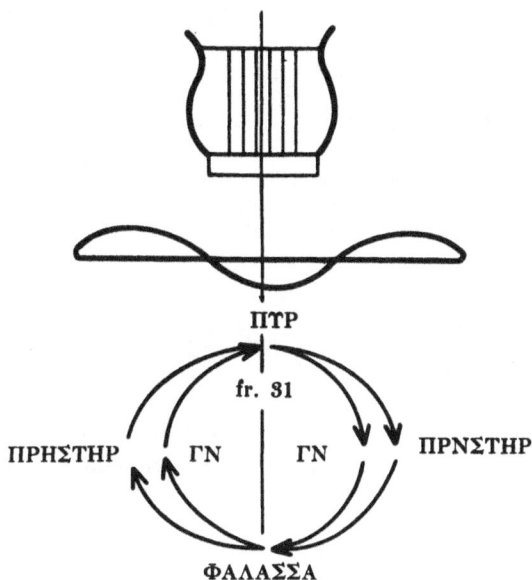

In Fragment 8 of Parmenides, the Heracliteans are called δίκρανοι, "double-headed people," and their view of the universe is termed, παλίντροπος (an epithet originally applied to ships forced home by adverse winds): an apposite parody of the symmetry which prevails in the Heraclitean system.

But already in the fourth century B.C., the visual picture originally intended by Heraclitus was misunderstood by the poet Scythinus, who, in a synesthetic vision, takes the lyre to mean the whole of the world, the plectron to be the sun: [τῆς λύρας] ἣν ἁρμόζεται Ζηνὸς εὐειδὴς Ἀπόλλων πᾶσαν, ἀρχὴν καὶ τέλος συλλαβών, ἔχει δὲ λαμπρὸν πλῆκτρον ἡλίου φάος (according to Professor Rüstow's explanation, "the lyre of Zeus was skillfully fitted together by Apollo, who brought together the beginning and end of all things; and it has as a shining plectron the light of the sun").

9. How genuine this concept must have appeared to the Romans, we may guess by the use of *symphonia discors* by Horace, who, in his *Ars poetica* (374–8), wittily applies it to bad music played at a banquet; in this way he parodies what is most abhorrent to his (Grecian) aesthetics; lack of proportion = tastelessness: "Ut gratas inter mensas *symphonia discors* / Et crassum unguentum et Sardo cum melle papaver [evidently a dyscrasia or bad mixture] / Offendunt, poterat duci quia cena sine istis, / Sic animis natum inventumque poema juvandis, / Si paulum summa decessit, vergit ad imum." Du Bellay, imitating Horace in his invective, "Contre les Petrarquistes," opposes poetic excesses by references to cosmic harmony:

> L'un meurt de froid et l'autre meurt de chault,
> L'un vole bas et l'autre vole hault,
> L'un est chetif, l'autre a ce qu'il luy fault,
> L'un sur l'esprit se fonde,
> L'autre s'arreste à la beauté du corps:
> On ne vid onq' si *horribles discords*
> En ce *Chaos*, qui troubloit *les accords*
> *Dont fut basty le monde.*

The *symphonia discors* as a principle of world harmony is found with Pontus de Tyard, the poet of the Pléiade and theoretician of music, in a bacchanal song from his *Erreurs amoureuses*: "Quel accord discordant bruit, / S'entremêle s'entrefuit, / Qui mes esprits épouvante! [the music of the bacchanalian evoe]"; Bacchus himself appears as victor accompanied by integrated appositions such as *la discord—l'amitié.* In this connection we must think of Pope's lines:

> Not, chaos-like together crush'd and bruis'd,
> But, as the world, harmoniously confused:
> When order in variety we see,
> And where, though all things differ, all agree.

In French Renaissance poetry, Catholic as well as Protestant, political discord is portrayed, after the manner of Cicero, as a perturbation of divine harmony: as an example of the former, cf. Ronsard, "Discours des misères de ce temps" (1564), who uses against the Protestants the argument of the pernicious *variations* to which Bossuet will later resort:

> Vous devriez, pour le moins, avant que nous troubler,
> Estre ensemble *d'accord sans vous desassembler*;
> Car Christ n'est pas un dieu de noise ny *discorde*;
> Christ n'est que charité, qu'amour et que *concorde*,
> Et monstrez clairement par la division
> Que Dieu n'est point autheur de vostre opinion.

An example of the latter is found in the *Tragiques* (I, 141) of D'Aubigné, who compares France, torn by religious wars, with the body of a giant, hitherto invincible, now afflicted with dropsy and dyscrasia: "Son corps est *combattu à soi-mesme contraire*, / Le sang pur ha le moins [= "the pure blood is conquered (by the impure); the explanation of the editors, Garnier-Plattard, is wrong], le flegme & le colere / Rendent le sang non sang . . . / La masse degenere en la melancholie; / Ce vieil corps tout infect, plein de sa *discrasie*, / Hydropique, fait l'eau, si bien que ce geant, / Qui alloit de ses nerfs ses voisins outrageant, / Aussi foible que grand n'enfle plus que son ventre." Similarly, Maurice Scève in *Le microcosme* writes, according to A.-M. Schmidt, *La poésie scientifique en France au XVIe siecle* (Paris, 1939), p. 153, "deux des plus beaux vers qu'il ait jamais imaginés" on the discordant accord in music:

> Musique, accent des cieux, plaisante symfonie,
> Par contraires aspects formant son harmonie.

These lines are among the most beautiful in French poetry because they not only define harmony but evoke it by means of a "symphony of vowels." Scève describes as follows the effect of the invention of the musical modes:

> De *discordant accord* mélodieux tesmoins
> Par les proportions des mouvements celestes
> Soulageans icy bas nos cures plus molestes.

The classical-minded Grillparzer, seeking to define the music of Liszt, who came into this world of passions "with an eye as though from Eden," states the principle of all art in the same terms, "*Eintracht in Zwietracht* ist das Reich der Künste."

10. A more conservative view is taken by B. L. v. d. Waerden in his article, "Die Harmonie der Pythagoreer (*Hermes*, 78 [1943], 163 seq.); this scholar would restitute to Pythagoras himself much of what Frank attributes to later scholars, and he insists much more on the empirical point of departure of Pythagoras than on the religious.

11. Later the numerical speculations became still more complicated. Plutarch reports on the cosmology of Petron of Himera, that, of his 183 "worlds" (κόσμοι), 60 were located on every side of an isosceles, with three in addition

at the corners, all of them touching each other as in a χορεία. In the neo-Pythagorean school, about the time of the birth of Christ, old Pythagorean speculation was revived: The seven planets which cause the harmony of the spheres are identified with the Greek vowels, αεηιουω, while Nestorius teaches that harmony originates from the consonance of seven vowels and seventeen consonants, which are roughly identified with the planets and the twelve signs of the zodiac; cf. H. Diels, *Elementum*, p. 45.

12. Milton has put this part of the *Republic* into verse in his *Arcades*, line 61 seq.: "... in deep of night when drowsiness / Hath lock'd up mortal sense, then listen I / To the celestial Sirens harmony, / That sit upon the nine infolded spheres, / And sing to those that hold the vital shears, / And turn the adamantine spindle round, / On which the fate of Gods and men is wound. / Such sweet compulsion doth in music lie, / To lull the daughters of Necessity, / And keep unsteady Nature to her law, / And the low world in measur'd motion draw / After the heavenly tune, which none can hear / Of human mold, with gross unpurged ear." Here we have the allusion to Ananke holding the spindle of adamant, while her three daughters wind the web about the spindle and sing along with the Sirens.

We find another treatment of the same theme in Chamisso's allegorical tale "Adelberts Fabel" (1806), in which Ananke is presented as an old man, clad in an azure robe beset with stars, who, as he plays on the harp (of the world) makes the stars fall in order, and whose chords are the texture of the poet's life, as it is woven by two female beings at cross-purposes. Here, the motif of the harmony of the spheres is combined with that of the Fates, whose weaving becomes a music of the stars.

13. The (eight) singing Sirens of Plato were easily able to become the (nine) Muses with Plutarch, Martianus Capella and Macrobius (cf. De Tolnay, *loc. cit.*, p. 89, who points out that in a thirteenth-century parchment of Reims, representing the harmony of the universe, the sky that encompasses the earth contains nine medallions with the nine muses who, at the same time, symbolize the nine planets).

14. Cf. in Philo Judaeus (ed. Cohn-Wendland, I, 196) the idea that the Creator made things to be consonant, as he made the tone of the lute consonant, in spite of the unequal sounds (λύρας τρόπον ἐξ ἀνομοίων ἡρμοσμένης φθόγγων εἰς κοινωνίαν καὶ συμφωνίαν ἐλθόντα συνηχήσειν ἔμελλεν —this whole chapter being an anticipation of Panurge's speech on the principle of borrowing and lending in nature). The soul is fitted together in a musical manner (II, 61: ὥσπερ τινὰ λύραν τὴν ψυχὴν μουσικῶς ἁρμοσάμενον) so that contrasts do not jar.

On the other hand, when Philo interprets the Jewish chandelier with its seven branches as the seven celestial strings of which the sun is the μέση, the middle string serving to tune (ἁρμόζεσθαι) the instrument (cf. Boyancé,

Étude sur le Songe de Scipion, p. 100), we see before us a world lute (μουσικὸν καὶ θεῖον ὄργανον) that corresponds macrocosmically to the human soul.

It is also in Philo that we first find the idea of God as a musician who plays, unseen, upon man: ὄργανον θεοῦ ἐστιν ἠχοῦν, κρουόμενον καὶ πληττόμενον ἀοράτως ὑπ' αὐτοῦ (cf. L. Schrade, "Die Darstellung der Töne an den Kapiteller der Abteikirche zu Cluni," *Deutsche Vierteljahrsschrift*, VII, 245). This simile appears again and again in modern literature in the secularized version of one *human* being playing upon the soul of another as on a musical instrument—the human "musician" par excellence being the inamorata who inspires the emotions of the poet's heart; the first attestations of this simile known to me are fourteenth-century examples from Machaut and Chaucer (each independent of the other, according to Karl Young's essay on the *Dit de la harpe*).

Quite different is the scene in *Hamlet* (III, 2) where the treatment of the human soul as an instrument is seen as a violation of the mystery of the individual (Hamlet to Guildenstern): "You would play upon me; you would seem to know my stops; you would pluck out the heart of my mystery; you would sound me from my lowest note to the top of my compass; and there is much music, excellent voice, in this little organ, yet you cannot make it speak. 'Sblood, do you think I am easier to be played on than a pipe? Call me what instrument you will, though you can fret me, you cannot play upon me."

It remained for the post-Romantic bourgeois Murger to debase this glorious metaphor to the description of the sexual conditioning of a woman (*Scènes de la vie de Bohème*, in the chapter titled "La crémaillère"): "Rodolphe s'approcha de Mimi et l'enlaça dans ses bras. Puis, comme un musicien qui, avant de commencer son morceau, frappe un placage d'accords pour s'assurer de la capacité de son instrument, Rodolphe assit le jeune Mimi sur ses genoux et lui appuya sur l'épaule un long et sonore baiser qui imprima une vibration soudaine au corps de la printanière créature. L'instrument était d'accord."—The chapter ends on this cheaply epigrammatic note.

The idea of the beloved playing upon the heart of the lover has been treated humorously, and in a manner far from medieval, by Gottfried Keller in his poem, "Geübtes Herz": the poet tells his sweetheart that she should not reject his heart because he has loved before; his heart is a violin that becomes more precious the more it is played upon. And, to illustrate this continuous practicing the poem is based on a sequence of sounds (and rhymes) in -i- (it may be noted that in Keller's native Swiss dialect, *gige*, not *geige*, is the name of the "fiddle").

A final step in the downward development of the metaphor is to be seen in its crystallization in reference to "playing on a person's nerves," as in Germ *auf den Nerven jem. spielen* (for "nerves" = "strings [of an instrument]," *vide infra*).

15. Certain of the later Greek writers conceived the idea of the wedding of music and chastity. We find this concept, perhaps for the first time, in the

fabulous tale of Achilles Statius, *ca.* 300 (who, according to legend, was converted to Christianity in his old age), that describes the invention of the pipes of Pan; in Book viii, 6, of his "Adventures of Leucippe and Clitophon," he tells us that a maiden, being pursued by Pan, was able to escape his grasp by melting into the ground, leaving in her place a clump of reeds which Pan then collected, "kissing them as though they had been her wounds," breathing upon them and groaning from love, and made into a musical instrument. This he suspended in a cave to be guarded by Artemis, on condition that only virgins should enter there; and from that time on, whenever a girl approached who had lost her virginity, a groan was heard, but a virgin was greeted by a divine note.

I would remark that the basic idea of Mallarmé's *Après-midi d'un faune,* the idea, that is, that art comes not from the actual sensuous experience (the capture of the naiads), but from longing and renunciation, is essentially that of the legend told by Achilles Statius.

16. There is a very moving passage in the final paragraph of Schleiermacher's "Monologen," IV, which deals with friendship in musical terms: "Es ist das Leben der Freundschaft eine schöne Folge von Accorden, der, wenn der Freund die Welt verlässt, der gemeinschaftliche Grundton abstirbt. Zwar innerlich hallt ihm ein langes Echo ununterbrochen nach, und weiter geht die Musik; doch erstorben ist die begleitende Harmonie in ihm, zu welcher ich der Grundton war, und die war mein, wie diese in mir sein ist." In the eighteenth century, friendship finds an accent which would seem to us more fittingly reserved for romantic love; compare A. G. Spangenberg (writing about 1750; cf. *Pietismus und Rationalismus,* p. 59): "[a member of the Herrnhut Brotherhood] kam durch Gottes Fügung zu mir. Wir *flossen* gleich *in Liebe zusammen,* und alle unsere Gedanken *harmonierten mit einander* . . . und ich werde dem Herrn noch in der Ewigkeit dafür danken."

17. The claim of "government by music"—well known also in the philosophy of Confucius—has been reiterated often in modern times. The music teacher in the *Bourgeois Gentilhomme* declares (I, ii): "Sans la musique, un état ne peut subsister . . . si tous les hommes apprenaient la musique, ne serait-ce pas le moyen de s'*accorder* ensemble, et de voir dans le monde la paix universelle?" The *Grand-ecrivains* edition, in a note to this passage, mentions a similar reference by Charles IX to Plato, on the occasion of the opening of the Royal Musical Academy (1570), as well as a passage from the *Harmonie universelle* of Père Mersenne, 1636.

18. The text is reproduced from Boyancé, *Étude sur le Songe de Scipion* (Limoges, 1936); see his commentary on pp. 104 seq.: the eight spheres produce seven musical intervals.

19. Such an accumulation of terms insisting, by means of the prefix, on a theme—perhaps they may be called "prefixal leitmotivs," and they may be placed within the more comprehensive "symphonic clusters"—illustrates

clearly the importance which the writer in question attaches to a concept. Any translation which would render *convenientia* by "harmony" and *consensus* by "agreement," and would omit the anaphoral *co-* appearing in the rest of the passage, would detract thereby from the full force of the "hammering." I may add that "symphonic clusters" are also a help in determining historically the presence of a *topos* or theme in a particular writer; in other words, history of ideas, as applied to a text, can greatly profit from the study of words.

I have never been able to understand how one could read a philosopher properly without recourse to the text in its original language (to my mind, the procedure of the *Journal of the History of Ideas*, which usually renders the words of the original philosopher in English, is one which shows more regard for the reader than for the philosopher who is being treated). A philosopher is, after all, only one special kind of writer, to whom the same procedure may be applied which is so often used by critics of "literature," who will, for example, point out the "key words" in Milton and Goethe, in Dante and Pascal, which give a clue to lyrical motifs: this is what Hans Sperber and I have called "Motiv- und Wortforschung." Anyone who reads Plato or Cicero in translation may, perhaps, grasp the general trend of thought; but how could he perceive the interwoven pattern of overtones, the density of thought in the making, the practical and energetic application of thinking at the moment the thought is being expressed, the recourse to favorite concepts as reflected by key words: the thinking *as action*, as practical realization? To think with words and in words is a procedure as old as human philosophy. In fact, the first attempt at philosophy is language itself; and language never loses its grip on the philosopher, however elaborate and refined his philosophemes may become. "Language thinks for him," as Schiller said. To try to separate thought from word is as illusory as to try to separate in linguistics semantics from phonetics. Professor Crane has recently shown the fallacies generally inherent as well in philological interpretation of texts as in history of ideas applied to texts (*College English* II, 764–5), and he advocates, although without revealing the particular nature of his particular synthesis, a "third alternative": "we may endeavor to acquire, in this field, a subject matter of our own—a subject matter which is neither words as the philologist treats them nor yet ideas as these are conceived by the dialectical historian, but rather some *combination of the two* . . . " Yes, I would say: *that* combination of the two in which the idea *and* the word are, at every moment of the reading, *seen* together (we may, of course, separate them temporarily for pedagogical purposes)—as is done in this study.

The importance of the combination of *con-* clusters is not sufficiently realized by editors and critics; when Dante (*Convivio*, 3.14) says in unison with Cicero, "... a quelle Atene celestiali, dove gli Stoici e Peripatetici e Epicurii per l'altre [virtù] de la veritade etterna, in uno volere *concordevolmente concorrono*," the commentators fail to insist on the presence of the *topos* indicated by the prefix. Again, the *dis-* cluster portrays disharmony: Agrippa d'Aubigné, describing in his *Tragiques* the *mère non mère* (i.e., France) torn by religious intestinal war, emphasizes the state of a nature *se desnaturant*, of a *mère desnaturée* (as embodied in Catherine de' Medici [I, 501, ed. Garnier]: "La mère du berceau son cher enfant *deslie*; / L'enfant qu'on desbandoit autres-fois pouv sa vie / Se desveloppe ici par les barbares doigts / Qui s'en vont *destacher de nature* les lois / La mère deffaisant, pitoyable et farouche . . . " (Disharmony floods everything, attracting into its whirlpool even such harmless verbs as *deslier*, *desbander*, *desvelopper*).

In George Herbert's *Cambridge Poems* (III: "The Church," ii), the harmony of the Bible is brought together with the harmony of the spheres. As the starry sky is a book written by God, so the book of God is also a starry sky: "Oh that I knew how all thy lights *combine*, / And the *configurations* of their glorie! / Seeing not onely how each verse doth shine, / But all the *constellations* of the storie . . . / This book of starres lights to eternal blisse." The edition Boston-New York, 1915 (II, 188) quotes by way of comment from Herbert's *Country Parson*, iv: "All Truth being *consonant* [italics mine] in itself, an industrious and judicious comparing of place with place must be a singular help for the right understanding of the Scriptures." And the editor notes: "To emphasize the theme, the prefix *con-* is used three times in the first four lines." There is no mention, however, of the fact that these prefixes in themselves are historically connected with the *consonare-harmonia topos*: that they themselves form a linguistic *topos*, inherited from antiquity and are not a feature of style particular to Herbert.

Again, our contemporary commentators have all extolled the particular vein in Paul Claudel of introducing punningly a *con-* prefix in such a word as *connaître* [= *co-naître*, according to Claudel]. But they have failed to observe that the same poet has imitated, in his *Art poétique*, the ancient accumulation of *con-* prefixes, in a passage dealing, in the ancient vein, with the "concert" that is contained in a moment of time: after long enumerations of all the things that "together" (*tout cela* is repeated several times) constitute *l'heure totale* (= *la durée réelle* of Bergson), we read (pp. 41-3): "à toute heure de la terre il est toutes les heures à la fois. . . . Les aménagements de la terre travaillée par le feu et l'eau, les réactions des acides et des sels, le tirement spirateur de la végétation, l'animal asservi à son instinct, l'homme debout: tout concourt au même dessin, reçoit d'un même moteur impulsion, mesure et vie. . . . Toutes choses dans le temps écoutent, *concertent* et *composent*. Les rencontres des forces physiques et le jeu des volontés humaines *coopèrent* dans la *confection* de la mosaïque instant" (for *concerter*, which is used as by Corneille, see below). Similarly, in *Positions et Propositions* (I, 11): "Nous procédons à l'émission d'une série de *complexes* isolés [if the poet is composing verses], il faut leur laisser, par l'alinéa, le temps, ne fût-ce qu'une seconde, de *se coaguler* à l'air libre, suivant les limites d'une mesure qui permette au lecteur de *comprendre* [this verb is italicized by the author] d'un seul coup et la structure et la saveur." *Ibid.* (p. 111): "Ce moule [the book] où viennent *se coaguler et se composer* les images du Passé, les témoinages du Présent et les impulsions du Futur." And it is no chance that, with Paul Valéry, too, formations cluster around *composer*, which is conceived, by Valéry as by Claudel, as a *com-ponere* (cf. R. Burkart, *Arch. f. neu. Spr.*, CLXI, 95); with Claudel there is a Catholic influence to be seen while Valéry followed more ancient models; with both we may find the traces of one unified, ultimately Ciceronian, tradition.

In Maine de Biran, *Les discours philosophiques de Bergerac* (1807; *Œuvres*, V, 5) we read the following passage (where the italics are in the original): "Le Chef-d'œuvre de la nature, l'homme, considéré sous les rapports d'une organisation admirable par la variété, la *complication* et le jeu de tous les instruments de la vie; plus admirable encore par *l'unité* de cette vie même et l'accord parfait de toutes les fonctions qui y *conspirent* et *consentent*, l'homme se trouve lié par l'ensemble de ses rapports avec tout ce qui l'entoure." (It is evident that the italics of the original indicate a quotation from Cicero: the *conspirare—convenire —concordare* found above.)

Finally, I may mention the passage of the Mayflower Covenant in which the Pilgrim Fathers pledged to "*covenant* and *combine* ourselves together into one civil body politic," thus imitating, by the "prefix of concord," the cosmic order and speaking Ciceronian in the middle of the seventeenth century. Confer the *con-* prefixes in the passage (quoted by G. L. Finney, *Jour. of the Hist. of Ideas*, VIII, 153–86) from the sixteenth-century writer, Stephen Gosson, *The School of Abuse*, who compares the well-governed commonwealth with musical harmony and the harmony of the elements: "the *concorde* of the Elementes and their qualyties . . . *con*curring togeather to the constitution of earthly bodies and sustenace of euery creature" (p. 156). This *topos* is not extinct in our own days. Winston Churchill during the last war on several occasions described the association of the Allies by means of combinations of *co[n]* nouns; in his speech to Congress on May 18, 1943, for example, he states: "we have . . . acted in close *combination or concert* . . ."; "this intimacy and *concert* . . ."; "the Northwest African campaign . . . is the finest example of the *co-operation* of the troops of three different countries and of the *combination* under one commander." And in a speech before Parliament concerned with the same events, June 8, 1943, he says: "the most complete *concord* and *confidence* prevails at General Eisenhower's headquarters, and the forces of the two great nations of the English-speaking world are working together literally as if they were one single army"; " . . . our growing *concert* and unity . . . ."

Our stylistic *topos* of *co-* clusters is also important for historical linguistics. Several Romance words, which long defied explanation, contain a *con-* indicative of (Christian) "harmony"; one example is that of *contropare* "to harmonize" (Biblical texts), "to interpret figuratively" (in Cassiodorus), which, according to me (cf. *Romania*, 1938), is underlying the word family of French (*con*) *trouver*, and is a late outgrowth of the *consonare-concordare-consentiri* family. The Romance (*cum*)*initiare*, "to begin," which Jaberg, *Revue de Linguistique Romane*, I, 128, rightly refers to the Christian "initiation" (though he fails to justify the *cum-* prefix), is to be explained, I believe, by the "togetherness" of the initiated; for the *cum-* prefix in Christian Latin, as an indication of Christian solidarity and fraternity, cf. a treatise of Erik Ahlman (Helsinki, 1916), which I know only from a quotation by Y. Malkiel. The Italian *congratularsi* (Eng *to congratulate*), and the words for "condolence" are rooted in an atmosphere of Catholicism, as this is expressed in the medieval trope: "*Congaudeant* Catholici / Laetentur cives celici / Die ista . . .".

20. In the German Romanticists we find a tendency to revive not so much the Latin *con-*, as its Greek prototype, *syn-*. Kluckhohn, in *Persönlichkeit und Gemeinschaft*, p. 13, speaks of "das romantische Syn," and lists the following terms found in the writings of this school: *Symphilosophie, Sympoesie, Synexistenz,* συνενθουσιάζειν, *Koaktivität, höchste Sympathie,* and even *Sympolemisieren* and *Symfaulenzen.* All of these are derivatives of συμπάθεια and of its congeners, including συμφιλοσοφεῖν, "philosophizing in sympathy."

21. In the following poem, attributed to Petronius (communicated to me by Professor Castro), it is the community of mourners sympathetically united in grief that is portrayed by the reiteration of *con-* (as well as by words suggestive of union):

> Naufragus eiecta nudus rate quaerit *eodem*
> Percussum telo, qui sua fata legat;
> Grandine qui segetes et totum perdidit annum,
> In *simili* deflet tristia fata sinu.
> Funera *conciliant* miseros, orbique parentes
> *Coniungunt* gemitus, et facit hora pares.
> Nos quoque *confusis* feriemus sidera verbis,
> Et fama est *iunctas* fortius ire preces.

22. Cf. in the *Cambridge Songs*, ed. Strecker, n° 3: "Voces laudis humane / curis carneis rauce / non divine maeiestati / cantu sufficiunt, // Que angelicam sibi militiam in excelsis psallere / *sanctam* iussit / *simphoniam.* // Necnon variam / mundi discordiam / se movendo *concordem* / dare fecit / *armoniam.*"

23. For the connection between "islands" and the Christian faith, cf. Rabanus Maurus (*De Universo* [*c.* 844]), Migne, III, 353:

Insulae dictae quod in salo sint, id est in mari positae [here we have an etymology of Isidore of Seville: *Etym.* XIV, vi, 1], quae in plurimis locis sacrae Scripturae aut Ecclesias Christi significant, aut specialiter quoslibet sanctos viros, qui tunduntur fluctibus persecutionum, sed non destruuntur, quia a Deo proteguntur. Nam in psalterio scriptum est: *Dominus regnavit, exsultet terra, laetentur insulae multae* (*Psal.* XCVI): Regnante itaque Domino per totum mundum dispositae laetentur Ecclesiae: quae merito insulis comparantur, quia mundi fluctibus ambitae circumlatrantium persecutionum numerositate tunduntur: sed sicut istae saevientibus fluctibus nesciunt laedi, ita nec sanctae Ecclesiae perturbationibus adversariorum probantur immunes: quin potius illos suis cantibus frangunt, qui in eas undosis culminibus irruerunt.

Here, too, we find an indication of a protecting *ambiens,* which resists the outward world that "hounds" the Christian (note the inimical flavor of *circum-* in contrast to the friendly one of *amb-,* and of world harmony triumphant over persecution ("illos suis cantibus frangunt").

24. I am not forgetting the poetry of the Psalms which praise the earth by way of praising God, revealing to us in the star-filled firmament the manifestation of God's glory (Ps. 19, 1–5; 147, 4–5; 148, 3). Charles de Tolnay, in his article, "The Music of the Universe" (*Journal of the Walters Art Gallery*, VI, 82–104), has shown that the identification of David's music with the Pythagorean harmony of the spheres made it possible for the figure of Orpheus (who was for the ancients the singer of world harmony and whose myth has a certain similarity with that of David) to be replaced in medieval art by that of the Jewish musician-king, who, with the magical power of music, tamed not beasts but a king. Thus, David the Musician will appear in the Middle Ages surrounded by the signs of the zodiac, by the animals he is supposed to have charmed, by the six tones, or by the allegorical figures of the seasons and the elements. In the painting by Lorenzo Ricci (now in the Walters Art Gallery) which has prompted Mr. de Tolnay's article, we are offered the scene of the Annunciation, which takes place beneath a *supercoelum* on which is painted a blue sky with golden stars, and a medallion showing David playing the harp—as though the scene below were accompanied, were motivated, by world music.

(As for the representation [in a miniature by Cosmas Indicopleustes] of David surrounded by six choirs, which are also figured as six stars, de Tolnay explains the number "6" by the six intervals between the seven tones. I would suggest also the pattern of "6" found first in Oriental, then in late Greek art [cf. Friedländer, *loc. cit.*, on the fifth-century tapestry representing Hestia surrounded by three figures on each side], and finally on twelfth-century stained windows [where, for example, the Virgin and Child are portrayed with three angels to left and to right].)

It was also to this role of a Christian musician that the "prefiguration pattern" (David as the precursor of Christ) was applied: David's musical conquest of the demon in Saul was an anticipation of Christ's victory over the evil in man. One ecclesiastical writer (Nicetius in *De laude et utilitate spiritualium canticorum*, cf. L. Scrade, *Dtsch. Vierteljahrsschr.*, VII, 248) even saw in the cithara, supposedly used by David, a "figura crucis Christi, quae in ligno et extensione nervorum mystice gerebatur jam tunc": David's instrument was "mystically attuned" to the cross. We find this theme as late as the seventeenth century: the frontispiece of Mersenne's *Harmonie universelle* (1637) shows a figure in ancient attire (that could be either David or Orpheus, or a synthesis of both) charming animals by music; below is inscribed a verse from the Psalms. In the preface, Mersenne refers to Tertullian's description of the sign of the cross as a musical performance (*modulabantur Christum*), and expresses the wish that "des Orphées chrétiens" would sing, in his time, "des airs spirituels." The fusion of the Christian and the pagan elements is here perfect.

In yet another manner did the Old Testament conform to the Christian concept of world harmony: I am thinking of the song of the three Hebrew children in the fiery furnace, which was inserted into Daniel 3, 51 (this is now a part of the Laudes in the Roman Breviary) by a Jew in the first century B.C., whose "jubilant tone . . . is in marked contrast to the despondency of the Prayer of Azariah," and whose mention of the "holy and glorious Temple" seems to indicate a flourishing condition of religious services, as has been pointed out by R. H. Charles, *The Apocrypha and Pseudepigraphica of the Old Testament*, p. 629. The litany of *benedicite*'s comprises the whole creation, and an introductory line contains an allusion to the unanimity of this chant in praise of God and His wondrous creation, uttered in the midst of deadly peril ("Tunc hi tres quasi *et uno ore* laudabant et glorificabant et benedicebant Deum in fornace").

A Benjamin Franklin, belonging to a civilization with a bent for visual apperception and rationalism, could only dismiss the manifold "repetitions" of the Psalms (cf. Van Doren, *Benjamin Franklin*, p. 438).

25. The difference between Jewish and Mohammedan symbolism on the one hand and that of Christianity, on the other, has been described in a masterly fashion by Mahnke, *Unendliche Sphäre*, p. 214:

> . . . das christliche Grunddogma der Menschwerdung Gottes vermag die substantielle Transzendenz des göttlichen Wesens durch die *wirkliche* Immanenz seiner Schöpferkraft und die *unmittelbare* Offenbarung seiner Persönlichkeit in irdischen Geschehen doch viel wesentlicher zu ergänzen, als dies in der jüdischen und islamischen Erhabenheitstheologie . . . möglich ist. Deshalb hat auch erst die christliche Mystik einen *echten Symbolismus* ausbilden können, der in der sinnlichen Realität nicht bloss äusserliche Allegorien oder Analogien der höheren göttlichen Wirklichkeit findet, sondern dem alles Irdische ein wahres σύμβολον, ein Erkennungszeichen des sich offenbarenden Himmlischen ist, ja ein von Gott persönlich "eingesetztes und geweihtes" *Sakrament*, das im Sichtbaren selbst unsichtbare Werte spendet.

What is here said of the visible Christian symbol pertains also to the audible.

26. These expressions have remained characteristic of the religious hymn, cf. *Cambridge Songs*, n° 23: "Vestiunt silve tenera ramorum / virgulta, . . . / canunt de celsis sedibus palumbes / carmina cunctis. // Hic turtur gemit, resonat hic turdus / . . . passer nec tacet . . . / aves sic *cuncte* celebrant estivum / *undique* carmen."

27. The world-embracingness of Ambrose's religious musicality is narrowed and adulterated by Maurice Barrès in his *Amitiés françaises* (1903), in which he depicts the ideal education of a "little Lorrainer." He first proposes to act on the imagination of the child through music: the task of the educator is to bring up the child *in hymnis et canticis* (a phrase borrowed from Ambrosius), in order to adapt the melody of the child's soul, without adulteration, to the symphony of the community. But, in the child's genuine melody, it is, of course, according to Barrès, the French race that sings, and it behooves the educator to strengthen this innate, potential French music. What was world music with Ambrose becomes nationalistic music with this would-be Christian of the twentieth century.

28. In contradiction to the Christian "synesthetic" liturgic performances, Jewish liturgy has remained austerely confined to monodic singing; there is a relative absence of mimics (an embryonic reminder of a mimic approach is the custom in the Kedushshah—which corresponds to the Sanctus of the Catholic

mass—to rise on one's toes thrice, at every utterance of the word "holy" in order to symbolize that "the mountains leapt like sheep").

I should think that Spanke's investigations on the origin of the dance-song *rondeau* would have been more fruitful if he had not posited the question in terms of "which is first: the lay or the liturgic dance-song?" For the idea of the Christian world harmony must have been ecclesiastic as well as lay in the early Middle Ages—a civilization pervaded by Christian feelings. The relative earlier date of a *rondeau* in Latin or in a vulgar language proves little: it is the common background we must reckon with. Even if Abelard knew the metrical form of the lay *rondeau*, we do not know whether the lay *rondeau* is not an outgrowth of religious feelings. In such cases, the *Volkslied* approach is more apt to obscure than to enlighten. In the Provençal epic poem on St. Fides (ed. Alfaric and Hoeffner, Paris, 1926), written as late as the eleventh century, we see a cleric listening to a (Latin) hagiologic *canczon . . . qu'es bella 'n tresca* ("a beautiful song for a dance"; line 14), and singing its Provençal paraphrase (probably also *bella 'n tresca*) in one of the ecclesiastical "tones" (·l *primers tons*). In the imaginative picture of this performance as visualized by Alfaric (II, 77): "Replaçons-la par la pensée, au temps des croisades, en une des églises de la région pyrénéenne, . . . devant une assistance très-croyante, qui s'est réunie en une nuit d'octobre, à la lueur des cierges, pour célébrer les vigiles de sa Sainte préférée, patronne des croyants, et à qui de pieux chanteurs font entendre, en des chœurs alternés (?), le récit émouvant du martyre, tandis que des acteurs bénévoles (?), dans un but religieux, en miment les scènes avec des gestes cadencés," I have introduced question marks in accordance with Spanke's doubts about factual attestation (see note 31, below); I do not, however, wish to imply that I believe that this poetic picture is not *basically* true: poetry may sometimes be truer to the spirit of an epoch than so-called history. A saint was celebrated by dances and hymns according to the principle of the *Gesamtkunstwerk*.

It is interesting to note the influence of the Ambrosian hymn on the narrative genre of the Christian legend, which became thereby a lyrical and musical genre. A specimen of such an "Ambrosian" hagiographical narrative is the Latin model of the *chanson de sainte Eulalie*, a sequence which is preserved along with that first poetic document of France in the same ninth-century manuscript: "Cantica virginis Eulalie / concine, suavissona cithara! / Est opere quoniam precium / clangere carmine martyrium, / tuam ego voce sequar melodiam / atque laudem imitabor Ambrosiam. / Fidibus cane melos eximium, / vocibus ministrabo suffragium. / Sic pietate[m], sic humanum ingenium / fudisse fletum compellamus ingenitum." This relatively long exordium (10 lines) of the poem (29 lines) states the literary descent of the poem (Ambrose), and insists deliberately on its audible qualities (*concine, suavissona cithara, clangere*, etc.); music is emphasized (the human voice will only "follow, give suffrage to, the instrument"), and this music is "praise," therefore "worthy," and its emotional content will be "love" and sympathy ("tears") for the saint.

The idea of the last couple of lines seems to be that music (with its order, probably the *numeri*) restrains (*compellamus*) the free flow of feeling. The narrative itself takes up only eight lines: because of her godly deeds, Eulalia, in a Christianized Ovidian metamorphosis, ascends to the sky (*idcirco stellis caeli se miscuit*). This feature seems to be the pivotal point of the poem: the last part of eleven lines is dedicated to the hope that the intercessor saint will protect those who joyfully sing her praise—and thereby do good deeds (*qui sibi laeti pangunt armoniam* and *devoto corde modos demus innocuos*)—and who would propitiate the Lord of the sky by placing in the sky the good deeds of His servants (e.g., the singing of this hymn). We may also note in passing the presence of synesthetics: Eulalia's soul is *lacteolus*; our deeds shall "scintillate" among the stars. (Prudentius' hymn, on the contrary, dwells nearly exclusively on colors.)

I believe that the idea of the harmony of the spheres, though not explicitly referred to, is implicit in the poem. The link connecting the parts of the poem (the "sonorous" praise of the saint, the "sympathy" for her martyrdom, the description of the heavenly abode of the saint, and the imploration of her intercession for the pious singers) is evidently to be sought in music = piety = heavenly exultation. It is the deed of love of Eulalia which provokes the music, and the musical praise is itself a good deed. The French Eulalia sequence has omitted all musicality and lyricism, presenting an epic account centered around the καλοκαγαθία, the moral beauty of the saint; her character which is first defined in the opening lines (beauty of soul) and elaborated (as in a French classical drama) in the subsequent ones; her concentration of will power on the acceptance of martyrdom and conquest of death, with Christ's aid; and the link with the intercessional prayer for the believers is the idea that we may be able to gain support from the Beyond for our hour of death, as she has done. Since, here, it is character which is stressed, there is a greater emphasis on logical development than on exultant feeling. The epic narrative is demusicalized, although it has retained the metrical (and perhaps also the musical) form; and instead of the ornate form of the Latin poetry, there has entered a note of devout simplicity and dogmatic precision.

29. There are listed in Margot Sahlin's work (*Études sur la carole médiévale*, Uppsala, 1940) many medieval expressions of "unanimism," of the will to spiritual unity on the part of a congregation, manifested by responds,—were they only such simple words as *kyrie eleison* and *gloria tibi domine*, which *simpliciores et idiotae* may be able to utter (p. 101): cf. from Paderborn (*ca.* 836): "Cumque clerus in hymnis et confessionibus Deum benediceret, et spiritualium carminum melodiam . . . concineret, populus vero *Kyrie eleison* ingeminaret, *cum ineffabili jubilo erectis ad Deum mentibus singulorum* " (p. 100); at the funeral of St. Wunebaldus (✠777): "cumque illi psallentes, *caelestia* modulantes portabant eum ad sepulchrum, omnis plebs comitantes *cyrieleizabant*, qui *consonantis* canentium vocibus, qui iocundis iuvenum iubilantionibus . . . *multis vocibus quasi uno ore psallentes glorificabant Deum*" (p. 109); a vision of

the angels in Paradise who sing Kyrie eleison: "et ego *eorum vocibus vocem adjunxi, et eadem laetabundus deprompsi*" (p. 102); a German preacher (*ca.* 1300) describes, among the six species of songs distinguished, the *cantus jubilancium, vreodenlied* thus: "hoc cantant angeli et sancte virgines coram deo et agno, *chorizantes alterutrum ad leticiam se provocantes*"—it is the *certamen* of musical elation over the paradisiac world harmony which will lead to the "concert" (cf. below). In a vita of St. Heribertus of Cologne (✠1200), a procession composed of Frenchmen and Germans, undertaken to avert drought is thus described: "ex omni ordine utriusque sexus, *lingua quidem diversa, sed una intentione et eodem sensu concrepando, Kyrie eleïson,* altitudo caeli pulsabatur" (p. 96)—the language of the liturgy, the supranational language, even in its minimum phrases, guarantees the *concordia,* the unanimity in the discord of languages.

30. This reading (instead of *colore acri adnectitur*) has been proposed to me by Professor Friedländer, as being more in harmony with Empedocles' idea that fire, by virtue of its warmth, is more akin to air; and by virtue of its dryness, to earth.

31. I take these quotations from p. 138 in the synthetic chapter on medieval ritual dances, in Miss Sahlin's book, a chapter which resumes the investigations of Dom L. Gougaud, *Rev. d'hist. eccl.,* XV (1914), of Alfaric, "La chanson de Sainte Foy," II, 71, and of H. Spanke, *Neuphil. Mitt.,* XXXI, 143; XXXIII, 1. But the next example which she gives, from St. Paulinus, has been misinterpreted by Miss Sahlin: "Hinc senior sociae congaudet turba catervae: / Alleluia novis balat ovile choris"—*balat* is surely not a Romance *baler, ballare, bailar,* "to dance", but *balare* = Fr. *bêler,* "to bleat" (*ovile*!). Thus the Paulinus passage testifies rather to the Alleluia respond. Miss Sahlin's rich collection of medieval texts shows that very often a choir is combined with dancing; thus the modern interpreter may hesitate whether to translate a *ducere choream* with the one or the other—or with both at a time; this is also the case with the OFr *caroler, carole* word family itself, whose semantic kernel is "to sing songs with a refrain, while marching in procession" (note also Dante's use of *carole: Par.* XXV, 97: "E prima, appresso al fin d' este *parole* / "Sperent in te" di sopra noi s' udi; / A che *risposer* tutte le *carole*": = dances + words ?). As for the etymology of *caroler, carole,* Miss Sahlin proposes the refrain *kyrie éleison* (> Fr *kyrielle*), which seems to me inacceptable for phonetic reasons, cf. MLN, 56, 222–5. We must needs go back to that *coraulis* (Sahlin, p. 76) in the line of Venantius Fortunatus (*clericus ecce choris resonat, plebs inde coraulis*); whatever the word may mean, there is in that line the clear idea of a "respond" sung. It has perhaps as yet not been observed that the current OFr epic phrases *mener joie, mener duel,* "to show exhilaration, grief," etc., must be explained by this *ducere chorum,* "to conduct a choir of jubilation or lamentation," said of the conductor of a choir. These phrases meant originally *solemn* or *formal* (public) manifestations of sentiments.

32. We find a reference to the flute as a pagan instrument used to tame and soothe, in the lines of Milton from *Paradise Lost*, I, 549–62: "Anon they move / In perfect phalanx to the Dorian mood / Of flutes and soft recorders, such as rais'd / To heighth of noblest temper heroes old / Arming to battle, and instead of rage / Deliberate valor breath'd, firm and unmov'd / With dread of death to flight or foul retreat, / Nor wanting power to mitigate and swage / With solemn touches, troubl'd thoughts, and chase / Anguish and doubt and fear and sorrow and pain / From mortal or immortal minds. Thus they / Breathing united force with fixed thought / Mov'd on in silence to soft pipes that charm'd / Their painful steps o're the burnt soil." The same theme also appears in the text of Mozart's *Magic Flute* (by Schikaneder-Giesecke), which offers a combination of heathen mysteries with the medieval atmosphere of Wieland's *Oberon*.

33. This scene is reflected by that in the German mystic, Seuse's *Des Dieners Leben*, ch. 5, where the servant (of God) sees a *himelscher spilman* resembling an archangel at the head of a group of similar heavenly youths, who invite him to join the dance ("er muste mit in och himelschlich tanzen"), to the merry tune ("froelichez gesengeli von dem kindlin Jesus"), *In dulci jubilo*: "dis tanzen waz nit geschafen in der wise, als man in diser welt tanzet, ez waz neiswi ein himelscher uswal und ein widerinwal in daz wilt abgrund der goetlichen togenheit" (with order and numbers in the midst of the wild abyss of God's grace). This quotation I have found in E. Benz's article "Christliche Mystik und christliche Kunst," *Deutsche Vierteljahrsschr.*, XII, 34 (Benz quotes also a contemporary anonymous poem with the lines: "Jesus der tanzer maister ist . . . er wendeth sich hin, er wendeth sich her si tanzet alle nach siner leye").

34. Hence Boethius, *Inst. Arithm.*, I, 2: "omnia quaecumque a primaeva rerum natura constructa sunt, numerorum videntur ratione formata"; Alanus de Insulis, *Anticlaudianus*: "[Arithmetic] Muta tamen totam numerandi praedicat artem: / Quae numeri virtus, quae lex, quis nexus et ordo, / Nodus amor, ratio foedus, concordia limes. / Quo modo *concordi numerus ligat omnia nexu*, / Singula componit, mundum regit, ordinat orbem / Astra movens, elementa ligans, animasque maritans. / Corporibus, terras caelis, caeleste caducis" (this is a sentence reminiscent of Archytas: στάσιν μὲν ἔπαυσεν, ὁμόνοιαν αὔξησεν λογισμός εὑρεθείς). Karl Fiehn, who quotes these texts in his article "Zum Troilus Alberts von Stade" (in *Ehrengabe Karl Strecker*, 1931, p. 55), shows how, in the medieval Latin epic poem, Philosophy holds in her hands the numbers 27 and 8, i.e., the geometric forms which correspond to the elements ($27 = 3 \times 3 \times 3$ [i.e., the figures developing from the triangle] is the pyramid or tetrahedron, corresponding to fire; $8 = 2 \times 2 \times 2$ is the cube, arising from the square, which corresponds to earth). In other words, Philosophy is represented as dominating the elements.

35. When Wordsworth said: "It should seem that the sonnet, like every other legitimate composition, ought to have a beginning, a middle and an end;

in other words, to consist of three parts, like the three propositions of a syllogism, if such an illustration may be used . . . ," and applied (as N. F. Maclean has shown in *The University Review*, 8 [1941], 202–9, at 205) a threefold structure to a sonnet of his own dealing with the "holy time—breathless with adoration," he was thinking in Augustinian terms: the sonnet, a unit of time and breath, in which the discovery of God by His creature takes place, is but a picture of the Timeless as captured by time-conditioned man.

36. It is in fact unbelievable that Bergson should have stated, for example, in the survey which he gave of his philosophy in 1934, in *La pensée et le mouvant*, that "no" philosopher before him had looked upon time as anything else than a spatial succession of states without any liaison between them—i.e., as having positive attributes. Did he not think of Augustine, whose very musical metaphors he uses, as, for example, when he states that a future event is unpredictable in its development because, precisely at the moment we think of it, we are separated from it by a lapse of time? As he says: "Pouvez-vous, sans la dénaturer, raccourcir la durée d'une mélodie? La vie intérieure est cette mélodie même"—the last sentence is purely Augustinian. But, evidently, Augustine was a Christian Platonist, as Bergson is not, and he thought that God, the divine artist, was able to have at least the idea of what would happen in time, before this time had come, while Bergson says (pp. 20–21): "on se figure que toute chose qui se produit aurait pu être aperçue d'avance par quelque esprit suffisamment informé, et qu'elle préexistait ainsi, sous forme d'idée, à sa réalisation;—conception absurde [!] dans le cas d'une œuvre d'art, car dès que le musicien a l'idée précise et complète de la symphonie qu'il fera, sa symphonie est faite. Ni dans la pensée de l'artiste, ni, à plus forte raison, dans aucune pensée comparable à la nôtre, fût-elle impersonelle, fût-elle même simplement virtuelle, la symphonie ne résidait en qualité de possible avant d'être réelle. Mais n'en peut-on pas dire autant d'un état quelconque de l'univers pris avec tous les êtres conscients et vivants? N'est-il pas plus riche de nouveauté, d'imprévisibilité radicale, que la symphonie du plus grand maître?" The analogy of the *musicum carmen* of the world is retained with Bergson—without the *archimusicus* God, and without the Platonic idea of the Perfect Being who could have in His mind the vision of the whole creation yet to be created. At this period, Platonism was an absurdity to the evolution-minded French philosopher, who, however, at the end of his life, when he wrote *Les deux sources de la morale et de la religion* (1932), had learned to understand it; the transcendental God can be understood, he finally realizes, only by the saint and the mystic. It has been said (e.g., by Léon Dujovne in *Logos*, [Buenos Aires], I, 115–6) that Bergson's philosophy began as Neoplatonic pantheism seen through the lens of biological evolutionism, but ended in transcendentalism; thus he came closer to Plato, and to his final conversion, shortly before his death.

Independently of Bergson, William James discovered that, in a sequence of musical notes, each single one, as it appears to the listener's mind, is affected by those before; thus the present phase of conscious life is shaped by the retention of phases past—and by extension into the future: "continuity and temporality are then two names for the same fundamental structure of conscious life," which has the nature of a stream (hence the "stream of consciousness"). Again, just as in the case of Bergson, one is surprised at the lack of familiarity with Augustine revealed by the modern philosopher James. (A. Gurwitsch, "'William James' Theory of the 'Transitive Parts' of the Stream of Consciousness," *Philosophy and Phenomenological Research*, III, 449, contrasts James only with Hume.)

37. Allers, p. 376, compares the function of music in such a philosophical system to the role played by modern mathematics, quoting Macrobius ("iure . . . musica capitur omne quod vivit, quia caelestis anima, qua animarum universitas animatur, originem sumpsit ex musica") and Robert Grosseteste, who states that music is higher than, and prior to, physics and mathematics.

38. Augustine, in line with the whole of ancient authors, includes poetry under music: Orion and Orpheus are conceived as singers and poets at the same time.

It may also be noted that Novalis, when retelling the story of Orion (in his *Heinrich von Ofterdingen* [ed. Kluckhohn, Leipzig, 1929, I, ii, last paragraph]), calls him "einer jener sonderbaren Dichter oder mehr Tonkünstler," adding parenthetically: "wiewohl die Musik und Poesie wohl ziemlich eins sein mögen und vielleicht ebenso zusammen gehören wie Mund und Ohr, da der erste nur ein bewegliches und antwortendes Ohr ist . . . " Orpheus, on the other hand, is to Novalis one of those early priest-doctors by whom "die mannigfaltigen Töne [the *numeri*] und die sonderbarsten Sympathien und Ordnungen" have come into being. Similarly, Nietzsche in his *Birth of Tragedy*, declares the natural identity between the lyric poet and the musician; this identity, which he postulates as necessary for Dionysiac rapture, is, to him, "the most important phenomenon of the whole lyric poetry of the ancients" (ed. Levy, 1910, p. 45); modern lyricism, lacking music, is like a headless ancient idol.

39. Ortega y Gasset, in his enlightening treatise "Apuntes sobre el pensamiento" (in *Logos* [Buenos Aires], I, 11 seq.), opposes to the presupposition of Greek philosophy (i.e., the axiomatic belief in a resting truth which exists since eternity and whose stable rules [numbers] must be unveiled by man: ἀλήθεια, "truth" = the state of not being hidden), the Jewish-Christian conception of God as the only reality, of a God who has once *in time* created the universe and can change its rules whenever He will; important in this connection is for Ortega the Hebrew *emunah*, "truth" = security, confidence (i.e., of something which will work out in the future). Thus it may be said that Augustine has adapted the *numeri*, which, with the Greeks, represented eternal manifestations of the *natura rerum*, to the Jewish-Christian belief in a temporal creation of the universe: thus his "numbers" are more abstract evidences (as

in the Trinity) than they are numbers underlying nature. Augustine sought to transplant something of the Greek search for cognizance (for the discovery of the eternally given, as Ortega says) into a climate of thought in which the universe was considered not as in Eleatic rest, but in a perpetual historical development willed by Providence. He created "temporal numbers."

40. It is also true that the realization of God's ineffability induces the believer to dispense with the scanning of syllables: the *jubilus* is a shout of joy which mocks all metrics: cf. P.L. 36, 283 [commentary on Ps. 32, 3: *Bene cantate ei in jubilatione*]:

> Quid est in jubilatione canere? Intelligere, verbis explicare non posse quod canitur corde. Etenim illi qui cantant, sive in messe, sive in vinea, sive in aliquo opere ferventi, cum coeperint in verbis canticorum exsultare laetitia, veluti impleti tanta laetitia, ut eam verbis explicare non possint, avertunt se a syllabis verborum, et eunt in sonum jubilationis. Jubilum sonus quidam est significans cor parturire quod dicere non potest. Et quem decet ista jubilatio, nisi ineffabilem Deum? Ineffabilis enim est, quem fari non potes: et si eum fari non potes, et tacere non debes, quid restat nisi ut jubiles; ut gaudeat cor sine verbis, et immensa latitudo gaudiorum metas non habeat syllabarum? [Similar passages are to be found in the same work, pp. 528, 1128, 1254.]

Here we have a justification of the *jubilus* of the Gregorian chant, and also of the *poesia per musicam* of the sequences based on the *alleluia*—that onomatopoeia of joy. Music, then, for Augustine is at the same time that which proves God by numbers and which testifies for God by the number-less irrationality of sound.

41. Professor Allers has drawn my attention to the *De trinitate* of Augustine in which the Church Father, in order to exemplify man's capacity for understanding his fellow man, describes the success of a comedian who, with a felicitous improvisation, was able to voice the unspoken feelings of his audience— because of "compatiente vel conspirante vitio seu natura" (P.L., 42, 1017). We recognize here Gr. συμπάθεια and σύμπνοια.

42. From *concinnus* is derived the verb *concinnare*, "to arrange" which is often glossed: συμπλέκω. In the Middle Ages, *concinnare* is confused with *concinere* (cf. Strecker, *Cambridge Songs*, ad n° 2)—not only for phonetic reasons, but also because of the inner relationship of συμπλοκή and συμφωνία. Ernout-Meillet assume an etymological relationship between *concinnus, concinnare* and *cincinnus*, "lock, curl" (cf. Columella: *capitum et capillorum concinnatores*, "hairdressers"); the *concinnus* word family would thus quite literally correspond to συμπλέκω.

43. The operatic Calderón, for example, opens an *auto sacramental* with a religious morning song: the spirits of Evil, Malice, and the *Lucero de la noche*, testify to the rejuvenating and unifying force of the morning in full accents and pictures of richness, quite similar to the Ambrosian morning hymns. *La viña del Señor* (1676), act I, lines 10 seq.: "¿Qué misteriosas voces / Saludan hoy al día, / Alternando veloces / Del ritmo de su métrica armonía / Las cláusulas suaves / Con las hojas, las fuentes y las aves?" // *Lucero de la Noche*: "¿Qué

misteriosa salva / Tan festiva hoy madruga, / Que al llorar de la aurora, al reir del alba, / Risas aumenta y lágrimas enjuga ? / A cuyo acorde acento, / En aves, fuentes y hojas calma el viento ?" // *Malicia*: "El orbe suspendido / Yace, al ver que en sus cóncavos más huecos / No hay parte en que no suene repetido / El balbuciente idioma de los ecos." // *Lucero de la Noche*: "Aun los troncos más aridos, más secos / Rejuvenecen al templado canto."—We shall see later how traditional are the phrases *templado canto, acorde acento,* and the reference to the choir formed of birds, fountains, leaves, echoes, salvoes, etc.; suffice it here to note how the *Gesamtkunstwerk* of Ambrose has survived, without change, until 1676! The Catholic art of Cervantes—just as so much of Catholic art which is well defined by Santayana as a *Santa Maria sopra Minerva*—perpetuates in modern times something of the Greco-Roman openness to the world of the senses.

44. It is strange to see that Wagner has totally misunderstood his own historical locus: he opposes his *Gesamtkunstwerk* to the ultimately baroque opera of which he saw the decadence in Rossini, Meyerbeer, and other contemporaries, and he would most energetically reject the common opinion of today that he himself, while enlarging and intensifying its range, has continued this genre. Nor has he seen that this *Gesamtkunstwerk* opera goes back, not to the *Volkslied* (which in his opinion expresses the "real" human being, and has alone preserved itself uncontaminated by the "dissective" and destructive influence of dualistic Christianity), but to that very Christian liturgy (and also to the Ambrosian hymn) which gathered together the community on the stage of the Church to represent the universe and to profess their gratefulness to the Creator.

On early Church singing, Wagner writes ("Oper und Drama," *Ges. Schriften . . . Dichtungen* [Leipzig, 1897], III, 310): "Im christlichen Kirchengesange hatte sich die Harmonie selbständig ausgebildet. Ihr natürliches Lebensbedürfnis drängte sie mit Notwendigkeit zur Äusserung als Melodie; sie bedurfte zu dieser Äusserung aber unerlässlich des Anhaltes an das Form und Bewegung gebende Organ des Rhythmus, das sie als ein willkürliches, fast mehr eingebildetes, als wirkliches Maass, dem Tanze entnahm. Die neue Vereinigung konnte nur eine künstliche sein." This harmony, out of vital need, looks for melody, this in turn seeks the rhythm of the dance; the three elements of music are not, in Wagner's opinion, primordially together. Wagner saw expressed in Christianity his own death-craving (and that of Tristan and Isolde), the death-love of an isolated individualistic soul striving back to community and unity; the Catholic community seemed to him detrimental to the expression of this (his) modern tragedy, only the *Volkslied* ("abseits von der grossen Heerstrasse des gemeinsamen Lebens") could, he thought, offer real music, real melody. The modern opera has betrayed the *Volkslied* by fitting the *aria* into an artificial frame; he himself was preceded only by Beethoven, who drew new flame out of poetry and music combined, thanks to his association with the poet Schiller. In historic reality, the *Bühnenweihfestspiel*, "Parsifal," is but a renovation of an *auto sacramental* of Calderón, and this, as well as some of the medieval *mystères*, goes back ultimately to the liturgy. Similarly, Wagner, striving to attain unity in a world of dispersal (the unity of the Greek drama), adds the gesture (mimics) of the theater to his *Musikdrama* because he feels the need of the complete expression of the "real man": he forgets that, as we have shown, gestures (dances) were inherent to the early Christian liturgic performances.

The synesthesias of *Isoldes Liebestod* ("In des Wonnemeeres wogendem Schwall, / in der Duftwellen / tönendem Schall, / in des Weltatems / wehendem All—ertrinken— / versinken— / unbewusst— / höchste Lust!") are Ambrosian in principle, though the theme of dissolution into nothingness is anti-Christian. Thomas Mann, in his article "Leiden und Grösse Richard Wagners" (in the volume *Leiden und Grösse der Meister*, 1935, p. 93), has sensed in Wagner's "art of sensualism and symbolistic formulae" the ritualistic element which is the strongest in *Parsifal*, his last and "most theatrical" work. He has seen in this theatrical art of a Protestant the craving back to Catholic liturgy: "Theater-kunst, das ist in sich selbst schon Barock, Katholizismus, Kirche" (it seems to me that this definition is better reversed: not all theatrical art is Catholicism, but Catholicism implies the *teatro del mundo*).

On the other hand, it is difficult to understand, given the statement just quoted, how Mann can see, in Wagner's aesthetic theory of the *Gesamtkunst-werk*, the "bad," mechanistic thinking of the nineteenth century which sought to establish artistic unity by adding several arts together. Apart from the fact that Wagner had in mind, not addition but fusion (and his *Musikdrama* in fact rests on fusion, as Thomas Mann himself has pointed out), it seems evident, from our historical discussion, that the *Gesamtkunstwerk* harks back, not to the mechanistic nineteenth century, but to the quite unmechanistic, the world-harmony-seeking fourth century of Ambrose.

Goethe, in his *Italienische Reise*, while expressing his aversion against the Catholic rites he had witnessed in the Sistine Chapel, still had to confess that the Catholics had had "all the arts" in their possession for centuries—which is tantamount to saying that the *Gesamtkunstwerk* is ever present in Catholic church service.

NOTES TO CHAPTER II

1. In medieval glossaries the identification of the two word families *concordia-consonantia* may be noted; compare, for example, the old French "Abavus" (M. Roques, *Recueil général des lexiques français du Moyen Age* [Paris, 1936], I, 290, 314): *Discordare-descorder; discordia-decorde; discors-decordable; dissonare-discorder; dissonus-descordable.* *Concordare-acorder; concordia-concorde; concors-acordant.* Also *discolus* (< Gr. δύσκολος) is glossed with *decordable*, the usual rendering of *discors*, *dissonus*, probably because of the phonetic assonance. The same tradition prevails also in the Spanish glosses, which A. Castro has edited (*RFE*, supp. 22): *discolus-cosa desacordable; discors-desacordable; disino* (probably to be corrected: *disuno = dissono*; Castro's suggestions are wrong) = *desacordar*.

2. A strange attempt at connecting morals and music by means of numbers has been pointed out by Allers, p. 375: Rupert von Deutz finds the numbers of the Just, mentioned in Genesis by Abraham, to correspond to the musical intervals.

3. This predominance of instrumental over vocal music can still be seen as late as the seventeenth century in Spanish plays. In Mira de Amescua's *El harpa de David* it would really seem that the harp is the most important element of the play, although for the public it is evidently the words of the song, destined to move King Saul, which make the greatest impression; but what is emphasized is the excellence of David's playing: "es tal la musica y armonía / de su arpa que podía / suspender la celestial" (i.e., his *musica humana* vies with the *musica mundana*). David himself concurs in the opinion that "mi arpa," since it is tuned to praise of God, must cure the king; and so he plays, singing to his accompaniment (this is managed in the theater by off-stage singing). King Saul's first reaction is to attribute his relief from pain to "O poderosa armonía! / ¡O celestial instrumento!"; it is only later that he speaks of David himself, the "Pastor que sana si canta" (line 155). Here there is precedence of the harp over the voice, which is theoretically purported to be *instrumentalis* (cf. also *Don Quixote*, I, 27: *música, músico* used of a song and of a singer, respectively). Another indication that the voice itself is conceived of as an instrument is to be found in the stage directions, in which the off-stage singer is called *músico*, not *cantor* (also in Molière's *Bourgeois Gentilhomme* the *musiciens* are "singers"). Similarly, in Shakespeare's stage directions (*Merchant of Venice*, III, 2) the singing of a song is indicated by the word *Music*.

In Ronsard's Pindaric ode to Michel de l'Hospital (1550), the Muses are defined as "Les filles qu'enfanta Mémoire . . . / En qui répandit le ciel / Une musique immortelle, / Comblant leur bouche nouvelle / Du jus d'un attique miel / Et à qui vraiment aussi / Les vers furent en souci; / Les vers dont flattés nous sommes, / Afin que leur doux chanter / Pût doucement enchanter / Le soin des dieux et des hommes" (12–34); Jupiter desires to hear "[les chansons . . .] de ces neuf musiciennes. / Elles ouvrant leur bouche pleine / D'une douce arabe moisson, / Par l'esprit d'une vive haleine / Donnèrent l'âme à leur chanson; / Fredonnant sur la chanterelle / de la harpe du Délien / La contentieuse querelle / De Minerve et du Cronien . . . / Puis d'une voix plus violente / Chantèrent l'enclume de fer . . . . / Après, sur la plus grosse corde, / D'un bruit qui tournait jusqu'aux cieux, / Le pouce des Muses accorde / L'assaut des Géants et des Dieux" (169–220). The music of these *musiciennes* consists of singing to the accompaniment of an instrument whose different strings ("chanterelle—la plus grosse corde") are used according to the *Stimmung* of the contents. But the singing, even the poetry, is subordinated to music.

Ultimately, there may be, in the theory which includes the human voice with the musical instruments, a remainder of a Latin (and perhaps Indo-European) lexicological fact: that *canere* was said both of instrumental (cf. *fidibus canere, tibicen,* etc.) and of vocal music (whereas *cantare* has been specialized in the meaning, "to sing").

4. Pontus de Tyard in the sixteenth century will word the same thought thus: "la musique . . . retenue comme image de toute *l'Encyclopédie.*"

5. It is in remembrance of the completeness and variety of tones of the heptachord of antiquity (Philo Judaeus, I, 64, calls this the most powerful of the musical instruments, just as the seven vowels are the most powerful in "grammar"), that Ronsard, in his Pindaric ode on Michel l'Hospital, says: "Faisant parler sa grandeur / Aux sept langues de ma lyre" (739–40), by which he would say that he wishes to celebrate his hero with *all* the strings of his lute—though he had shown us the Muses (cf. n. 3, above) using different strings for their different songs.

6. Browning who, in his "Abt Vogler," recognizes the "finger of God" more clearly in music than in painting or poetry and, in this poem, voices the medieval feeling that music is the particular expression of God (" . . . But God has a few of us whom he whispers in the ear; / The rest may reason and welcome: 't is we musicians know"), justifies the pre-eminence of music by the miracle of the chord (Stanza 7):

And I know not if, save in this, such gift be allowed to man
That out of our three sounds he frame, not a fourth sound, but a star.

Consider it well: each tone of our scale in itself is nought;
It is everywhere in the world—loud, soft, and all is said:
Give it to me to use! I mix it with two in my thought:
And there! Ye have heard and seen: consider and bow the head!

Before A.D. 1200 the finger of God could not be sensed in the mixture of the triple chord. Today this chord is a promise of harmony: such a sentence as the following from Duhamel "Ce sont de tout petits enfants. L'un a deux ans, l'autre un peu plus de quatre. Ils me font penser à l'*accord de tierce*. J'espère bien qu'un jour nous entendrons l'accord parfait"—would not have made sense in the Middle Ages.

There is still a reminiscence of the predominance of the ancient diapente in the symphonic *a cappella* singing found in the compositions of Palestrina; the fifth constituted with him a favorite opening chord: "Pierluigi's usual method of procedure is to sound one or the other of the requisite notes alone, completing the chord on the entry of the second voice." Even in our own time the Belgian musician Gevaert "defended the cause of the fifth in parallel voices vigorously, claiming that, although without an accompanying third, the effect was characteristic and not inartistic" (Pyne, *Palestrina, His Life and Times* [1922], p. 226).

As late as the eighteenth century Rousseau, in his *Dictionnaire de musique*, makes himself the advocate of Greek prejudices by calling the chord an "invention barbare et gothique" of Northern peoples who possess harsh organs and a sensibility without finesse—a statement for which he was rebuked by Schopenhauer. The physiologist T. Billroth ("Wer ist musikalisch ?," 1898) expresses the obvious truth that no mathematical or physical formulae, no "Laplacian attitude" can explain why the third should please today and not have pleased formerly: in art, he says, "erlaubt ist was gefällt."

7. In the "Coronation of the Virgin" by Gentile da Fabriano (fifteenth century), the idea of the completeness of world harmony is indicated by eight angels (representing the Gregorian musical tones) playing various musical instruments and seated within the *primum mobile*, above the starry sky, sun, and moon (cf. de Tolnay, p. 93). Cf. also the six tones of world music figured by "women playing music" in Tintoretto's painting (*ib.*, p. 101).

8. In modern times Victor Hugo, in his most paganistic poem, *Le satyre*, endows the satyr (who becomes the god Pan whom the Olympian gods must obey) with a gigantic lute, capable of expressing all moods: "la lyre, devenue . . . géante, / Chantait, pleurait, grondait, tonnait, jetait des cris, / Les ouragans étaient dans les sept cordes pris" (Part IV). The poet himself boasted of having added a "corde d'airain" to his lute by his invectives against Napoleon III (with Donne, the "new string" God had added to the world lute was Christ).

The idea of the complete lute is again echoed in the title of Hugo's posthumously published collection of poems, *Toute la lyre*, of which one section is called "Les sept cordes," and another, "La corde d'airain"—by which the lute (and, it might be added, the collection) is made overcomplete. (George Sand, in 1839, wrote a fantastic play called *Les sept cordes de la lyre*.)

9. The ideal completeness of a human being could be figuratively compared to a musical instrument: this has been done by Machaut (fourteenth century)

in his *Dit de la harpe*, published by Karl Young in *Essays in Honor of A. Feuillerat* (New Haven, 1943). Young analyzes the poem as follows:

> The design of the piece is a comparison of the poet's lady to a harp of twenty-five strings, each of which represents one of her virtues. Since her excellence exceeds this number, however, the writer attributes to her five additional graces, thus enlarging the total to thirty. By way of apology for the bold comparison of a lady to a harp, Machaut, the musician, emphasizes the potency of this instrument, and its association with aristocracy. For its effective sweetness it was chosen above all other instruments by David, Orpheus and Phoebus. . . . The poem, then, may be regarded as a pleasant fancy of a graceful versifier rather than as the utterance of a passionate lover or a moving poet.

In the last sentence we have one of those supercilious remarks of which modern "unmusical" commentators of medieval poetry are so fond. But the idea of the poem is no personal fancy of Machaut's: it is connected with the themes of the completeness of David's psaltery and of the musicality of virtue (the seventh string, for example, is "Charité que Saint Pol tint en si grant amité"). And we will not be surprised to find the word family *acort—acorder* represented here several times in order to denote musical and moral harmony (the "quarteron" [=τετρακτύς] of *Humeur, Sens, Raison,* and *Mesure* is necessary in order that "les cordes soient bien en acort / si qu'on n'i puist trover aucun descort," etc.). One cannot understand the poem without "sympathizing" with the medieval delight in perfection and completeness: the Beloved, the *summum bonum*, is analyzed into a sequence of *summa bona*, of virtues made visible (and, in our case, audible) by allegorical art. In the idea that the virtues of a lady are as various as the strings of an instrument, and form a unit like a harp, we have a graceful play on a very serious medieval concept.

10. This term has been coined by H. Hatzfeld for such summarizing descriptions as, for example, Calderón's résumé (*Mágico prodigioso*, II) of his description of a beautiful woman: "Al fin *cuna, grana, nieve,* / *Campo, sol, arroyo, rosa,* / *Ave que canta amorosa.* / *Risa,* que . . . , / *Clavel,* que . . . " etc., etc. Curtius, in his article "Mittelalterlicher und barocker Dichtungsstil" (*Mod. Phil.*, XXXVIII, 325–33), has traced this baroque *Summationsschema* back to a poetic description of a landscape to be found with the contemporary of Constantine, Tiberianus: "Sic euntem per virecta pulchra odora et musica / *Ales amnis aura lucus flos et umbra* juverat" (p. 330). For us it is interesting that the first occurrence in poetry of this summary should be attested in a passage evidently inspired by world harmony and depicting, by means of enumeration, the riches of the created world—as is characteristic of the enumerations of Calderón (cf. my remarks in *Rev. de filología hisp.*, III, 91, and, particularly, those of Dámaso Alonso in *Rev. de la Bibl., Arch. y Museo*, XIII, 147, and *RFE*, XXVIII, 145, on the verses of "disseminación y recolección" as he calls them). What I would stress most, at the present time, is the fact that Augustine offers, in the passage quoted in the text, essentially the same stylistic device long before Tiberianus; in fact, the Calderonian résumé is in line with what Jean Bayet, *Littérature latine*, p. 733, finds characteristic of Augustine's style: "une prose

harmonieuse allant d'un trait au but, mais revenant ensuite sur elle-même
avant de repartir plus loin; cette suite de glissements et de reprises finit par
produire une sorte d'incantation." (We shall see later the same qualities of
incantation in his definition of peace.) The "Calderonian résumé," with all
its richness, is already present in Augustine—with whom it represents the final
peak (or better, abiding place) attained after many a tentative, impatient forward
and upward striving. With Calderón, this artist of the Counter Reformation,
the impatience preparatory to the crowning effect has disappeared, so that what
remains is really a *Summationsschema*, a more schematic device.

The mental procedure of the artist Augustine, consisting of this forward
movement, retreat, and final *épanouissement* is that of a musician working with
motifs, if we are to accept the words which Bettina von Arnim (in *Goethes
Briefwechsel mit einem Kinde*, 1835, *Sämtl. Werke*, ed. Oehlke, III, 457) puts
into the mouth of Beethoven [who has been carried away by the poetic rhythm
of one of Goethe's poems]: "Da muss ich denn von dem Brennpunkt der
Begeisterung die Melodie *nach allen Seiten hin ausladen, ich verfolge sie, hole
sie mit Leidenschaft wieder ein, ich sehe sie dahinfliehen, in der Masse verschiedener
Aufregungen verschwinden, bald erfasse ich sie mit erneuter Leidenschaft,* ich kann
mich nicht von ihr trennen, ich muss mit raschem Entzücken *in allen Modulationen sie vervielfältigen, und im letzten Augenblick da triumphiere ich über
den ersten musikalischen Gedanken, sehen Sie, das ist eine Symphonie;* ja, Musik
ist so recht die Vermittelung des geistigen Lebens zum sinnlichen."

11. He transmitted certain Neoplatonic ideas to the Middle Ages. For
example Plotinus, *Enneads,* IV, 4, 4, states that the prayer addressed by the
astrologer to the stars, takes effect on them not by direct influence, but because
of the sympathy ruling throughout the universe. World harmony is comparable
to a vibration which propagates itself from one part of the lute to the other, and
from one lute to the other (a simile we shall meet with in the works of the
Renaissance Neoplatonists, Marsilio Ficino, Donne, etc.); world harmony is
based as well on συγγενῆ as on ἐναντία, "adverse elements" (as in Heraclitus'
simile of the bow). And in III, 2, 16–17, Plotinus offers a theodicy based on
the theory that the evil in the world is necessary because Intelligence acts with
reason as to the plan of the whole world, but does not impart perfection to all
the parts; on the contrary, πόλεμος καὶ μάχη obtain in the parts, just as in a
play there are conflicts in the plot, though the whole of the play is one and
harmonious. Just as the high sounds and the low (ὀξὺ καὶ βαρὺ) become one
and harmonious by numbers (συνίασιν εἰς ἕν ὄντες ἁρμονίας λόγοι εἰς
αὐτὴν τὴν ἁρμονίαν), so the oneness of reason stems from the fact that the
latter makes the parts not διάφορα μόνον, ἀλλ' εἰ καὶ ἐναντία—not only different
but adverse (the black and the white, the cold and the hot etc.) . . . οὐδ' ἐν
σύριγγι φωνὴ μία . . . ἄνισοι μὲν οἱ φθόγγοι πάντες, ὁ δὲ τέλεος εἷς ἐκ
πάντων. The flute of Pan, with its unequal tones, is the symbol of world
harmony. Along with the more famous symbolism of light there is, in Plotinus,

a string of musical similes which has strongly influenced medieval and (particularly) Renaissance writers.

12. A similar feeling seems to be that expressed in Robert Browning's "Abt Vogler," the hero of which is known for having advocated the use of discords, such as the seventh, ninth, and eleventh, at any place of the scale, and for composing a symphony whose finale was built up on the C major scale. It is Abt Vogler himself who speaks in the poem, praising the glory of music; he is presented to us "after he has been extemporizing upon the musical instrument of his invention" [an organ which he called "orchestrion"]. The last stanza reads: "Well, it is earth with me; silence resumes her reign. . . . / Give me the keys.   I feel for the common chord again, / Gliding by semitones, till I sink to the minor—yes, / And I blunt it into a ninth, and I stand on alien ground, / Surveying awhile the heights I rolled from into the deep; / Which, hark, I have dared and done, for my resting-place is found, / The C-Major of this life: so, now I will try to sleep."   His willingness to return from his wanderings in heaven to the earthly tonic of C major, because he has brought back with him the solace of God-inspired music, is reminiscent of the return to the *tonus* in Erigena.

In another vein Pontus de Tyard had explained the invention of musical notation (by the "musical hand") as due to a desire to perpetuate the music of the heavens after it has ceased: the Pythagorean "musical silence," the return to silence after the supernatural enjoyment, is rendered creative: "Les voix et instruments en leurs accords plaisans / Ravissoient l'Escoutant: mais enfin se taisans, / Luy par eux transporté en l'ame de l'ouïe [the "inner ear"] / *Retourne à soy confus de l'harmonie ouïe,* / Où plus ne se sentit et moins vivre eust il cru / Sans le chantre cessant, et le Sonneur recru / *Qu'il ne peut oublier . . .* "

13. It is this musical theorist of the eleventh century who took the decisive step of inventing the modern names for the tones of the hexachord (whereas the Greeks had known such names only for the tetrachord: τε τα τη τω): *ut re mi fa sol la.*   He took these from the words of a hymn of Paulus Diaconus (eighth century) on St. John the Baptist, which were sung on an ever-higher tone of the scale: "*Ut* queant laxis / *re*sonare fibris / *Mi*ra gestorum / *Fa*muli tuorum / *Sol*ve polluti / *La*bii rectum / Sancte Johannis."   This historical fact, which made possible the preservation of musical composition, is interesting to us for two reasons: the hymn on St. John brings into relief the *junction* of music and grace; its ascension to the higher tones of the scale must evidently have depicted the gradual ascension of the soul from sin to grace.

14. Once we have realized the importance of *musica mundana* for the medieval world, we should not allow ourselves henceforth to take lightly any allusions to music in the literary works of the Middle Ages, to accept them as mere metaphors, or even as *topoi* in the sense of Curtius.   There is always behind them a universal and transcendent meaning which reminds the reader of the whole, unsecularized

complex of a world harmony accessible as well to feeling as to reason. When, for example, the Spanish Arcipreste de Hita, in his *Libro de buen amor* (fourteenth century), has his book say (str. 70): "De todos instrumentos yo, libro, soy pariente, / bien o mal cual que puntares, tal te dirá ciertamente ... / si me puntar supieres, siempre me habrás en miente," the musical term *puntar*, "to sing according to notes" > "to interpret" (as we would say, "Toscanini interprets Mozart excellently"), has the function of suggesting not only the glossing technique applied to biblical texts, but the variation of a musical motif, which was conceived as a glossing; cf. Bukofzer, *loc. cit.*, and the present writer, *ZRPh*, LIV, 37, and *Modern Philology*, 41, 96. The reader is thus asked to collaborate with the author at the "musical interpretation" of a text which is supposedly susceptible of various meanings, but offers an ordered whole shaped in unison with world harmony. To give another example, Suolahti, *Neuphil. Mitt.* (Helsinki), XXXIII, 207, has explained the MHG *salfisiren*, "to discuss (a problem)," and the OFr *solfier*, "to discuss a juridical case," by solfeggio-singing (ML *solfizare*, "to sing the notes *sol, fa* according to the system of Guido d'Arezzo"); here a rational procedure is thought of in terms of the singing of a musical scale, and through the comparison with music, it is disintellectualized; at the same time, the particular discussion takes its place within an ordered whole (as does the gloss within the frame of the totality of the artistic work). Since the universe is a *musicum carmen* shaped by the Divine Artist, any intellectual work of man, whether artistic or not, participates somewhat in the orderedness and completeness of this universe (and we may also mention the parallel offered by medieval *declinare*, "to explain," drawn from grammatical declension which places the particular intellectual work within the frame of a whole, cf. above).

Another example of the metaphorical use of musicological terms is offered by medieval French idioms with *gamme*: *entendre la gamme*, "to understand"; *entrer en la haute gamme*, "to be excessive"; *changer de gamme*, "changer de conduite"; *mettre hors de gamme*, "déconcerter"—all based on the idea of a self-contained rationale which must be grasped as a whole. Life itself was, in the Middle Ages, a scale on which man reaches now a high note, now a low (*ut*, being the lowest note, had the meaning "pain": *estre assis en gamme ut* = "to be miserable"; cf. Schultz-Gora, *ZRPh*, XXVI, 721).

How much the audible prevailed in the Middle Ages is apparent not only from what knowledge we have of the way that books that would be read today were recited in that period (accompanied by music, as, for example, in the case of the epic poems), but also from such casual remarks as that which opens the Alexander fragment of Albéric de Besançon: "Dit Salomon al primier pas / quant de son libre *mot lo clas*" (the German version of Lamprecht says similarly of Albéric, "Dô Elberîch daz liet irhub"); according to the medieval author, Solomon *sang* his "Vanitas vanitatum," he "fit résonner la voix de son livre," as P. Meyer rightly translates. Here, *clas* > *classicum*, "trumpet signal"; perhaps we could even think of the Fr *sonner le glas*, "he rings the death knell for the vanity of life." On the other hand, since the Bible was a written text, it was possible to conceive of something oral as also "written": in the Old French *Mystère d'Adam* (which is evidently destined for performance, as is shown by the carefully-worded *rubricae*), to Abel's admonitions that God should be given the title which is his due, Cain replies that Abel has well preached and well written: *bien escrit*; obviously, since Abel is a character of the Scriptures, any word of his partakes of the "It is written."

Otfrid (ninth century) justifies his German translation of the Gospels in *Ad Liutbertum* by his intention, "ut aliquantulum huius *cantus* lectionis ludum secularium vocum deleret et in evangeliorum propria lingua occupati dulcedine *sonum inutilium rerum* noverint declinare." F. P. Magoun Jr., in *PMLA*, LVIII, 875, writes, "*sonus inutilium* [*rerum*] very likely refers to the disturbing noises of everyday life ... The interpretation of *cantus* ... is important for an understanding of Otfrid's intention as to the oral delivery of the poem.... Is one to understand the phrase as the 'singing melody' or merely as the 'sound of the text'?" It is obviously the second interpretation which we must accept; the text of the Bible partakes of the heavenly *dulcedo* of music. How could there be an *Evangelienharmonie* if the Bible did not sing?

15. Thus rhyme belonged to the *numerus* of prose. It is well known that the particular rhythm of prose is called ἀριθμός by Aristotle (*Rhetoric*, 3, 8) and *numerus* by Cicero (*De Oratore*, III); subsequently we find *nombre oratoire* used by Batteux, *Cours de belles lettres* (1753), 4, 114, and *numerus* by Sulzer and others. In general, the prose *numerus* is a looser or more flexible rhythm than is that applied to poetry; "Distinctio et aequalium aut saepe inaequalium intervallorum percussio numerum conficit," says Cicero (cf. Walzel, *Gehalt und Gestalt*, p. 207 seq.). Since both ἀριθμός and *numerus* are evidently echoes of the Pythagorean world music, they must have been originally identical with ἁρμονία and *concentus*, being only secondarily specialized for prose rhythm. In the Ode to Michel l'Hospital, Ronsard says (strophe 23) of his hero, who encourages the arts of the Muses, "Par lui leurs honneurs s'embellissent, / Soit d'écrits rampant à deux pieds [= verse], / Ou soit *par des nombres* qui glissent / *De pas tous francs et déliés* [= prose]."

16. The destiny of alliteration in Romance poetry is in contradistinction to that of rhyme: the former originally appeared in late ancient prose and medieval *Reimprosa* along with the rhyme as an equally intellectual device; later it penetrated into poetry (of which the Old French *Chanson de Roland* is a late witness), and began to disappear from the later medieval poetry (the pseudo poetry of the late medieval *rhétoriqueurs* is no exception to this rule). In Germany, on the contrary, where it was probably genuine, it was retained in medieval poetry (*Stabreim*), and has been revived, if with dubious success, by Wagner, its deficiencies offset by the music with which it was bound up. In fact the similes used by Wilhelm Scherer and Wagner, who compare the vowels to the organic body and the consonants to the skeleton of language (Wagner

speaks of the *Fellfleisch*, the visible skin), would suggest that the consonant is the characterizing, distinctive, limiting element, as compared with the organic and expansive element of the vowel. A. Heusler sees in alliteration a dynamic *Ausdrucksgebärde*; in rhyme, harmonious song. I would say that the consonant is more intellectually expressive, and thus it is only logical that it was alien to the Christian musicalization of language (and to the Italian *bel canto*). In Wagner's *Musikdrama* the intellectual element of the *Stabreim* poetry of the text is, so to speak, overwhelmed by the power (also the physical power) of his music: we could not, for example, imagine alliteration in a Mozart libretto. It is obviously wrong to declare, as does Julius von Schlosser, "Magistra Latinitas und Magistra Barbaritas" (*Bayr. Sitzgsber.*, 1937), that alliteration (*Stabreim*) is the typically "barbarian" and rhyme (*Klangreim*) the typically classical, given the historical fact that the two are found together in late ancient prose and medieval *Reimprosa*.

17. Schopenhauer, *Die Welt als Wille und Vorstellung* (Book 3, 51), explains rhyme and rhythm by the fact that "unsere an die Zeit wesentlich gebundenen Vorstellungskräfte hiedurch eine Eigenthümlichkeit erhalten haben, vermöge welcher wir jedem regelmässig wiederkehrenden Geräusch innerlich folgen und *gleichsam mit einstimmen*"—whereby is produced in us "ein blindes, allem Urtheil vorhergängiges *Einstimmen* in das Vorgetragene." He did not know how well his feeling concorded with the meaning of the medieval *consonantia* based on *numeri*.

The word "rhyme" itself (or, rather, Fr *rime*, OProv *rim(a)* from which the English word and the Ger *Reim* are borrowed) is etymologically connected with OHG *rim*, "number, series," according to the convincing paper of Nils Törnquist, *Zur Geschichte des Wortes Reim* (Lund, 1935), which disposes of the older *rhythmus* etymology offered by Kluge-Goetze. Törnquist, it is true, starts from the OHG meaning "series" rather than from "numerus," and sees as the basic meaning of Romance *rim(a)*, "a series of rhymes" (*rimar*, "to arrange in rhymes")—the OFr *tirade* (*laisse monorime*) being a series of rhymes. But in view of the existence of such ancient OFr texts as the *Alexis*, the *Passion*, *St. Léger* and *Eulalia*, all without tirade, it can hardly be said that the *laisse monorime* is the oldest rhyme-form in Romance. I would modify Törnquist's theory by starting from the meaning "numerus" of the OHG *rim* : *rimer* = "in numero disponere" (to arrange in order); cf. OFr *arimer ce beau latin*, "arranger"; Poitevin *s'arimer*, "s'accorder ensemble"; Fr *cela ne rime à rien*, *ni rime ni raison*. The MHG uses of the word family, *ze reimen richten*; *wie kan er rime limen* ("to 'glue' together rhymes"), *als ob si gewachsen sin!*, are consonant with those in French (cf. also MHG *wie reymt sich daz in den wind*?, Ger *das reimt sich wie die Faust aufs Auge*, etc.); the main idea, that of "rhyme," is then "(harmonious, reasonable) arrangement." The poetics of reason and order underlying medieval rhyme has been defined by Jaufre Rudel: ". . . Ni conois de rima co·s va / Si razo non enten en si."

18. And see also the significant title of the work which first endeavored to bring the multilayered sources of canon law into a scholastic system by harmonizing thought, and thus became the basic text of ecclesiastical jurisprudence in the later Middle Ages: Gratian's *Concordia discordantium canonum* (c. 1140). Jurisprudence is an art, too, according to the Roman classical definition: *jurisprudentia est ars boni et aequi*. (Communication of Prof. Kuttner.)

19. This *concordium* is evidently a coinage after the pattern of the *consortium* which occurs in the same sentence. The passage is not listed in the ThLL, which contains only two quotations from juridical texts. It is significant that in Romance it has been preserved: in OProv *concordi*, "agreement" (coupled once with *patz=pax*). I cannot understand why *concordium* appears with an asterisk in A. Thomas, *Essais de philologie romane*, Index, and in the *REW* (the former attests a *discordium* with the bucolic poet of the first century, Calpurnius). It is no chance that Provençal should have preserved the learned forms in -*i*: *concordi*, *discordi*, also †*acordi*, †*coveni* (< *convenium*), *termini* (< *terminium*), †*tempori* (< *temporium*) [the words marked with a dagger are not found in Levy's Provençal dictionary—Ed.]—all of which are words related to our well-known idea of order (term). In general, historical grammarians who deal with word formations have a tendency to reason only on the basis of patterns of formation (e.g., the pattern -*i* in Provencal = -*ium* in Latin), without taking into consideration the ideological patterns: it is the latter which bring about the development of the former. Without the emotional appeal of *consortium*, *concordium*, the Prov -*i* < -*ium* word-formational pattern could probably not have crystallized. Language forms do not evolve and function without an emotional content (which may, of course, be connected with intellectual values).

20. In the Middle Ages, the "harmony of the Bible" spread from the precincts of theology to other walks of life; I have shown, in my article on *trouver* (*Romania*, LXVI [1940], 1–11), that the *contropare*, *adtropare*=τροπολογεῖν, "to explain or compare biblical passages by harmonizing them," led to *contropare*, "to compare, corroborate legal documents" found in the Visigothic laws. Similarly, *consonantia* came to mean "contract, stipulation" (cf. *RFH*, VIII, 131). And Ger (*es*) *stimmt*, "it is right" (i.e., a calculation, an assertion, etc.) is nothing but the translation of scholastic Lat *consonat*.

21. Cf. Dryden's *Song for St. Cecilia's Day* (1687): "From harmony, from heavenly harmony, / This universal frame began ... [the 'jarring atoms' of nature were aroused by music; 'cold, and hot, and moist, and dry' took their stations—all ancient ideas] / From harmony to harmony / Through all the compass of the notes it ran, / The diapason closing full in man"—here we have the idea of *musica mundana* being completed by *musica humana*.

St. Cecilia achieved more than Orpheus, who enraptured only nature: when she touched the keys of her organ, an angel descended "mistaking Earth for Heaven"; in opposition to the older idea that Cecilia listens to heavenly music while playing earthly music, Dryden would suggest that heaven listens when man makes music—an idea worthy of the Age of Enlightenment.

22. De Tolnay—who speaks so eloquently of the panel by Cima da Conegliano in which "the three saints Peter, Augustine and Nicholas, each apparently isolated by his meditation, are none the less united intimately by the melody [played by an angel] which in each of them evokes the same mood"—does not, surprisingly enough, mention Raphael's painting of St. Cecilia which portrays that fullness of feeling evoked by music, in an artist-become-saint, overwhelmed by the artistry of God.

23. The idea that language is a kind of music, and that the organs of human speech are comparable to the plectron is much older than this poem.   Gregory of Nyssa (in Gilson-Boehner, p. 107–9) explains that, just as musicians play music in a manner adapted to their instruments (they do not, says Gregory, flute on the lute or lute on the flute), so the organs of human speech had to be created in view of their function; the human hands were developed in a manner unknown with the animals, thus freeing the organs of the mouth for the performance of speech; the human tongue would have had to be more fleshy and resistant, or wet and dissolving, in order to perform what the animal's tongue is called upon to do.   God shaped man after His own image, endowing him with gifts reflecting Himself: his *nous*, given as a spiritual principle, would have been unfit to manifest itself unless God had given man an "organic device" enabling this principle to manifest its movement to the outside world: πλήκτρου δίκην—that is, in the manner of the plectron of the cithara.   Thus, just as an expert musician who has lost his voice may, in order to show forth his art, lend the songs he has composed to the voices of his fellow men, or practice his art on the flute or the lute, so the human mind, καθάπερ τις ἁρμοστής ἔντεχνος, like an expert musical performer, uses the "living organs" (ἐμψύχων τούτων ὀργάνων) in order to make manifest his secret thoughts to which he could not have given utterance by his "naked soul."   It is evident that the *plectra linguae* metaphor with Fulbert grows out of Gregory of Nyssa's comparison of the human organs of articulation with the plucking of strings by human hands, and of the division of labor which he assumes between hands and articulatory organs.   The mind at work in these analogies is that of a scientist who sees as well as thinks.   Otfrid, *Ad Liutbertum* says that God has given man the *plectrum linguae* that he may praise his Creator.   The phrase evidently is a patristic echo.

24. In a goliardic song of the *Carmina Burana* (ed. Schmeller, p. 137), the word *concinit* is used of the nightingale (as often = "sings [in a harmonious way]"), in a setting of pagan *Elementargeister*; it is not too rash to assume that this is the introduction of a Christian note (one may observe the discreet expression *his alludens*: only the slightest allusion to things pagan is permitted): "Estivantur Dryades, / colle sub umbroso / prodeunt Oreades, / cetu glorioso, / Satyrorum

concio / psallit cum tripudio / Tempe peramena; / *his alludens concinit,* / cum jucundi meminit / veris, filomena." The Christianization is also effected by the use of the biblical *psallere* in reference to satyrs.

25. There is something of this, too, in Strecker's remark (which Errante makes his own, p. 261) in *Cambridge Songs* (p. 32), on the possible attribution of our poem to Fulbert: "was ich im Interesse des Bischofs von Chartres nicht hoffen möchte." I rather concur with P. S. Allen's judgment expressed in *The Romanesque Lyric* (1928), chapter XIV, that, with the *De musica,* "we have come into the fullness of a world of poetry that is our own"—and incidentally, ancient as well.

But it is important to emphasize as do Strecker and Errante, that the whole collection of the *Cambridge Songs* is based on musical criteria (the insertion of *De Luscinia* between sequences may be due to its musicological *exordium*) which testify to the return to fervid belief—and, consequently, to music—in the tenth century.

26. When Jean Paul in *Titan* writes of a nightingale, "die geflügelte Zwergorgel riss auf einmal alle Flötenregister heraus," he evidently had in mind such medieval texts that applied the word *organum* "instrument" to the little bird which is a microcosm. (The fanciful writing of Jean Paul is saturated with a medieval tradition.)

27. The modern poem of Fr. von Schober, *An die Musik,* which has been made famous by Schubert's song, is based on the same triad—though reflecting the Romantic feeling of a "Paradise Lost" of grace:

> Du holde Kunst, in wie viel grauen Stunden,
> wo mich des Lebens wilder Kreis umstrickt,
> hast du mein Herz zu warmer Lieb' entzunden,
> hast mich in eine bess're Welt entrückt.
>
> Oft hat . . . ein süsser, heiliger Akkord von dir
> den Himmel bess'rer Zeiten mir erschlossen

There is also a reflection of this trinity in a passage from the modern French author Balzac, otherwise so worldly: "La religion, l'amour et la musique, ne sont-ils pas la triple expression d'un même fait, le besoin d'expression dont est travaillée toute âme noble ? Ces trois poésies vont toutes à Dieu, qui dénoue toutes les émotions terrestres. Aussi cette sainte trinité participe-t-elle des grandeurs infinies de Dieu."

28. Cf. the Old French passage from *Romanzen und Pastourellen,* ed. Bartsch, I, 30a: "An avril a tans paskour / Ke nest la fueille et la flour, / L'aluete a point dou jor / *chante e loie son signor,* / por la dousour / dou tans novel / si m'en entrai an un jardin, / s'oi chanteir sor l'arbrexel / les ozeles *an lour latin*"—how but in Latin could the birds sing the praise of the God who created spring ?

Jaufré Rudel contends (III, 1): "Pro ai del chan *ensenhadors* / Entorn mi e *ensenhairitz*: / Pratz e vergiers, albres e flors, / Voutas d'auzelhs e lays e critz . . . "—birds (meadows and flowers) are the school-masters and -mistresses in the spring. Teachers of what? Of music, forsooth—and with music the school element is given.

H. Pongs, *Das Bild in der Dichtung*, I, 186, states that in these lines of Gottfried von Strassburg's *Tristan* romance: "die wilden waldvogelîn / hiezen sie willekommen sîn / viel suoze in ir Latîne" (cf. the OFr *les oiseles an lour latin*) the "Überströmen des Gefühls . . . sich sozusagen aufhebt, indem es ins Geistreiche verspruht." But there is precisely nothing facetious in the idea that loving birds should greet human lovers in Latin: that choice language, that private language for choice beings. It is not advisable for the modern German critic, whose sensibility has been fed on the spontaneous lyricism of an Eichendorff, to apply his standards to medieval lyricism, which is naturally saturated with didacticism. For the medieval ear, Latin could be "sweet."

The motif of "learned birds" occurs in Gottfried's *Tristan* (vv. 4749 ff.), when he compares poets to nightingales: "[The Minnesingers are] Nachtigallen . . . sie kunnen alle ihr ambet wohl"; now that their former conductor (leitfrowe), the "Nachtigall von Hagenau," has become silent, it is the "Nachtigall von Vogelweide" who will conduct the choir: "ir meisterinne kan ez wol / diu von der Vogelweide. / Hei, wie diu über heide / mit höher stimme schellet! / was wunders sî gestellet!"

29. This scene is evidently inspired by Augustine, *De civ. Dei*, XIII, 21: "[one should understand] paradisum scilicet ipsam ecclesiam, sicut de illa legitur in cantico canticorum; quattuor autem paradisi flumina quattuor evangelia, ligna fructifera sanctos, fructus autem eorum opera eorum"—though the Beloved of the Song of Songs, who is for Augustine the Church, is for Berceo the Virgin. Cf. for the sources of the prologue to the *Milagros*, Luís Alfonso, *Boletín de la Acad. Argentina de las Letras*.

30. There must have been in existence a tradition contrary to the Augustinian, which emphasized the (natural) *art* of the birds' song and was based on the line of the Psalms (104, 12): "Super ea volucres caelum habitabunt: de medio petrarum dabunt voces"; Luther comments on this line (reading " . . . in medio ramorum" instead of " . . . petrarum") as follows: "divinus psaltes David cum ingenti stupore et exultante spiritu praedicit mirabilem illam volucrum *peritiam et certitudinem canendi*." (From this "volucres in medio ramorum dantes voces" of the Psalmist are ultimately derived such sayings as, "Ich singe wie der Vogel singt, der in den Zweigen wohnet" [Goethe]; or "Un oiseau c'est un rameau qui chante" [Mme de Sévigné].

We may think also of the classification of Isidore, *Etym.* III, 20, who puts on one plane the voices of men and of birds: "Proprie autem vox hominum est seu inrationabilium animantium." The idea appears also in *Cambridge Songs*, n° 6: " . . . multimodis gutture canoro idem sonus redditur plurimarum faucium, *hominum volucrum animantiumque"* (incidentally, I do not find the *idem* surprising, as does Strecker: *multimodis . . . idem* renders the idea of unity and variety, which exist together in a chord). The same mode of classification appears to survive in OFr *lai*, "song [of man]" < OIr *lóid, laid*, "bird's song"—if the etymology offered by D'Arbois de Jubainville (*Romania*, VIII, 422) is correct. We may also find in Christian poetry a reminiscence of the ancient technique of describing natural phenomena as if these were works of art, figments of the imagination (e.g., Pliny says of the nightingale, "perfecta Musae scientia modulatus editur sonus"). "*Milvus tremulaque voce aethera pulsat*" (*Cambridge Songs*, no. 23) is in this ancient vein. Huyzinga, in his treatise on Alanus de Insulis (*Mededeelingen K. akad.v. wet.*, 74, B, n° 6, p. 64), mentions such phrases as "the wood imitates [*mentitur*] the shape of a wall," "the lark imitates a cithara"—while the cithara " . . . cantus varii faciem variando colorans / Nunc lacrymas in voce parit, *mentita* dolorem / Nunc *falsi* risus sonitu *mendacia* pingit"; again (p. 25), the lute imitates the nightingale [*philomenat*], etc.

In the Renaissance, Luis Vives, when treating, in his Dialogue *Vestitus et deambulatio matutina* (1539; ed. W. H. D. Rouse, Oxford, 1931), the delights accessible to the senses, re-edits the medieval theme of "scholarly birds," by presenting these singers as familiar with classical metrics (with which Vives would inculcate his pupil):

> Animadverte accurate, et annotabis varietates omnium sonorum; nunc non interquiescit, sed continuo spiritu in longum aequabiliter, sine mutatione; nunc inflectitur; iam minutius et concisius canit; nunc intorquet et quasi crispat vocem; nunc extendit, iam revocat; alias longos concinit versus, quasi heroicos; alias breves ut Sapphicos; interdum brevissimos ut Adonicos. Quin etiam quasi *Musicae ludos et scholas habent.* Meditantur aliae iuniores, versusque quos imitentur accipiunt. Audit *discipula* intentione magna, utinam nos praeceptores nostros pari; et reddit; vicibusque factis reticent. Intellegitur emendatae correctio et in docente quaedam reprehensio. Sed illos ducit natura recta, nos voluntas prava (p. 56).

The medieval pattern survives also in Scaliger's definition of poetry (Prologue to *Poetices libri septem*, 1560) as that which "materias ipsas animet numerosa concordia dissimilium momentorum, quae in levissimae dictionis flexionibus continentur" (the modulations of human speech are birdlike, cf. Vernon Hall, *MLN*, LX, 452). Indeed, as late as Góngora we may recognize this artificial bridging of the gap between the human artist and the bird artist: " . . . el que algún *culto ruiseñor me cante* / *prodigio dulce que corona el viento* / en unas mismas plumas escondido / el músico, la musa, el instrumento." The *cultismo* of Góngora applied to the birds is based on the conception of the "human artist in the bird."

Mme M. R. Lida (*RFH*, VII, 381), purports to find an opposition to this love of "learned birds" in the praise expressed by Garcilaso and Fray Luis for "untutored singing" (in this case, that of human artists). For her, the nightingale of Berceo "que canta por fina maestría" is only one more example of that medieval emphasis on learning which is to be explained by the respect for classical traditions and which was intensified by a deliberate opposition to the barbarism of the times. But, when Church Fathers become birds, and birds sing Latin—it seems to me obvious that Berceo's emphasis on learning, in such a connection, shows rather an ideal of fusion: the artistic and the natural become one.

31. The same is true of the dancing saints in Dante's *Paradiso* (Thomas Aquinas, Albertus Magnus, Gratian). A modern positivist such as R. von Mises states (*Kleines Lehrbuch des Positivismus*, p. 342) that today, "for reasons of good taste," a scholar would not be presented in so "extreme an artistic attitude" as that of dancing. What he evidently has before his eyes is a picture of bodies in ecstatic gyration, whereas Dante is depicting the dance of the soul: the souls of his scholar-saints are communing with the divine.

I am also astonished to find E. Auerbach in that society of worldly scholars who cannot imagine holy dancing: in *Dtsch. Viertaljahrsschr.*, V, 72, dealing with Thomas of Celano's report on St. Francis who, when speaking the first time before the pope, was overcome by fervor and joy and moved his feet as if dancing. Auerbach can see only the empirical person, Francis of Assisi, an oratorically and musically gifted Italian, endowed with "the freedom of the great and masterful actor." But, in Celano's biography, we should see the exemplary saint who dances when moved by the spirit: that person who, while still dwelling on this earth, had become an instrument of the divine, or who (in the words of Celano, quoted by Auerbach) "de toto corpore fecerat linguam," in whom a "*concordia* utriusque hominis" (i.e., harmony of body and soul) was miraculously established. He was not an "actor of himself" but an "agent of God, who enacts God."

For what is Francis but an impersonation of God, of that Divine Being who has impressed Himself into the sensitive wax of the saint's body (in the form of the stigmata)?

32. Professor Allers mentions to me the legend, of late origin, of St. Rose of Lima: she is reported to have sung the Psalms alternatively with the birds sitting on the trees before her window; she alone however could understand what the birds were responding.

33. This passage reflects the *parva et magna pulchritudo* of Augustine, *De natura boni contra Manichaeos*, I, 13: "omnis mensura *et magna et parva*, omnis pulchritudo *et magna et parva*, omnis pax *et magna et parva* . . . omnis modus, omnis species, omnis ordo, *et magnus et parvus*, a Domino Deo sunt." The *ordo amoris* embraces animals, small and great, and man. In Augustine's eyes, the Christian orator knows not of "minimum aliquid atque vilissimum," because all small subjects are susceptible of greatness (cf. E. Auerbach, *Neue Dantestudien* [Istanbul, 1944], p. 10. Eckhart, commenting on Exodus 16, 18, and Genesis 2, 2, explains also that in God there is no "plus aut minus," and that He is "totus . . . in sui minimo" (Mahnke, p. 135; cf. also the sentence quoted from Weigel, p. 126: "im geistlichen unsichtbaren Wesen ist die Grösse und Kleinheit ein Ding, *magni et parvi eadem est mensura et divinitas*").

From the *parva pulchritudo* of Augustine branch off all the numerous attempts at apologetics for the small creatures in nature, from the glorification of the mosquito as a *milagro del mundo* by Luis de Granada, to the Loewe song of the cricket and the monk, which ends with the exclamation of the latter, "Wie gross bist du, o Gott—im Kleinen!".

34. Such representations in art are called by De Tolnay (*loc. cit.*, p. 90) "cosmic integrations of a Biblical scene"; and he points out that, in medieval art, Christ's death was brought into agreement with world harmony. For example, in a miniature of a Munich codex of the eleventh century, there is "a Crucifixion surrounded by the representations of the harmonies of medieval music. The sacrifice of Christ here becomes the symbol of the harmony of the universe. With the death of Christ all opposing elements are reconciled." Again, in fifth- or sixth-century mosaics at Ravenna, there appears, "in the middle of the starry sky . . . either the monogram of Christ or the cross. The combination of these features with the starry sky expresses the harmony of the universe, since the sacrifice of Christ was considered its symbol."

35. We are reminded here of the stanza in William Dunbar's poem, "The Nativity of Christ" (fifteenth century):

> Sing, hevin imperial, most of licht!
> Regions of air mak harmony!
> All fish in flud and fowl of flicht
> Be mirthful and make melody!
> All Gloria in excelsis cry!
> Heaven, erd, se, man, bird and best—
> He that is crownit aboue the sky
> *Pro nobis puer natus est.*

36. From lyric poetry (mainly Provençal) the *Natureingang* extended to the epics; for example, to the Prologue of the *Canterbury Tales*. Lines 1–11, according to Manly, have the practical purpose of stating the time of year at which pilgrimages usually took place, while serving also to set the tone of pagan joy, inspired by the coming of spring. In reality, Chaucer's prelude offers another image of world harmony—here appropriate because the theme of the pilgrimage itself was inspired by the idea of love.

As for the last three of these lines (9–11), given to the description of the singing birds, "And smale fowles maken melodye, / that slepen al the nyght with open eye— / So priketh hem nature in hir corages," the commentators suggest that by "smale fowles" are meant the nightingales, who, according to Pliny, sing ceaselessly during the mating season (comparing thereto line 98, "[a lover] slepte namore than dooth a nyghtyngale"). They confess, however, the uniqueness of the reference contained in line 10 ("with open eye"). In my opinion, the nightingale, the bird that is the symbol of love-inspired song, can, given the *forma mentis* of the Middle Ages, easily become the symbol of vigilance (thereby sharing a traditional attribute of the hare): Philomela is here as lovingly watchful as are those guards of Modena who call out: "Vigila!"

Another extension of the *Natureingang* from lyrical to narrative poetry is to be found in the lai, "L'aüstic," of Marie de France (and we may note that the lai itself, as developed by Marie, represents a transposition of musical and lyrical poetry, of the *lai breton*, into narrative poetry; cf. my article in *Rom. Stil- u. Literaturstudien*): in the springtime, when "cil oiselet par grant dulcur / mainent lor joie en sum la flur," when every being sensitive to love gives heed thereto, the married lady and the knight talk to each other lovingly, the night through, from their adjacent dwellings. When the husband, who has been told by his wife that she had been listening to the joyful song of the nightingale, kills the bird on the pretext that her sleep must not be disturbed, he kills not only a tiny, singing bird, but the *ordo amoris* (and, therein, "fist que vilains"), that *joie* pervading the whole universe which the bird had glorified. Thus, it was only fitting that the body of the bird, which had been a martyr of loveless villainy, should become a holy relic for the knight to carry with him all his life, wrapped in velvet, enclosed in a jewel-studded golden case (Marie's lai itself is a commemoration, in lyrical music, of the singer of Love). The crime of the husband can be sensed by the modern reader only if he remembers the sacred function of the nightingale, the musician of God.

37. It has not yet been remarked that the very word "refrain" for a repeated part of a poem has to do with our concept of world harmony; the word referred originally to all kinds of echoes, of response, especially to the response of the birds. As Schultz-Gora, *ZRPh*, XI, 249 points out, the Prov *refranh* hardly occurs at all during the twelfth and thirteenth centuries in the meaning "refrain"; it means regularly "the birds' song"; OFr *refrait* (< *refractu*) has both the meaning "birds' song" and "refrain," while OProv *refrach* means only "birds' song." Schultz-Gora starts from *refrangere*, "to start on one's way back" [i.e., "to break tracks"] (Lat *frangere iter*), comparing with it the *refloit*, "refrain," in Gottfried von Strassburg, which must echo an OFr representative of *reflexu (cf. the abbreviation *refl* in the *Carmina Burana* for refrains). Gaston Paris thought rather of the breaking of the melodious line by modulation. (Cf. Jaufré Rudel: "Quan . . . ·l rossinholetz el ram / volf e refranh ez aplana / son dous chantar et afina, / dreitz es qu'ieu lo mieu refranha"). Schultz-Gora mentions, without explanation, the OProv *refrim*, "chant des oiseaux, son d'une trompe frémissement d'un penon, cliquetis d'armes" (hence *refrimar*, "to echo"); *FEW* again mentions only OProv *frim*, "frémissement, son des cloches," s.v. *fremere*; evidently we have to do with a *refremere, in which the re- indicates the echo, as in *résonner*, *retentir*. With Jaufré Rudel (III, 4) we came across the line *voutas d'auzelhs e lays e critz*, where *voutas* is translated by Jeanroy as "roulade," and thus commented on: "refrain, ritournelle; le mot est souvent appliqué au chant des oiseaux et associé à lui" (cf. also Appel in Levy, *Prov. Suppl.-Wb.*). Evidently *vouta* is a "response" of birds, and a refrain in poems.

Finally, I submit the Sp *requebrar*, "to flatter (esp. a woman)," which *REW* explains from a hypothetical meaning, "die Stimme beugen" (to modulate the voice); it referred originally to the song of an amorous bird, and reflects a "*cantibus ecce* tuis recrepant arbusta canoris, consonat ipsa suis frondea silva comis" ("the thicket echoes his songs") in Eugenius of Toledo's hymn on the nightingale (Raby, *Secular Latin Poetry*, I, 151). It would not be too rash, perhaps, to assume that birds' song and refrain were both conceived of as echoes, responses, "refractions" of the world harmony (note the *consona resultatio* of Ambrose, to which may be compared the Calderón passage cited in note 43 of Chap. II). Guido Errante, *loc. cit.*, p. 79, lists the various explanations given hitherto to our word, and points out that in the *Leys d'Amors* the refrain is called *respos*, i.e., "response," and that the refrain in troubadour poetry goes back to the psalmody (the coloratura resting on the final syllables of Kyrie and Alleluia), that is, to the oldest form of liturgical Christian chants which unite the community in a common cultic action. But he fails to give a clear semantic explanation of *refrain > refrangere*, or to mention the refrain of the birds, which, to my way of thinking, is just as truly as in the response in the church, an "echo to the music of the world." There is, however, a very significant quotation to be found on p. 310 of his book: we learn that Amalarius, *De ecclesiasticis officiis* (ninth century) makes the difference between the *responsorium* (where the soloist is answered by a choir), and the *tractus* (where the soloist sings alone), comparing the two with the song of the pigeons (gregarious animals, representing active life) and of the turtle dove (a bird which prefers to be alone and represents speculative life). This comparison seems to me to indicate how closely the birds' song and the church songs were associated; they have in common the "response." One may also quote from the *Tierstimmengedicht* (n° 23) in the *Cambridge Songs*, which starts with the pigeon and the turtle dove, and continues with other birds, rendering some of the bird sounds thus: "*resonat* hic turdus ... gracula *resultat*." On "Klangspielereien im mittelalterlichen Liede," cf. H. Spanke in *Ehrengabe Karl Strecker*, p. 171–83; he mentions the solfeggio added to Latin stanzas as a kind of reversion of the process obtaining in the sequences, replacing the alleluia by words and series of vowels that served as transitions between musical sections (the AOI of the *Roland* evidently belongs here). Thus the refrain is a kind of rhyme within the poem, picturing the responds of the world.

The refrain as an imitation of world music may well go back to antiquity; R. Peiper, *Rhein. Mus.*, XXXII, 523, has published an ancient *celeuma* (sailor's song) with the refrain "Heia viri! *nostrum reboans echo sonet heia!*" This seems to represent the human echo (that of the rowers to their leaders), parallel to that of nature (cf. the last line of the poem: "Vocibus adsiduis *litus resonet*: heia!"). This song has been imitated in Christian poetry: in the (perhaps allegorical) watch-song of Modena (*ca.* 802, cf. Beeson, *Primer of Medieval Latin*, Chicago, 1925) which contains an echo-refrain ("*Resultet* echo: 'comes, eia, vigila' / Per muros 'eia' dicat echo 'vigila' "), and in a religious poem on

St. Columban (tenth century), which borrows the refrain of the ancient song (the last stanza of this poem suggests a *certamen* of Christians vying for the prize of virtue granted by God: "Rex quoque virtutum, rerum fons, summa potestas / *Certanti* spondet, vincenti praemia donet. / Vestra, viri, Christum memorans mens personet: Heia!").

Thus we see how a pagan refrain, an echo to pagan world harmony, has become Christianized.   The *celeuma*, the mariners' song, was especially well fitted to lend itself to the new contents.   Augustine, *De cantico novo*, II (Migne, 40, 680), writes: "Adsit nostra tutela Christi gratia, *celeuma nostrum dulce cantemus Alleluia*, ut laeti ac securi ingrediamur sempiternam ac felicissimam patriam."   Now the human echo (to nature) will be replaced by nature's echo to the prayers of Christians (as in Ambrose).   Sidonius Apollinaris (Migne, 58, 488) tells us of sailors who, having taken refuge in a church, sing their *celeuma* (that is, the alleluia), to which nature responds: "Curvorum hinc chorus helciariorum [*sc.* se reflectit], / Responsantibus alleluia ripis. / Ad Christum levat amnicum *celeuma*. / Sic sic psallite, nauta, vel viator: / Namque iste est locus omnibus petendus / Omnes quo via ducit ad salutem."   (I would suggest that the [*h*]*eia* found in Latin mariners' songs survives in the *eia* of the jubilus of the Church, and in Old Romance [Provençal, Spanish, Portuguese] poetry; for the connection between the *celeusmata* and It *vogare*, "to row" < Lat *vocare*, "to call out," cf. my article in *Italica*, XXIII, 23.)

The refrain appears in a derivative manner in a poem of Jaufré Rudel, in which the *a a* that echoes the last rhyme of every stanza seems (in my opinion) to suggest the "response" he hopes the poem will elicit from his audience. Cassella has pointed out (in *Jaufré Rudel, Liriche*, 1946) that this poem contains the "poetics" of the author, who would insist on the unity, the rationality, and convincingness of his work; and the echo-verses, as I believe, would stress this last quality: "Com plus l'auziretz, mais valra, a a" (the more you will hear, the greater value will it have); "Bos es lo vers e faran hi [the princes of Cahors and Toulouse] / Calque re don hom chantara, a, a" (this last line is translated by Cassella: "essi, là, ne faranno materia di canto").   I would also point out that the lyricism of Jaufré, as of other troubadours, is basically communal, appealing to the audience in a manner strange to us, who are wont to enjoy lyrical poetry in the isolation of private rooms.   And since it was the echo that the poet was most pleased to anticipate, the first stanza contains the line: "mas lo mieus chanz comens' aissi (com plus l'auziretz, mais valra): a a." That is, while general poetics, as he says, requires (only) a knowledge of music, composition, and rhyme, he will introduce a new element: the prospective echo of his readers—the noble resonant "a" (which is far from being the "mocking" sound that commentators have thought to discern in it).

38. F. Schalk, in *Neuere Sprachen*, and in his volume, *Französische Aphoristen*, explains the birth of the aphorism in modern literature by the unsystematic approach of Renaissance writers such as Bacon and Erasmus, in contrast to the

scholastic *summae.* Since he defines the aphorism as an entity reflecting in its fragmentariness the whole, we must obviously think him wrong in dating the aphorism so late; it is, in fact, as the aphorisms of Lull show, a medieval find, generated at a time, that is, which saw in detail the great connection of all things. The aphorism was born at a time when world harmony seemed to be reflected by all phenomena. One can be aphoristic only when one trusts in the consistency of all detailed truths. Fichte who demanded of the romantic "fragment" that it be a microcosm, separated from the surrounding world, and "in itself perfect as a hedgehog," recognized, by his definition, that the artistic microcosm reflects the macrocosm of the world. Even in a Nietzsche the aphoristic rests on confidence in his "system," without taking sufficient care in establishing the connections of the details with the whole—and this because of the basic modern fragmentariness. These modern writers have used a literary form which presupposes the existence of a system, in order to express an unsystematic approach to life—the approach which is really more genuine with them.

39. The same thinker sees in the song of the bird in the garden the supraintellectual language of love, by means of which *Amic,* the lover, communicates with *Amat,* the Beloved (p. 31, ¶ 26):

> Cantava l'aucell en lo verger de l'amat, e venc l'amic, qui dix a l'aucell:—Si no ens entenem per llenguatge, entenam-nos per amor; cor en lo teu cant se representa a mos ulls mon amat ("in thy song my Beloved is represented to my eyes": i.e., to the 'inner senses' [Augustine]).

The look which achieves the union of the mystical lovers is identical with the song of the loving bird; this song is the mystical look of union become sound (p. 33, ¶ 40):

> Ab ulls de pensaments, llanguiments, de sospirs, e de plors, esguardava l'amic son amat; e ab ulls de gràcia, justícia, pietat, misericòrdia, liberalitat, l'amat esguardava son amic. E l'aucell cantava lo plaent esguardament damunt dit.

And there is always present the situation of the Provençal *Natureingang* along with the Christian melancholy that strives to regain the paradise lost of divine harmony.

40. It would be astonishing not to find our concept in Middle High German; and, indeed, it is present in the poem of Walther von der Vogelweide entitled, by Wilmanns, "Schlechte Musikanten" (n° 44): "Owê, hovelîchez singen, / daz dich ungefüege doene / Solten ie ze hove verdringen! . . . *frô Unfuoge,* ir habt gesiget . . . Ich enwil niht werben zuo der mül, / dâ der stein sô riuschent umbe gât / und daz rat sô mange unwîse hât. / merkent wer dâ harpfen sül [a clearly Pythagorean reminiscence!]." Later, the poet speaks of "ungefüegen sachen," with which he compares the croaking of frogs. The three occurrences of the *Unfug* word family have been translated as "ungefüge," "Unfug," "ungelenke," respectively, whereas the right translation, for them all, would be "disharmony" or "disharmonious"; the German words (which are related to Lat *pango— compages,* etc.) continue the original meaning of the Greek word ἁρμόζειν which was, as we have said above, a joiner's term. Walther wishes to assert

the unity of aesthetic and ethical values, of musical harmony and courtly love. The German word family has today entirely lost its medieval aesthetic connotation, and has become restricted either to the technical (*Fuge, Gefüge, fügen*) or to the moral sphere (*mit Fug und Recht, Unfug, ungefüge, sich fügen, befugt*). Goethe was still conscious of the medieval tradition when he rendered the Greek concept of harmony, in which love and political order are implied, by a member of this word family:

> Die zum grossen Leben
> *Gefügten Elemente* wollen sich
> Nicht *wechselseitig* mehr mit Liebeskraft
> Zu stets erneuter Einigkeit umfangen [= *ambire!*].
> Sie fliehen sich und einzeln tritt nun jedes
> Kalt in sich selbst zurück.

(*Kalt* may suggest lack of temperedness.)   Stefan George has restored, in recent times, the ancient value of *Fug*: in a phrase which combines the meaning of *Fügung* ("the [harmonious] will of God or Fate"), and *Fug* (as in *Fug und Recht*), he speaks of "eherne Fug"—the abridged form evidently having for him a more manly ring (cf. also his coinage, *Tucht* = *Tugend* + *Zucht*).

An evident parallel to German *fügen* is the Slav word family лад, for which Berneker gives the original meaning as "[Zusammen-] Gelegtes, Lage, Schicht" (things laid together: layer), positing a development to that of "order, harmony, love (beloved)," and comparing the semantic development of the клад family ("Lage, Schicht" > "Einklang, harmonisch"; cf. Slov *sklàd*, "Lage, Schicht; Falte, Fuge; Einklang"). It is regrettable that in this statement the original *musical* reference is ignored, although such words as Russ разлад, "Missklang," ладить, "passen, stimmen" (to tune); ладиться "mit jemand auskommen, sich vertragen" (to attune oneself to s.o.), and Czech *ladìts*, "stimmen [ein Instrument]," clearly point in that direction. It may be remarked in general that in this, as in so many etymological dictionaries of modern European languages, the semantic developments are presented abstractly: as logically explicable possibilities, with no particular determination by the particular moral climate. In our case, the Greek and Christian semantic ancestry of the Slavic word is ignored.

I may point out here that the Russian word family represented by согласие, "harmony, unison, concord, consent, assent"; согласить, "to conciliate"; ————ся, "to consent, agree" (whose phonetic aspect characterizes it as a borrowing from Paleoslav; cf. the genuine Russ голос, "voice") is evidently patterned on συμφωνία–συμφωνεῖν—another fact unmentioned by Berneker.

41. With this theory which in turn goes back to the Greek and Augustinian preference given to the eye as the sense par excellence, the ear, as an incentive to love (*musica amoris incitamentum*), was relegated to second place. Tasso gave a new turn to the secondary role of the ear in matters of love, when he

says that, the great danger being the eye, the lover shuts his eyes in order to avoid the temptation of loving—forgetting the more insidious danger coming from the ear: "i detti andaro ove non giunse il volto" (Sonnet; published 1565). In his dialogue, *Il Minturno o vero della Bellezza*, he has Minturno quote these lines, to which Ruscellai makes answer: "... alcuna volta vorrei mille occhi *e mille orecchi* per mirare *e per udire* a pieno la bellezza *e l'armonia* de la mia signora, la qual a guisa di sole ci dimostra una obliqua via di salire al cielo e di tornare a noi medesimi" (*Dialoghi*, ed. Ezio Raimondi [Florence, 1958], II², 939). *L'armonia* is added to *bellezza* because it is musical harmony emanating from the beloved. Nevertheless the following metaphor of the sun is again a visual one.

NOTES TO CHAPTER III

1. The telescoping of reality and of speculation, which I call "harmonizing" is in fact just what was achieved by the earliest Greek thought—an achievement for which Gomperz, from the point of view of modern science, finds only words of blame: "Xenophanes had figured out a theory according to which sea and land will gradually be mixed up with each other until a state of universal 'muddification' is reached. . . . Then, sea and land will little by little be separated again. . . . Now, *in support of this theory*, Xenophanes adduced two series of observations. First, shells are found in mid-land and even on hilltops. Secondly, in certain places . . . the rock exhibits imprints of fossils that could only have originated at a time when the rock was mud . . . Xenophanes did *not* see that these facts do not bear out either his assumption that 'muddification' took place everywhere at the same time, or his contention that a new period of 'muddification' is impending. . . . This was because he compared *his theory as a whole* with the evidence of *one element* of his hypothesis."

Granted that in our case, the Pythagoreans, acting on the assumption— unsupported by evidence—that vibration must *always* produce a sound, reached the conclusion that a sound may be produced by revolving stars, is not this telescoping and harmonizing, even when leading to conclusions which cannot stand up under modern scientific analysis, the corollary of synthetic thought, of the urge to seek unity in the variety of the world ? And are modern "scientists" less prone to speculation resting on insufficient factual evidence ?

2. The word family of κρᾶσις was revived in Romance in the Renaissance period: "L'âme d'ung homme indebté est toute hectique, *dyscrasiée*" (Rabelais); compare also in Chap. I, note 9, the passage from D'Aubigné; Brissaud, *Histoire des expressions populaires relatives à . . . la médecine* (Paris, 1892), p. 85, lists *dyscrasie* as common among physicians as late as the nineteenth century; *discrasia* in Italian is listed for Francesco Redi, seventeenth century, in Tommaseo-Bellini (= *stemperamento di umori*); the Greek compound Ιδιοσυγ- κρασία (Ptolemy, Galen) appears in 1604 in English as *idiosyncrasy*, "a peculiarity of constitution or temperament"; in French with Charles Nodier (*Histoire du roi de Bohême* [1830], p. 20): "Que de siècles n'auroit-il pas fallu pour remettre mes molécules constitutives en harmonie, pour raccrocher mes atomes, pour *idiosyncraser* mes monades"; in German since 1750 (Schiller: "wenn es mir erlaubt wäre von *Temperamenten, Idiosynkrasien, und Konsensus* zu reden"; cf. Schulz-Basler), where it has a more pejorative meaning, e.g., "the loathings of a pregnant woman."

3. His views, however, are (implicitly) contradicted by Allers, p. 333, who objects strongly to the assumption of the πόλις (social order) as the origin of κόσμος (cosmic order), on the grounds that world order is a primary experience of man.

4. The ideal form represented by the square (defined by Clarembaud d'Arras [twelfth century] as the primary form which comes out of the One, i.e., Christ, *figura substantiae patris*; cf. Schrade, *Dtsch. Viertelj.*, VII, 250) is often brought into connection, in medieval art, with that other ideal form, the circle; the *mandorla* of Romanic churches, which usually contains the representation of the Saviour is somehow "completed" by a square formed by the symbols of the four Evangelists, or by four angels holding the *mandorla* (compare, for example, the picture on the façade of the cathedral of Angoulême, reproduced by R. Hamann in his *Geschichte der Kunst*, p. 144). Again, in that thirteenth-century representation at Rheims, of the harmony of the spheres, which I mentioned in an earlier chapter as an example for the περιέχον (=Air, or world soul), the circles formed by Earth and Sky are, so to speak, counterbalanced by the square formed by the four winds and the four extremities of the gigantic figure of Air. In such representations there is no attempt to square the circle, or to "circle" the square: the two ideal forms rather tend to complement each other.

5. The same development from four to ten took place in Jewish and medieval cabalistic speculation: the tetragrammaton, or the four letters of the name of Yahweh, led to the ten *sephiroth*, the spiritual emanations of God. Cf. Mahnke, *loc. cit.*, p. 120.

Mersenne, in one of the prefaces to his *Harmonie universelle* (1637), mentioning on one level Plato and David as the great promoters of music, says of the latter that he drove out the demons of Saul "en appliquant les dix noms de Dieu ... avec leur dix Sephiroths, aux dix chordes de son instrument."

6. In another speculation, man is presented as a microcosm formed out of the four elements. Honorius of Autun says, in his *Elucidarium*: "unde corporalis [homo] ? De quattuor elementis, unde et microcosmos, id est minor mundus, dicitur. Habet namque ex terra carnem, ex aqua sanguinem, ex aere flatum, ex igne calorem. Caput eius est rotundum, in caelestis sphaerae modum, in quo duo oculi ut duo luminaria in caelo micant ... ; pectus, in quo flatus et tussis versantur, simulat aerem, in quo venti et tonitrua concitantur. Venter omnes liquores ut mare omnia flumina recipit. Pedes totum corporis pondus ut terra cuncta sustinent." (Migne, 172, 1116.)

This passage is quoted by Karl Fiehn (p. 54) in *Studien zur lat. Dichtung des Mittelalters (Ehrengabe Karl Strecker)*, order to explain the description of the allegory of Philosophy in the medieval Latin epic poem *Troilus* of Albert of Stade: "Terra pedes, aqua venter, habet [is related to, signifies] par pectoris aer, / Ignis frons capitis ... " A similar passage from Honorius, equal in content but slightly different in wording, is cited by Allers, p. 348 (cf. also the comparable example from Hildegard of Bingen, p. 378), who points out a twofold symbolistic parallelism: one between the organs or functions, and the elements; and another between the parts of the body and the parts of the universe. This symbolism has had the greatest consequences for poetry: representation of the human body (particularly that of the beloved lady) by means of the elements thus became possible. We have examples of this pattern in many descriptions of feminine physical beauty as late as Calderón.

The same pattern came also to be extended to other beautiful objects—for example, to horses; in *La vida es sueño*, III, 485-94, the horse is said to be a "map" (=a reduced globe): its body corresponds to the earth, its fiery nature to the soul, its foam to the sea, its breath to the air, "en cuya confusion un caos admiro; . . . pues . . . mónstruo [=a hybrid] es de fuego, tierra, mar y viento." Krenkel notes that this speech is put into the mouth of the *gracioso* and that, in other cases, Calderón offers the same metaphorical description quite seriously. May not this ambiguous procedure on the part of the Spanish poet stem from his attitude which is at the same time humanistic and Christian? He had before him two possibilities: he could take over from the ancients, simply and without comment, the idea of the creation of the four elements—or else he could scorn the non-Christian cosmogony. In the passage in question, his attitude was Christian, so that he saw in this cosmogony a "chaos" peopled by hybrids (cf. *caos animal* in one of Krenkel's parallels; and, in the *Mágico prodigioso*, the designation of a certain mountain by the devil as "mónstruo de elementos cuatro": II, 975).

7. Cf. Thomas, *Mélanges*, p. 156 and *REW*, s.v. *trinio* (the word, a variant of *ternio*, is attested in Isidore, XVIII, 65, as "trice in dice" along with *binio*, *quaternio*). Du Cange, *s.v.*, has also a *trinion*, "chimes," attested for Mâcon in 1495; he refers to *trasellum* (*trisellum*), "chimes" in Burgundy (in 1497), evidently a diminutive of *tres*, and to a "tintinnabulum seu Tricodonum bene ordinatum melodiosum" (in which *tricodonum* is evidently a Greek *τρικώδω-νον*), in a papal bull of 1482. All these examples make me doubt the correctness of the etymology usually given for It *trillo*, *trillare*, "trill, to trill" (from which Fr *trille*, Ger *Triller*, and Eng *trill* are ultimately derived): the *REW* suggests an onomatopoeic origin, evidently in view of such onomatopoeic formations as Fr *tralala*, *turelure*, *tirelire*, *torelore*. But It *trillare* never shows the characteristic vocalic variants of an onomatopoeia, and Sp-Prt-Catal *trinar*, "to trill," are evidently not to be derived from onomatopoeias. Since It *trillare* has the additional meaning "to shake," and Eng *to trill* that of "to tremble," one might think of an origin semantically parallel to It *tremolare*, "to quaver"—but, in that case the Iberian *-n-* forms would again be unexplained. Thus I would assume for the Iberian *trinar* a Lat **trin-are* meaning first "to play a trio," "to chime" (parallel to *trinio* > O Prov *trinho*, "chimes of three bells"), then "to twitter, to trill," and for It *trillare* a **trinulare* (cf. phonetically, *cunula* > It

culla) with the same semantic development. For the derivation as such, cf. Sp *trinca*, "number of three" (whose formation is not at all unclear, *REW*, s.v. *trinus*; cf. the *trinicum sacramentum* attested for Marseille in Du Cange, evidently a "threefold oath"). For the semantic development of OFr *trebl(oi)er*, "to sing in three voices," "to sing in treble" (probably also "to trill"; cf. the quotation in Godefroy from Gautier de Coinci, "Qui lors oy chanter archangres, / Deschanter puceles et angres, / Traibloier virges, sainz et saintes, / Beles notes y oist maintes"; and from H. d'Andeli: "Li douz ton diatesalon, / Diapanté, diapason, / Sont hurtees *de divers gerbes* / Par quarreures et par *trebles*"), derived from Lat *triplus*, "threefold" (the highest voice of the soprano or treble making the trio complete). The meaning "chimes" is not lacking (Renard: "Les sains sone de grant air, / A glas, a treble, a carenon" [= *triplus*]; Eng *treble-bell*).

8. In the passage from Hamlet (III, i), referring to the protagonist's derangement: "Oh, what a noble mind is here o'erthrown! / The courtier's, soldier's, scholar's eye, tongue, sword . . . / The glass of fashion, and the mould of form, / The observed of all observers, quite, quite down! / And I . . . / That suck'd the honey of his *music* vows, / Now see that noble and most sovereign reason, / *Like sweet bells jangled out of tune and harsh*; / That unmatch'd form and feature of blown youth / Blasted with ecstasy," we may assume a metaphor drawn from the carillon with three bells; the chimes of reason are out of tune, the music of proportion and equilibrium is destroyed.

9. In Longfellow's *The Carillon*, written in Bruges, 1845, we meet with "chimes in sweet collision [!] / mingled with each wandering vision"; here is reflected the paradox of the μάχη of the elements of the Greeks. Compare the mixture of contrasting feelings in Longfellow's *Voices of the Night*: "I heard the sounds of sorrow and delight, / The manifold, soft chimes."

10. In this poem, the casting of the harmonious bell is compared with the well-temperedness of a good marriage; Schiller's words are to be explained by a Latin-Romance *temperare* background, which comprehends music and temper:

> . . . Jetzt, Gesellen, frisch!
> Prüft mir das Gemisch,
> Ob das Spröde mit dem Weichen
> Sich vereint zum guten Zeichen!
>
> Denn wo das Strenge mit dem Zarten,
> Wo Starkes sich und Mildes paarten,
> Da gibt es einen guten Klang.

It is evidently in remembrance of Schiller's *Glocke* that Rudolf Borchardt writes, in *Die grossen Trobadors*, "Die Provenzalen sind ein himmelbegünstigtes *Gemenge* gewesen, das nie wieder, auch in den ähnlich *gemengten* Brudernationen, der altcatalanischen und altsavoischen nicht, so herrlich läutete. Einmal

und nicht wieder geriet den Mächten der Geschichte diese Glockenspeise der Geblüte" (*Gesammelte Werke*, ed. M. L. Borchardt and E. Zinn [Stuttgart, 1959], *Prosa*, II, 343–4). The same idea of "tempering" is underlying Schiller's *Punschlied*: "Vier Elemente, / Innig gesellt, / Bilden das Leben, / Bauen die Welt. // Presst der Zitrone / Saftigen Stern! / Herb ist des Lebens / Innerster Kern. // Jetzt mit des Zuckers / Linderndem Saft / Zähmet die Herbe, / Brennende Kraft."
The note in the edition of the *Bibliographisches Institut* comments on these lines as follows: "Das Gedicht führt drei Begriffsreihen vor: (1) Die vier Bestandteile des Punsches; damit werden verglichen (2) die vier sogenannten Elemente, welche 'die Welt bauen'; (3) Elemente unseres Gemütslebens, welche 'das Leben bilden': die Herbheit und die Süssigkeit des Lebens, die Seelenruhe und der feurig angeregte Geist. Der Dichter hebt aber nur die Vergleichungspunkte hervor, die sich ungezwungen darbieten, und verzichtet z.B. darauf, der Zitrone und dem Zucker ein Gegenbild unter den materiellen Elementen zu geben . . ."—This explanation fails to take into account the presence of the ancient *tetraktys* (hence the reduction of the traditional five ingredients of the "punch" to four) or the fact that Schiller has also introduced the four basic qualities of antiquity ("cold-warm" being represented by the "calm water" and the "glowing spirit" of the last three stanzas, while the couple "dry-moist" is replaced by "sweet-acid"). With the "lindernde Saft" of sugar which "zähmet" the "brennende Kraft" of the lemon, we arrive at the unity of temperament—temperature—temperance.

11. The ensemble ringing of the bells of Rome has been brought to the modern operatic stage at the end of the first act of Pfitzner's *Palestrina*. According to Thomas Mann's description, however, in *Betrachtungen eines Unpolitischen*, p. 412, this is only an orchestral imitation of the bells, offering a deafening variety, but little suggestion of "well-tempered" world harmony: ". . . so, wie hundertfach schwingendes, tönendes, dröhnendes Kirchenglockenerzgetöse überhaupt noch niemals künstlerisch nachgeahmt wurde—ein kolossales Schaukeln von abenteuerlich harmonisierten Sekunden, worin, wie in dem vom Gehör nicht zu bewältigenden Tosen eines Wasserfalls, sämtliche Tonhöhen und Schwingungsarten, Donnern, Brummen und Schmettern mit höchstem Streichergefistel sich mischen, ganz so, wie es ist, wenn hundertfaches Glockengedröhn die Gesamtatmosphäre in Vibration versetzt zu haben und das Himmelsgewölbe sprengen zu wollen scheint."
The well-known passage in Victor Hugo's *Notre Dame de Paris* (so different, in its sympathetic approach to the bells, from the *Isle sonnante* of Rabelais), in which we are given a bird's-eye view of Paris at the moment of the "éveil des carillons," contains rather the idea of the symphonic concert (which degenerates, with this poet, into an "opéra"), and of the synesthetics ("l'oreille a aussi sa vue"; "colonne de bruit, fumée d'harmonie"; "flûtes de pierre") offered by the ensemble of the carillons, rather than a picture of each single

carillon reflecting world harmony: "D'abord la vibration de chaque cloche monte droite, pure, et pour ainsi dire isolée des autres, dans le ciel splendide du matin, puis, peu à peu, en grossissant, elles se fondent, elles se mêlent, elles s'effacent l'une dans l'autre, elles s'amalgament dans un magnifique concert. ... Cependant cette mer d'harmonie n'est point un chaos ... elle n'a pas perdu sa transparence: vous y voyez serpenter à part chaque groupe de notes qui s'échappe des sonneries ..." (Book III, Ch. 2).

12. Such a line may throw light on the semantic development of the Slav word family мир, "peace" and "world" (ultimately connected with мил, "friendly"); the intermediate concepts must have been: "cosmos" > "cosmic order" > "orderly, peaceful community" (in Russian, the meaning "community of peasants" is attested for our word by Berneker).

13. Distinctions such as that between *temperamentum innatum* and *t. influxum* have gone over to Descartes: *tempérament acquis* and *t. inné*; compare also his *cerveau mal tempéré*. Similarly Goethe writes of Newton as a "wohlorganisierter, gesunder, *wohltemperierter* Mann, ohne Leidenschaft, ohne Begierden," and we shall have occasion in another study to read a passage from Rousseau in which the harmonious mixture in the soul is compared to that in the climate.

14. In the case of words once belonging to a field which since has been broken up, the problem of translating is a vexing one: "accord" no longer calls to mind "temper," and "temper" is now far away from "temperance" and "temperature" (though the act of translating, itself, must always involve, to some extent, cutting through the fields established in the original language). In this connection, Franz Rosenzweig has graphically described the perplexity confronting him in his attempt to translate the Hebrew Bible into German (*Die Schrift und ihre Verdeutschung* [1936], p. 125):

Das Flugbild der Wortlandschaft einer Sprache [he uses this term for "etymological family"] aber scheint zunächst einmal von dem jeder andern Sprache geschieden und unterschieden; und auch die Landkarten dieser Landschaften, die Lexiken mit ihrem 1., 2., 3., a, b, c, beschreiben um das Wort der einen Sprache nur je einen grossen Kreis, der mehrere Kreise um Worte der anderen Sprache schneidet, so dass eine Anzahl gemeinsamer Flächen entstehen, die aber alle anscheinend beziehungslos und unverbunden auseinanderliegen. Anders wird das Bild erst durch die geologische Betrachtung. In der Wurzelschicht der Worte finden sich die oben getrennten Flächen zusammen, und in noch tieferer Schicht, des Wurzelsinns, der Wurzelsinnlichkeit, zeigt sich, jenseits allen Fragens nach etwaiger Urverwandtschaft der Sprachen, die an der Wortoberfläche nur erahnbare Einheit alles menschlichen Sprechens. In diese Schichten also muss der Übersetzer sich hinunterwagen, wenn er die in der einen Sprache eng zusammenliegenden Worte, in denen sich ein Begriffskreis schliesst, in der andern Sprache, ungeachtet dass sie da oberflächlich, lexikalisch, weit auseinanderliegen, ebenfalls als geschlossenen Anschauungs- und Begriffskreis entdecken will. Bei dieser Einfahrt muss er ausgerüstet sein mit der Grubenlampe der wissenschaftlichen Etymologie; aber auch von dem Aufschimmern der Adern des Texts selbst darf er das Auge nicht hochmütig abwenden.

A significant example of Rosenzweig's procedure is offered by his translation of a Hebrew passage containing three words from the same root (*'ad 'od*) by a German phrase which offers the same threefold variation: "Gott gegenwärtigt sich [a] im Zelt der Gegenwart [b] über dem Schrein der Vergegenwärtigung

[c]"—where the familiar version of Luther had only a twofold variation (of another root): "sich im Offenbarungszelt [c] über der Gesetzeslade [b] offenbart [a]."

15. Language is a kind of organic music for the German Romantics, who were given to organological thinking: Schleiermacher, toward the end of his *Monologen*, III, after offering a metaphor comparing "Sitte" (*mores*) with clothing, which is organically fitted to the body, whose genuine nobility it reveals, speaks of language as "concealing and revealing" the individual mind— this time, using a carefully-elaborated musical metaphor, applying to language what Augustine had said of music:

Abbilden soll die Sprache des Geistes innersten Gedanken; seine höchste Anschauung, seine geheimste Betrachtung des eigenen Handelns soll sie wiedergeben, und ihre wunderbare Musik soll deuten den Werth, den er auf jedes legt, die eigene Stufenleiter seiner Liebe. Wol können andere die Zeichen, die wir dem Höchsten widmeten, misbrauchen und dem Heiligen, das sie andeuten sollen, ihre kleinlichen Gedanken untershieben und ihre beschränkte Sinnesart: doch anders ist des Weltlings Tonart als des Geweihten; anders als dem Weisen reihen sich dem Knechte der Zeit die Zeichen der Gedanken zu einer andern Melodie; etwas anderes erhebt dieser zum Ursprünglichen und leitet davon ab, was ihm unbekannter und ferner liegt. Bilde nur jeder seine Sprache sich zum Eigenthum und zum kunstreichen Ganzen, dass Abteilung und Übergang, Zusammenhang und Folge der Bauart seines Geistes genau entsprechen, und die Harmonie der Rede den Accent des Herzens, der Denkart Grundton wiedergebe. Dann gibt's in der gemeinen noch eine heilige und geheime Sprache, die der Ungeweihte nicht vermag zu deuten noch nachzunahmen, weil nur im Innern der Gesinnung der Schlüssel liegt zu ihren Charakteren; ein kurzer Gang nur aus dem Spiele der Gedanken, ein paar Accorde nur aus seiner Rede werden ihn verraten.

Less from the standpoint of the single individual and more from that of the speaking community, Humboldt elucidates, by means of a musical simile, the particular characteristic of speech, which, in its loose but energetic symbolism, consists of an understandable ununderstandability: "Die Menschen verstehen einander nicht dadurch, dass sie sich Zeichen der Dinge wirklich hingeben, auch nicht dadurch dass sie sich gegenseitig bestimmen, genau und vollständig denselben Begriff hervorzubringen, sondern dadurch dass sie gegenseitig einander dasselbe Glied der Kette ihrer sinnlichen Vorstellungen und inneren Begriffserzeugungen berühren, *dieselbe Taste ihres geistigen Instruments* anschlagen, worauf alsdann in jedem entsprechende, nicht aber dieselben Begriffe hervorspringen" (cited in Delbrück, *Einleitung in das Studium der idg. Sprachen* [5th ed., Leipzig, 1908] p. 46). (I have opposed, in *AJPh*, LXIII, 318, the materialism of the antimentalists who assume that "trigger effects" are unleashed by "speech habits," to Humboldt's "keys of the inner spiritual instrument" which bring about understanding in human speech.)

NOTES TO CHAPTER IV

1. The relationship of *temperare* with the climate (as we have it in English, cf. Laurence Sterne: "God tempers the wind to the shorn lamb," etc.) appears in the Middle Ages, for example in a Mozarabic Good Friday rite (cf. H. Rheinfelder, *Volkstum und Kultur der Romanen*, II, 137): "Pestem et famem abluat: Indulgentia / Medelam aegris conferat: Indulgentia / Captivos reddat patriae: Indulgentia / *Vices aërum temperet*: Indulgentia / Te deprecamur Domine: Indulgentia" (the plural of *aër* in the meaning of "climate" is Greek, and is attested in Lucretius as well as in the Late Latin *Expositio Mundi*, fifth century [?]: "civitates aeres temperatos habent"). Note also *temperantia aeris* in *Carmina Burana*, ed. Schmeller, n° 55: "Sol tellurem recreat, / ne fetus eius pereat; / ab aeris temperantia / rerum fit materia, / unde multiplicia / generantur semina." According to Benveniste, *Mélanges Ernout* (1940), p. 11, the original meaning of Lat *tempus* itself was "mixture of the elements composing the atmosphere." (I know of this paper only through R. O. Kent, *Language*, XXII, 262.)

2. Here belongs the dialectal phonetic variant of Eng *to temper*: to *tamper*, = "to work with clay, to machinate, to plot, to meddle, to interfere with" (which is also a semantic, more materialistic, variant of *to temper*), and dialectal Fr *étremper*, "élever ou abaisser la charrue suivant que la terre est plus ou moins profonde. On dit qu'une femme étrempe suivant qu'elle relève plus ou moins sa robe, d'après l'état du chemin" (in Vendôme, according to Martellière, *Glossaire du vendomois* [Orléans, 1893]), which shows a somewhat materialized meaning still inspired by the moral idea of "modifying according to decency."

3. Another word for "temper" is *complexio* attested in Firmicus, fourth century (*Math.*, 5, 9): "Tranquilli, quieti, alacres, bonae complexionis"; it is found earlier in Seneca as *complexio aëris*; in Cicero as "*complexiones* et copulationes et adhaesiones atomorum inter se," an expression which pictures the loving sympathy of nature, and the sexual copulation (*amplexus*, Gr συμπλοκή) of the atoms contained therein; similarly the combination of four elements, extant in any body, was portrayed as a manifestation of cosmic love (Cassiodorus, *ThLL*). Thus everything had a "complexion" (Ps. Apuleius: "invenitur quandoque nigra mandragora complexionem frigidam et siccam habens"). From philosophers and physicists the word went over to grammarians and rhetoricians, as was the case with *consonantia*: "mira verborum complexio"; "brevis complexio totius negoti" (Cicero), after a similar use of the Greek model συμπλοκή. The meaning of Eng *complexion* goes back to the idea

that the temperament manifests itself in the color of the face (we may remember the dark face of Dürer's *Melancolia*). *Complexio* and the following words have their part in the history of *Stimmung*:

Lat *constitutio* followed part way the development taken by *complexio*: Cicero has *corporis firma constitutio*, translated by Forcellini "buona complessione"; then from the "robust constitution" we come to "(good) quality of the body"— but throughout there is no idea of the mixture of elements!

Lat *dispositio*, which was first used in reference to the disposition of elements in the body, and the resultant energy, came, with the Schoolmen, close to the meaning of *inclinatio* (*intellectus dispositio*, Albertus Magnus), hence Fr *dispos*, *disposé*, Eng disposed, Ger disponiert (*indisposé, indisposed, indisponiert*, "slightly ill"), and such loan-translations as Ger *aufgelegt*, which as late as the eighteenth century could be used of the capacity ("disposition") for learning, the attitude ("disposition") of gratitude, and even of the "power of vibration" of strings.

In the following passages from Montaigne I have italicized the expressions for the good natural constitution of the human body—sometimes impaired by man: *structure et composition* is synonymous with *complexio, constitutio*: the re-formations are accumulated in order to stress that reintegration which, in the meaning of the writer, is the duty of man in conformity with the purposes of nature (2, 17): "Le corps a une grand' part à nostre estre, il y tient un grand rang; ainsi *sa structure et composition* sont de bien juste considération. Ceux qui veulent desprendre nos deux pièces principales, et les sequestrer l'un de l'aultre, ils ont tort; au rebours, il les faut *r'accoupler* et *rejoindre*; il faut ordonner à l'âme non de se tirer à quartier, de s'entretenir à part, de mespriser et abandonner le corps, ... mais de se *r'allier* à luy, de *l'embrasser* ..., *l'espouser* en somme, et luy *servir de mary*, à ce que leurs effects ne paraissent pas *divers et contraires*, ains *accordans et uniformes*. Les Chrestiens ont une particuliere instruction en cette liaison; ils sçavent que la justice divine embrasse cette *société* et *joincture* du *corps et de l'âme* ..." (cf. ed. Villey [Paris, 1922], II, 419). Similarly, *de- dis-* show the willful counteracting of nature by man (3, 13): "A quoy faire *demembrons* nous en *divorce* un bastiment tissu d'une si *joincte et fraternelle correspondance*? Au rebours, *renouons* le par mutuels offices: que l'esprit esveille et vivifie la pesanteur du corps, le corps arreste la legereté de l'esprit et la fixe" (Villey, III, 448).

4. In Latin, the plural *chordae*, "strings" was used to refer to the lute itself; cf. Porphyrius in his commentary on Horace, *Carm.* I, 17, 18: "fides autem chordae dicunter"; Cassiodorus, commenting on Psalm 150, 4, "laudate eum in chordis et organo," writes: "quoniam praeter psalmum et citharam ... alia inveniri potuerant, quae *chordarum tensionibus* personarent, generaliter *chordas* posuit, ut omne ipsum instrumentum musicum domini laudibus imputaret."

5. This passage is a reproduction of Latin mnemotechnic lines concerned with the four temperaments; they are to be found in the *Regimen sanitatis salernitanum*, which was often translated into Romance (cf. Morawski, *Neuph.*

Mitt. [1927], 199, and C. V. Langlois, *La connaissance de la nature et du monde*, p. 314). We may compare the Italian passage, quoted above, on the sanguine temperament, with the following lines of the Latin model: "Largus, amans, hylaris, ridens, rubeique coloris, / cantans, carnosus satis audax atque benignus." It is characteristic of the harmonizing tendency of the popular songs of the Singleton collection, that a "Trionfo delle quatro scienze matematiche" (*loc. cit.*, p. 510) ascribes to Music the color red—that is, associates her with the sanguine temperament (evidently because of the *cantans* of the Latin verse), while Arithmetic appears as a yellow old woman, a choleric, because the corresponding Latin verse on the choleric temperament contained the epithets: "hirsutus . . ., astutus . . ., siccus, croceique coloris." Here we have to do with a harmonizing quite in the manner of the Pythagoreans.

6. In the *Vita nuova*, which is still shaped after the traditional pattern of a Provençal troubadour novel, the poet, who has displeased his lady, is advised by Amor (XII) to reconcile her with a poem—but a poem which will not speak to her directly (*immediatamente*), but uses the intermediary of music (*fa che siano* [the words] *quasi un mezzo*): "falle adornare di soave armonia, ne la quale io sarò tutte le volte che farà mestiere." Scartazzini explains, "falle dare il suono da un musico valente." This is surely wrong; it is the reconciliatory and curative power of music that must be meant, as well as the omnipresence of love in music (in accordance with the Augustinian and troubadour equation). The *ballata* which follows is thus quite in line with the mediatory part that Amor would have the words play: "Con dolze sono quando se' ['when thou (sc. the Ballad) art before her'] con lui [Amor the mediator], comincia este parole . . . ['Say, Ballad, to Amor'] / Per grazia de la mia nota soave ['in reward for my sweet music'] reman tu qui con lei"—all these expressions are the devices of the flattering, mediating attitude of a "go-between" (cf. *Travaux du séminaire roman d'Istanbul*, I). To our modern mind such an allegory may appear shocking, but it must be remembered that in the medieval civilization the use of intermediaries with highborn persons was quite usual (cf. the examples furnished by K. Lewent, *Mod. Lang.*, XXXVIII, 44), necessary because of the hierarchical position occupied by the lady—and what nobler intermediary than music could Dante find?

7. The ticking of the clock has often been compared to the human heartbeat, as for example in the song "Die Uhr" by J. G. Seidl, set to music by Loewe, where we find the suggestion that the divine Maker has put it in order ("Es ist ein grosser Meister, der künstlich ihr Werk gefügt"). This is, ultimately, the "machine theory," used so often by the Church Fathers to prove the existence of God; Gregory of Nyssa, in his dialogue with Macrina, states that just as an engine is to be explained, not by the "elements" but by the mind of its maker, so the functioning of the world can only be retraced to the mind of God.

The first clock with bells was, according to Rheinfelder (*Kultsprache und Profansprache* [Geneva, Florence, 1933], p. 355), set up in Milan 1336, but our passage itself, which must have been written before 1320, offers an earlier attestation; in any case, *l'orologio . . . tin tin suonando* was really a modern device for Dante.

8. We must remember that Jupiter, the "jovial," was called *Serenator* by the Romans. Orpheus, too, had the quality of appeasing nature; thus we find with Maurice Scève a verb *serainer* used of the beloved who, like Orpheus, is able to charm nature (*Délie*, st. 160): "Elle a le Ciel *serainé* au Pays . . . Et son doulx chant . . . A *tranquillé* la *tempeste* par l'air . . ." The Augustinian *moderator* is the Christian version of the *Jupiter Serenator*. We shall later find in a passage from the Spanish *siglo de oro* a similarly Christianized version of *serenar*.

9. According to an article of Joan Murphy in MLN, LVIII, 375-7, the first English imitation of any part of the *Gerusalemme liberata* to be published was Thomas Watson's *Italian Madrigals Englished* (1590), which happens to be a paraphrase of our stanza. But the English imitation ("Evry singing bird, that in the wood reioyces / come & assist me, with your charming voices : / Zephirus, come too, & make the leaues & the fountaines / Gently to send a whispring sound unto the mountains: / And from thence pleasant Echo, sweetly replying, / stay here playing, where my Phyllis now is lying") has suppressed the references to world music (the *temprare*, air the musician), and introduces a madrigal element ("where my Phyllis now is lying"—and the remainder of the poem) unwarranted by the original. If source chasing have any value, it would be to show the banality of an imitation which erases all the intellectual content of a poem in favor of lyrical commonplaces.

10. Here I may quote just one passage from French Renaissance poetry (J. Lemaire de Belges, *Description du temple de Vénus*): "Les neuf beaux cieux que Dieu tourne et *tempere* / Rendent tel bruit en leurs sphères diffuses / Que le son vient jusqu'en notre hémisphère. / Et de là sont toutes grâces infuses / Aux clairs engins, et le don célestin / De la liqueur et fontaine des Muses" (cf. *Œuvres*, ed. Stecker [Louvain, 1885] III, 111). The temperate climate of the heavens, the harmony of the spheres and the grace (with a Christian tinge: *grâces infuses*!) of the Muses—*temperantia* and *consonantia*—are fused with this poet who is able to render acoustically the clarity of classical music (one cannot fail to hear the crystalline sound of the line "aux clairs engins et le don célestin").

11. Cf. Tillyard, *The Elizabethan World Picture* (1943), a most glorious book, whose conclusions I am happy to make mine:

> People still think of the Age of Elizabeth as a secular period between two outbreaks of Protestantism: a period in which religious enthusiasm was sufficiently dormant to allow the new humanism to shape our literature. . . . They do not tell us that Queen Elizabeth translated Boethius, that Raleigh was a theologian as well as a discoverer, and that sermons were as much a part of an ordinary Elizabethan's life as bear-baiting . . . the Puritans and the courtiers were more united by a common theological bond than they were divided by ethical disagreements. . . . The greatness of the Elizabethan Age was that it contained so much of new

without bursting the noble form of the old order.   It is here that the Queen herself comes in: somehow the Tudors had inserted themselves into the constitution of the medieval universe (pp. 1–6).

On nearly every page Professor Tillyard offers Elizabethan literary specimens of "medieval" world harmony; most revelatory to me were the excerpts from Sir John Davie's *Orchestra* (1596), representing the concept of the dance of the universe, in which figure the queen and her court; so that, as Tillyard says, the "cosmic dance is represented in the body politic."

12. A commendable exception is F. Baldensperger's edition of Shakespeare's sonnets (*Les sonnets de Shakespeare*, Univ. of California Press, 1943).   But why must he explain the musical similes of one sonnet "biographically," by the poet's frequentation of "aristocratic society," instead of relying on that Platonic and Christian tradition of world music which Baldensperger's parallel texts serve to establish ?   It is not "aristocratic society" that suggests phrases such as "the true concord of well-tuned sounds."

13. One may oppose to Gundolf's characterization of Shylock the passage in which this character describes himself, the Jew, as a human being with all the qualities of such a one (III, 1): "Hath not a Jew eyes ? hath not a Jew hands, organs, dimensions, senses, affections, passions ? fed with the same food, hurt with the same weapons, subject to the same diseases, healed by the same means, warmed and cooled by the same winter and summer, as a Christian is ?   If you prick us, do we not bleed ? if you tickle us, do we not laugh ? if you poison us, do we not die ? and if you wrong us, shall we not revenge ?"   That is, the Jew has the same κρᾶσις and δυσκρασία as the Christian (and his revenge is the logical effect of the latter), but he has no "music," i.e., no grace.   One may think that Shakespeare borrowed here from Jewish apologetic literature of the type of the Portuguese Samuel Usque's "Consolaçam ás tribulaçoens de Israel" (Ferrara, 1553; quoted by Vossler, *Poesie der Einsamkeit*, p. 365) in which the "harmony" of the Jew with other rational beings was emphasized:

Que *desemelhầça* ha de minha natural razaõ e entendimento aquella [= a aqu.] que a todolos outros animaes de minha especia foi ynfluido ? . . . Que *disformidade* ha em minha figura, e que *desconueniencia* em meus membros das outras racionaes criaturas ? . . . O alta e noua marauilha que em mi vejo, que enjeita a terra a simesma em minha forma; que aborrece o ceeo seu esprito em meu peito; que estranham as criaturas o seu propio treslado em minha figura; pois nam vedes que *toda ordem de naturaleza trastornais* ? em nam amardes aquilo que he a vos outros semelhằte, como todalas cousas amẫ seu semelhauel ?

In this truly Aristotelian-Christian argumentation, of a Jew who unlike Shylock fails to conclude that the violation of human rights justifies revenge, Vossler is able to see a "new spirit" of "arming oneself against the world" (*sich wappnen, sich verteidigen*) inspired by an "extreme consciousness of being rejected" (*Verstossenheit*): a transition to the spirit of "enlightened aggression toward nature," as this was to be expressed in *Robinson Crusoe*!   Obviously, this whimsical misjudgment of Vossler's was prompted only by the necessity to find a transition to the next chapter of his treatise—which was dedicated to

Robinson Crusoe. But should the literary critic not have forgotten his clever transitions, when faced with the plight of Israel in the Germany (his Germany) of 1938, a situation no less critical than that of 1553? And should he not have been moved to contrition by the four-hundred-year-old accusation of Samuel Usque, "Ye upset all the order of nature in loving not that which is similar to you..."?

I must also, of course, dissociate myself from the stand of Gundolf, that highly-gifted Jewish-born pre-Hitlerian German critic who would exculpate Shakespeare from "das moderne empfindsame oder anklägerische Mitleid"; from "jede politische oder soziale Parteinahme für die 'Erniedrigten und Beleidigten'" (note the quotation marks); from any "nachfühlen-wollen mit russischer Brüderei"[!]. It is one thing to state that Shakespeare saw Shylock the Jew as the incarnation of "unmusical," unredeemed disgrace, rather than as a victim of the social order (although this aspect is not missing in the play); it is quite another ironically to dismiss all modern attempts at alleviation of social injustice with the slur [?] of "Russian fraternalism." Has he a truly musical soul that cannot hear the voice of human justice?

14. Portia, the incarnation of grace, can not be unconnected with music. When Bassanio has to choose between the caskets, a choice on which her own happiness depends, she suggests (III, 2): "Let music sound while he doth make his choice. / Then, if he lose, he makes a swan-like end, / Fading in music... He may win; / And what is music then? Then music is / Even as the flourish when true subjects bow / To a new-crowned monarch: such it is / As are those dulcet sounds in break of day / That creep into the dreaming bridegroom's ear / And summon him to marriage." Thus she trusts music (=grace) to influence his choice, while accepting beforehand the particular sound of music (the decision of Providence: death or a new life).

The equation music=love=Christian grace, as opposed to the Jewish "lack of Grace" (=unmusicality) was a medieval *topos*. The religious service of the Synagogue seemed to the Christians noisy and discordant; since the Synagogue had been conquered by the Ecclesia, how could the Christian Church music not excel Jewish "disharmony"? (For the Italian dialectal expressions *baruccabá*, *tananai*, "noise," taken from Jewish liturgical phrases, as well as the German *Lärm wie in einer Judenschule*, cf. my article on "noise" in *Word*, II, 260 ff.) The idea of the Grace-forsakenness of the Jewish service is found as late as the eighteenth century, with the Deist J. C. Edelmann (1749; cf. the volume "Pietismus und Rationalismus" of *Deutsche Selbstzeugnisse* [Leipzig, 1933], p. 115), who offers a description caricaturizing a synagogue service at a *Judenschule* in Frankfurt. At the moment of writing his sketch, such a ceremony appeared to him as exemplifying the obscurantism of *all* religious services (including the Christian adoration of the Crucified); while he was witnessing the service, however, his impression was quite different: these "Bocks-Triller" and "Kater-Geschrei" appeared to him (according to the prejudices of that period) as the "lieblose Music" of a "von Gott verworfenes Volk." It is significant that the "prejudices" included seeing grace-forsaken music as characteristic of the Jews—though not exclusively characteristic of them, since the service of the sect of the "Homburghäuser Inspiratem" was, on a later occasion, similarly described as a "heiliger Übelklang dieser himmlischen Nachteulen."

15. Cf. also *Paradise Lost*, I, 550 seq., 711 seq.; III, 345, 365 seq.

16. T. Warton's commentary on the parallel passage in Milton's poem "At a Solemn Music," line 18 ("[that we on earth with undiscording voice] May rightly answer that melodious *noise*") points out the many contemporary passages where *noise* means "music" (also Spenser, *Faerie Queene*: "a heavenly noise"; Shakespeare, *The Tempest*: "[the] isle is full of noises" = "musical sounds"). The original meaning of *noise* being "strife" (as in Old French), we have here one of the numerous synonyms of "concert" (see the following discussion of this word) = "rivaling performance." In Old French, *noise* had already been used of the birds' song, which was also conceived of as a kind of orchestra sounding the praises of God *à l'envi*. Cf. a forthcoming article in *Word*. [This article appeared in 1945, *Word*, I, 260–76 (cf. also IV, 128).]

17. D. Masson writes: "It is rather difficult to say whether in 'the bass of Heaven's deep organ' Milton had a precise reference to his optical diagram of space and the Universe [as expressed in his academic oration *De Sphaerarum Concentu*, written about the same time as the *Ode*], or merely brought in a musical effect as such. Warton's notion that it was a recollection of the organ he had heard in his school-time in St. Paul's Cathedral is very bald [sic]. An organ was no rarity with Milton." *O sancta simplicitas!* what anarchy in the table of values of these prosaic commentators! It is evident that the theme of the organ was given with the conception of world music (see below Kepler's basso of Saturn), that the "musical effect" is there, but subservient to the *idea*, and that the autobiographic clues supposedly revealing where Milton may have heard an organ are superfluous and silly.

18. We may compare Milton's poem to Campanella's *Salmodia che invita il cielo, le sue parti e gli abitatori a lodar Dio benedetto*, which presents a synthesis of the biblical and the Greek elements fused in a Neoplatonic vision of light-emanation:

> Dal ciel la Gloria del gran Dio rimbomba:
> Egli è sonora tromba a pregi tanti;
> I lumi stanti, e que' ch'errando vanno
> Musica fanno.
>
> Musica fanno per ogni confino,
> Dove il calor divino il ciel dispiega,
> Ed amor lega tanta luce, e muove
> Altronde altrove.

Altronde altrove tutti van correndo,
Te Dio benedicendo e predicando,
Dolce sonando, ch'ogni moto è suono,
Com' io ragiono.

Così io ragiono.   Ahimè, ch'udir non posso;
Ch'innato rumor grosso è che m'occupa
L'orecchia cupa, ed un molino vivo
Me ne fa privo.

Se mi fa privo, voi spiriti eletti,
Che non siete soggetti a corpo sordo,
Fate un accordo al suon di ta' strumenti
Co' vostri accenti.

Co' vostri accenti sacri intellettuali,
D'una spiegando l'ali in altra stella,
Vostra favella,
"Santo, Santo, Santo," Dicete in tanto.

And the poet continues by invoking the nine hierarchies of angels (according to Dionysius, the Areopagite), the patriarchs of the Old Testament, the apostles, martyrs, confessors, virgins, the blessed souls, the stars with their different powers of light—calling upon them to chime in with the "salmodia di Davide canoro" that ends with the words: "Mia squilla [pun usual with Campanella on his name] è ebra per troppo desío / Di cantar vosco, o stelle, il grande Dio; / Gloria all' onnipotente Signor mio."   One may have noticed the contrast of the "rimbomba" of the first line (which renders "Coeli enarrant gloriam Dei") with the Adonic line 4: "Musica fanno"—creation echoes to God and is answered by *musica mundana*.   And the concatenation of the *terzine* ("Musica fanno. // Musica   fanno . . ."; "Altronde   altrove. // Altronde   altrove . . ." somewhat reminiscent of Dante's *differente-mente*) suggests the uninterrupted "chain of beings" emanating from God.   The particularly Neoplatonic element has found its stylistic equivalent in the fusion of a song which "flows like music."   There cannot be in Campanella that relative separation of cultural worlds which was found in Milton, who linked three civilizations with the thread of time.

I may add here that the Adonic verse with its echo effect is a Renaissance device used to depict the "respond of the world" to music; we find, for example, in Ronsard's *De l'election de son sepulchre* (Ode IIII, vol. II, p. 315, in the Marty-Laveaux edition):

> . . . Et vous forests & ondes
> Par ces prez vagabondes,
> Et vous rives & bois
> *Oyez ma vois* . . .

Que tu es renommée
D'estre tombeau nommée
D'un, de qui l'univers
Chante les vers ! . . .

Mais bien à noz campagnes
Fist voir les Sœurs compagnes
Foulantes l'herbe aux sons
De ses chansons.

Car il fist à sa lyre
Si bons accords eslire,
Qu'il orna de ses chants
Nous & noz champs . . .

Là, là i'oiray d'Alcée
La lyre courroucée
Et Sapphon qui sur tous
Sonne plus dous.

Combien ceux qui entendent
Les chansons qu'ils respandent,
Se doivent resiouir
De les ouir ? . . .

La seule lyre douce
L'ennuy des cœurs repousse,
Et va l'esprit flatant
De l'écoutant.

This echo-poetry of the Renaissance (which is ultimately derived from the repetition of Narcissus' words by Echo in Ovid's *Metamorphoses,* and which has been revived in modern times by Hugo and Banville), is only another of the many aspects of the poetry of world music.

I shall mention here also the scene of Guarini's *Pastor fido,* I, 1, where Echo ("o piuttosto Amor") contradicts the loveless Silvio, and the monologue of Erasmus about the young scholar who receives advice from the echo about his studies. The echo, the "respond of nature," is also easily the impersonation of love—originally, as we have seen, of divine, later of secular love. It is interesting to see how Guarini, who represents love as the primordial design of nature, inserts some lines on the birds' song of love which are conceived precisely in echo form:

Quanto il mondo ha di vago e di gentile
Opra è d'amore: amante è il cielo, amante
La Terra, amante il mare . . .
Quell' augellin che canta
Sì dolcemente, e lascivetto vola

> Or dall'abete al faggio
> Ed or dal faggio al mirto,
> S'avesse umano spirto,
> Direbbe: *ardo d'amore, ardo d'amore*; . . .
> Ed odi, appunto, Silvio,
> Il *suo dolce desío*
> Che gli responde: *Ardo d'amore anch'io.*

There is a double echo play here: Silvio, who does not love, *should* chime in with the love song of nature: "Alfine ama ogni cosa, / Se non tu, Silvio: e sarà Silvio solo / In cielo, in terra, in mare / Anima senza amore ?" (i.e., a response-less soul). In Tasso's *Gerusalemme liberata*, canto XI, 11, where a Christian religious service is described with the familiar epic periphrases suited to the aesthetics of the time, the hymns of the believers ("alternando facean doppio concento") are echoed by nature in the form of the ancient Echo:

> . . . ne suonan le valli ime e profonde,
> E gli alti colli e le spelonche loro,
> E da ben mille parti Eco risponde;
> E quasi par che boscareccio coro
> Fra quegli antri si celi e in quelle fronde;
> Sì chiaramente replicar s'udìa
> Or di Cristo il gran nome, or di Maria.

The most touching examples of echo-poetry are the religious compositions of the German baroque, characterized by the conceptual sophistication of that age. The *Trutz-Nachtigal* of the seventeenth-century Catholic mystic Friedrich Spee (no. 4: "Ein anders Liebgesang: und ist ein Spiel der Gespons Jesu mit einer Echo oder Widerschall") contains a dialogue between the soul of the poet (the "spouse of Jesus") and the echo. To such a query as "Bist du denn Jesus nicht?" the echo answers, "Jesus nicht"; in this play of question and answer (which the poet himself compares to a ball tossed back and forth), always concerned with the name of Jesus, the soul finds itself more and more conscious of its love for Jesus. And concludes:

> In diesem Wald, bei diesem Thal
> Gar oft ich will spazieren
> Und mich mit dir, o Widerschall,
> Gar freundlich verlustieren.
> O süsser Schall!
> O weisser Ball!
> Mit dir will vielmal spielen . . .
> Mein Jesum will nun tausend mal
> In Wälden lan erklingen,
> Mit mir auch sollen überall
> Die Bäum und Stauden springen;

Heck, Laub und Gras,
Wans merken das,
Mit müssens auch zum Reihen ...
Nun bitt ich dich, doch lass es sein ...
Dass Tag und Nacht
In steter Wacht
Die Welt nur Jesum singe
Und immerdar
Das ganze Jahr
Vor ihm in Freuden springe.

The whole world should join the echo to form one song and one dance in Jesus' honor.

In number 5 ("Anders Liebgesang der Gespons Jesu, darin eine Nachtigal mit der Echo oder Widerschall spielet"), an inquiry into the religious nature of the echo takes place in the heart and mind of the nightingale, the bird of love (who is endowed, quite in the medieval tradition, with all the musicological knowledge of the poet himself): "Dann kurz, dann lang / Zieh deinen Klang, / All *Noten* greif zusammen ... die *Färblein* schon sich melden [the edition of G. Balker, 1879, explains *Färblein* as "die Töne, welche die Färbung ihres nachfolgenden Gesangs angeben; Vorspiele"; but we have evidently to do with the medieval *colores*, the rhetorical terms transferred to music that survives in "coloratura"] ... sie sucht es in B Moll, B Dur, / Auf allerhand Gestalten, / Thut hundertfalt / Den *Bass und Alt*, / *Tenòr und Cant* durchstreichen." The devout nightingale vies with the echo in calling out the name of Jesus, in a bitter struggle inspired by ἔρις καὶ φιλία:

Da recht, du fromme Nachtigal,
Du jenem Schall nit weiche!
Da recht, du treuer Widerschall,
Du stets dich ihr vergleiche,
Zur schönen Wett
Nun beide trett,
Mein Jesum lasst erklingen
Obschon im Streit
Der schwächsten Seit
Am Leben sollt misslingen.

And in this sweet war ("in schönem Krieg"), in which the ever louder, higher notes of the bird are surpassed, each time, by the echo, the nightingale finally dies with a sigh so soft that the echo cannot give it back. The nightingale, in death, has conquered. The bird is a mystical soul that dies in love and through love; the piercing sound of the echo (that sophisticated voice of nature: "so subtil dein Widerpart") is an instrument which, like the arrow of St. Teresa, helps the soul fulfill its ultimate desire of death in God: "Hoff, mich mit ihren *Pfeilen* bald / Begierd und Lieb entleiben."

In Gottfried Arnold's (seemingly Anacreontic, but in reality deeply serious) song, "Die Seele erquicket sich an Jesu" (*Deutsche Barocklyrik*, ed. Wehrli), the echo of religious love is understood as twoness-become-one, as strife-become-love, and as a heavenly device that gives delight by multiplying the joy of love:

> So spielen die lieblichen Buhlen zusammen, . . .
> Das eine vermehret des anderen Lust
> Und beiden ist nichts als die Liebe bewusst.
> Sie *kämpfen im Lieben*, sie geben sich eigen,
> Die *Vielheit* muss endlich dem Einen hinweichen.
> Er singet, sie spielet; . . .
> Er sagt: Wie bist du mir ewig erkoren!
> Sie rufet: du bist mir zur Freude geboren!
> Die beide verdoppeln das Echo *in ein*
> Und schreien: mein Freund ist vollkommentlich mein!
> Echo: Ich mein!
> So recht, so vermehrt sich der göttliche Schein!

We find the motif (though not the actual device) of an echo playing its part in love-strife, in the song "Antwort Mariä auf den Gruss der Engel," in the *Mariale festivale* of Father Procopius (included in *Des Knaben Wunderhorn*, ed. Bremer, p. 281): The angel of the Annunciation and the Virgin Mary vie with each other in harmonious song, like nightingales echoing each other:

> Was war nicht für eine Echo da,
> Wie *stimmten sie zusammen* . . .
> Kein süssres Lied im Himmelreich
> Wird nimmermehr gehöret,
> Als wenn die Selgen allzugleich
> Wollen, was Gott begehret.

In a baroque drama of the eighteenth century, "Glorreiche Marter Joannes von Nepomuck" (I, 14), the echo becomes what the Spaniards of this period called "aviso del cielo": the villain echoes fragments of certain sentences uttered by his prospective victim, these fragments forming a pattern which allows the public to anticipate the latter's death.

19. Miss G. L. Finney, in her article "Chorus in 'Samson Agonistes' " (*PMLA*, LVIII, 649–64), explains the existence of the chorus in Milton's drama (while Corneille, in France, in the name of *vraisemblance* omitted it, seeing in it only the advantage it offered of furnishing songs to cover up the sounds of stage machinery being adjusted) by the interest which Milton took in music ("most poetry of the time—much of Milton's included—was thought in relation to music" [p. 653]), and by the association of the chorus with music. The Florentine circles which, in the late sixteenth and early seventeenth centuries, revived the interest in Greek drama, had believed that this drama was sung in

its entirety; in order to offer a modern parallel to this supposed Greek melodrama, they had to invent a new style which would emphasize the dramatic flavor of the words: this could no longer be the contrapuntal style which drowned out the words, but the recitative. Thus the new opera (of Rinuccini, Peri, etc.) is born, in which pseudo-Greek reminiscences, the Renaissance pastoral, and the medieval *mystère* are strangely intertwined in order to celebrate the musical beauty of the world. One need only read Milton's statement, in his *Reason of Church Government* (quoted by Miss Finney, p. 655): "... the Apocalypse of St. John is the majestic image of a high and stately tragedy, shutting up and intermingling her solemn scenes and acts with a sevenfold chorus of hallelujahs and harping symphonies," in order to see how Milton projects back into Christian antiquity the modern musical tragedy or opera and makes again a synthesis of Hebrew (hallelujahs), Greek (symphonies) and the Christian elements.

In a second article (*Journal of the History of Ideas*, VIII, 153–186: "Ecstasy and Music in Seventeenth-Century England"), in which Miss Finney devotes a chapter to Milton's conception of music as it developed from Greek and Christian sources, we learn that Milton's idea of the wedding of Voice and Verse was anticipated by the Italian musicologist Gioseffo Zarlino, *L'Institutioni harmoniche* (1558): "The most notable effects do not come from mere [musical] harmony, he insisted, but from harmony combined with verse: Harmony alone gives merely pleasure; harmony joined with number (which is determined by the rhythm of the verse) suddenly has a great power to move the soul; but join speech to these two and it is impossible to say what force they have" (p. 171).

As for Milton's synthesis of biblical and classical motifs, in his praise of music pointed out above, we may see an anticipation of this in the passage, quoted by Miss Finney, from William Slatyer (1643) who defines David as "Israelitish Orpheus, or Judean Arion" (p. 159).

NOTES TO CHAPTER V

1. It is remarkable that in German a *certiren* is attested in 1687 (cf. Schulz-Basler, s.v. *Konzert*) in the meaning "to rival in playing music": "Ist eine Concerten Art, da eine Stimm mit der andern gar annehmlich nach wenig Pausen *certiret*." *Konzertieren* (... *und mit allerhand Instrumenten zugleich in einander zu musiciren*) is first attested in German in 1619. As late as 1838 Hegel uses *konzertieren* in the meaning "to rival in a kind of musical dialogue" (*Vorlesungen über die Ästhetik*, III, 171); he compares the change of instruments in Mozart's symphonies to "ein dramatisches Koncertiren," "eine Art von Dialog," "ein Zwiegespräch des Klingens und Wiederklingens." And, according to Novalis, love of two beings can be either *Konzertierend* or *akkompagnierend* according to whether the two have equal weight, or one outweighs the other.

2. So much, at least, is clear, that Cuervo cannot be right when he states, in his *Diccionario de régimen*, that Sp *concertar* must be kept separate from Lat *concertare*, "to fight," and should be considered a derivative of Sp *cierto* (= "to make sure," cf. *acertar*), formed on the pattern of *concordar*, *conformar*. For, in either case, whether our *concerto* is based on the meaning of "harmonious striving" or of "contriving (a musical composition)," we would have to do ultimately with *concertare*.

3. The meaning of Sp *concertar*, in reference to music (of birds) appears to be slightly different in a passage from Barahona de Soto, *Fabula de Acteón* (quoted in Rodríguez Marín's edition of the *Don Quixote*, V, 255): "Por la suave *armonía* / Que la frecuencia confusa / De los pájaros hacía, / Parece que alguna musa / La *concertaba* y regía." Here, the idea is rather "to put order into music."

4. I may add that I found *concerto* in Italian, used precisely of the angelic concert and coupled with *armonia*, in Tasso's dialogue, *Il Rangone o vero de la Pace* (1584). Since Tasso, in his dialogue on love of the preceding year, had defined love as "una quiete nel piacevole," a divine repose in pleasance, his definition of "peace" is not surprising. In the dialogue on this subject, peace, which should emulate divine justice, and which, like justice, rests not on the unification of the discordant but on a unity pre-existent to multiplicity, is defined as "silence": "perché di lei [of divine peace] non si può ragionar convenevolmente, si chiama convenevolmente silenzio. Questo è quell' alto, profondo, quel dolce, quel divino silenzio nel quale tutte le ingiurie sono taciute e tutte dimenticate; questo è quel mirabile silenzio, tanto superiore *ad*

ogni armonia, e ad ogni concento che facciano gli angioli lodando il creatore, quanto la divina caligine è più luminosa del sole, e de le stelle, e d'ogni altra luce che sia nel cielo" (*Dialoghi*, ed. Raimondi [Florence, 1958], II, 543). Silence is here superior to the angelic concert, as is the night sky, void of stars, to any particular constellation. Thus we find here the same connection for It *concerto* as we will find for Sp *concierto*.

5. The idea of the *descort* still prevails in a *romance* of Lope de Vega, in which he protests against his enforced exile as he addresses his lute: "Aora vuelvo a *templaros,* / *desconçertado* ynstrumento, / que de una vez no se acavan / los muchos males que tengo. // . . . Cantemos nuevas ystorias / de aquellos pesares viejos. . . . // Ayuden *cuerdas templadas* / a un loco de penas cuerdo [pun with *cuerda,* 'string'—*cuerdo,* 'wise']" (cf. *Rev. hisp.,* LXV, 349). And the *canción desesperada* which Cervantes puts in the mouth of Grisóstomo, the suicide of love (*Don Quixote,* I, 14), is also a disguised descort which must contain the word family (*des*)*concierto.* The unfortunate poet proposes: "Haré que el mesmo infierno comunique / Al triste pecho mío un son doliente / Con que el uso común de mi voz tuerza . . . / De la espantable voz irá el acento, / Y en él mezcladas [unharmoniously mixed], por mayor tormento, / Pedazos de las míseras entrañas. / Escucha, pues, y presta atento oido, / *No al concertado son,* sino al ruido / Que de lo hondo de mi amargo pecho, / . . . Por gusto mío sale y por tu despecho [then follows an enumeration of all the sounds of monstrous animals, summed up in the lines:] / Mezclados en un son, de tal manera / Que se confundan los sentidos todos." And at the end of the song he invites Cerberus "Con otras mas quimeras y mil monstros / Lleven el *doloroso contrapunto.*" The allusions to music run through the whole poem.

A descort "après-la-lettre" has been composed, quite in the medieval manner, involving the metaphorical use of musicological terms, by the seventeenth-century German poet Weckherlin, in his poem, "Musicalische lieb," of which I shall quote the first and last stanzas (ed. Goedeke [Leipzig, 1873] p. 65):

> Meinen geist, mut, seel und herz
> Amor mit klag, forcht und schmerz
> Recht *componieret;*
> In leid ändert sich mein scherz,
> Angst mit mir accordieret . . .

> Ach Herzlieb, thu doch mit mir,
> *Greifend den ton* nach gebühr,
> Nu *moderieren;*
> Und alsdan will ich mit dir
> Schon tief gnug *intonieren.*

The *mit dir intonieren* is equivalent to *mit dir übereinstimmen.* This amorous musicology betrays its derivation from Romance models by the Romance loan words; the baroque artificiality should not blind us to the fact that the concepts —and conceits—of this poem are essentially medieval.

Somewhat similar to the poem of Weckherlin, motivated by a longing for harmony, as it was, is the popular composition, "Liebes-Noten" (in *Des Knaben Wunderhorn*, ed. Bremer [Leipzig, 1878], p. 624):

Wahres Lieben, süsses Leben,
Wo *zwei Herzen eins* nur sind,
Wie zwei Turteltäublein schweben,
Die ein treues Band verbind,
Wo *die Lieb den Chor anstimmet*,
Und die Treue giebt den Takt,
In dem Blut die Freude schwimmet,
Und der Puls auf Lauten schlagt.

Wo die Spröde muss pausiren,
Wenn die Lust ein Solo singt,
Wenn die Aeuglein *pizikiren*,
Bis der Lieb ein Saite springt,
Wenn die Herzen *konkordiren*,
Und schön *singen in dem Ton*,
Wird der Mund auch *sekundiren*,
Und ein Kuss giebt ihm den Lohn.

Will *ein Ton ins Kreuzlein steigen*,
Will ein *B* wie Weh erschalln,
Mag aufs Herz der Finger zeigen,
Und Musik ganz leise halln,
Weil die *Noten in zwei Herzen*
Einfach *stehen in der Terz*,
Lass uns ganz *piano scherzen*
Und *allegro* leiden Schmerz.

6. Very often birds appear in poetry, particularly in Provençal poetry, as musicians peacefully competing to express the mirth of spring; in such a connection our "concert" is implicit. Compare the lines from Camoëns: "Vi já das altas aves a *harmonia*, / que até aos montes duros *convidava* / a um modo suave de alegria" (ed. Da Costa Pimpão [Coimbra, 1953], p. 258) and the following passage from Lope's *Barlaán y Josafat, Apendice*, Act III:

Aquí sin libros quiero
Entretener los días
Que libros son las hojas de las flores
Adonde hallar espero
Altas filosofías
En la diversidad de sus colores.
¿Qué concetos mejores

Que ver sus diferencias
Y fábricas hermosas,
Y entre flores y rosas
De las aues las dulces competencias?
Todo a su Autor alaba
Y nunca el hombre de alabarle acaba.

mistranslated by Vossler (*Poesie der Einsamkeit in Spanien*, p. 112). It is, indeed, amazing to see how a translator with the philological training of Vossler has failed to grasp our topos—or, any topos of this passage; his translation is:

So will ich meine Stunden
Hier ohne Buch vertreiben,
In Blumen statt in Büchern fleissig blättern,
Dann hab ich bald gefunden
Ein hohes Weisheitsschreiben
Zu lesen in den bunt gefärbten Lettern.
Wo gibt es zu erklettern
Ein höheres Studieren
Als Rosen zu betrachten,
Auf ihren Bau zu achten
Und sanfte Vogelstimmen zu notieren?
Dem Schöpfer gilt es droben,
Kein Mensch vermag ihn je genug zu loben.

This is a striking example of the inadequacy of a so-called "poetic" translation to convey to us the impetus of philosophical thought.   All the conceptual content of Lope's poem has been ironed out in this translation, at once commonplace and *burschikos*, in the Uhland-Geibel vein (on the one hand, *sanfte Vogelstimmen*; on the other, *erklettern / Ein höheres Studieren*).   Vossler omits the idea of the *musicum carmen* in the Book of Nature (a book which makes all others superfluous, a book whose leaves are the leaves of flowers—this is a conceit which is followed by the word *concetos*, which contains in itself a conceit, since *conceto* is both "concept" and "conceit"); it is characteristic that Vossler should suppress the key word of the passage, the self-definition of this poem: the allusion to its conceptual nature.   Gone also is that variety of the world integrated into the Oneness of the Creator (the *todo* in line 12 is indispensable: "omnia in majorem Dei gloriam"), the idea of the flowers as samples of the varied creation (*fábricas hermosas* suggests the idea of the divine Maker, the Architect; *flores y rosas* means "lilies and roses" [cf. Fr *fleur de lys*; in Old Sicilian poetry, *più bella che rosa e che fiori*], and, above all, the idea of the loving rivalry in the "concert" as implied in the *competencias* preceding the all-inclusive line, *Todo a su Autor alaba*.   Already at the beginning of this poem (which is of the *soledad* type), there was a suggestion of the variety integrated into unity, of the fullness of the world which the poet leaves behind him in order to lift his soul to the Creator: *"Calladas soledades, apacible silencio* [the Pythagorean music of silence], / que el alma levantáis a bien más alto; / *centro* de las verdades / adonde *diferencio* / el bien . . . / yo he dado un grande salto, / pues dexo el mundo en medio / del cetro deste polo."

I cannot understand how, in this Augustinian, deeply Christian meditation of a princely ascetic, Vossler can detect any "buddhistische Duft" (this expression is to be explained only by Vossler's extraneous knowledge that the Buddha legend is underlying the medieval Barlaam and Josaphat legend), or how he can state that, with Lope, "the expiating saint becomes an Indian fairy-tale prince" (rather the reverse is true). It is sad to see literary impressionism destroy, not only the text, but the whole cultural climate of this classic.

We might compare with Lope's passage on the Book of Nature the speech of King Basilio, the mathematician and astrologer in Calderón's *La vida es sueño*, I, 624 sq. There the stars and crystalline spheres are "los libros / Donde en papel de diamante / En cuadernos de zafiro, / Escribe con líneas de oro, / En carácteres distintos, / El cielo nuestros sucesos" and his mind is "de sus márgines comento / Y de sus hojas registro." See also Curtius' study on the book motif in Dante (*Festschrift P. Clemen*). Any silent source of knowledge recalls, to the poets of the *siglo de oro*, the *música callada* of the Pythagoreans. There is a sonnet of Quevedo on the studying of books which reminds us of the *Barladn y Josafat* passages of Lope, which has, just as in the case of the latter, been altered by Vossler's translation (*Poesie der Einsamkeit*, p. 333):

> Retirado en la paz de estos desiertos
> con pocos, pero doctos libros juntos,
> vivo en conversación con los difuntos,
> y escucho con mis ojos a los muertos;
>
> Sino siempre entendidos, siempre abiertos,
> o enmiendan o secundan mis asuntos;
> y en *músicos callados contrapuntos*
> al sueño de la vida hablan despiertos.

Vossler translates the second stanza:

> Oft unverstanden, liegt doch fort und fort
> das Buch bereit, mir Trost und Rat zu geben,
> mit schweigender Musik mich zu umschweben,
> und weist dem Traume hier sein waches Dort.

Again the precise has been diluted into Neoromantic vagueness: "mit . . . Musik . . . umschweben," where the original has a (silent) counterpoint lay "instrumentalized" by the dead, who, having waked from the dream of life, "second" (*secundar* has a double meaning) the "dreaming" voices of the living. This Pythagorean music of books is first indicated by the paradox *escucho con mis ojos*; the double chessboard on which the poem plays (reading = listening to music of the immortal dead) should be reproduced in the translation; it is as though the Beyond orchestralized the Here. (The music of books has been well understood by the English humanist Gilbert Murray who, in his *Religio Grammatici* [1918], seems to hear the Pythagorean overtones of the *grammata* [i.e., of the classical texts]: "From him [the Philistine latent in us] and his influence we find our escape by means of the Grammata into that calm world of theirs, where stridency and clamour are forgotten in the ancient stillness, where . . . the great things of the human spirit still shine like stars pointing Man's way onward to the great triumph or the great tragedy . . .")

Stillness, music, and books are combined in a seventeenth-century poem of the Königsberg professor Johann Peter Titz (*Neudrucke deutscher Literatur-werke* 44/5, ed. L. H. Fischer, [Halle, 1883], p. 182), entitled "Christliche Stille Music," which bears the motto, "Non clamor, sed amor psallit in aure Dei":

> Wilstu in der Stille singen,
> Und ein Lied dem Höchsten bringen,
> Lerne, wie du kanst allein
> Sänger, Buch und Tempel seyn

—mind, heart, and body, if pure and concentrated on God, can be singer, book, and temple (although the harmony of the spheres is not mentioned here, the identification of stillness with music is ultimately Pythagorean).

7. How often does it not occur in the night scenes of Lope's dramas that music resounds as a reminder, however faint, of the eternal laws of Providence; in the last act of *El caballero de Olmedo*, for example, the hero, at midnight, hears a peasant sing a song about him, a song predicting his death—which, in fact, occurs soon after. On hearing the song, Don Alonso is immediately aware that this is a warning from heaven; but he fails to heed the message and, as he dies, blames himself for having disregarded the *avisos del cielo*.

While in these cases the connection, music – night – laws of Providence is preserved, other dramatic passages insist on the totality of the world expressed by music. In Calderón's *La vida es sueño* I, 5, there is again a concert, but this time mixed with birds' songs, rivers, trumpets, drums, and salvos:

> Bien al ver los excelentes
> Rayos, que fueron cometas,
> Mezclan salvas diferentes.
> Las cajas y las trompetas,
> Los pájaros y las fuentes:
> Siendo con *música* igual,
> Y con maravilla suma, . . .
> Unos clarines de pluma
> Y otras aves de metal;
> Y así os saludan, señora,

Como á su reina las balas,
Los pájaros como Aurora,
Las trompetas como á Palas
Y las flores como á Flora.

This courtly compliment to a lady called Estrella is evidently built in the
pattern of the world concert: the appearance of a heavenly (celestial) star
(which could be Our Lady: *salve, regina* . . . *stella maris*) is greeted by music
composed of ("mixed," as with the Greeks) the music of nature and of man
(the latter including the most modern music of salvos—but salvos are *salve's*), a
música igual which is the result of a loving rivalry (a "concert") between unequal
instruments (*mezclan salvas differentes*).   The characteristic conceits of Calderón
are due to the synesthetic devices typical of baroque art: the exchange of forms
between those beings which are devoted to the one common purpose (the birds
are musical instruments with feathers, the bullets birds of metal), as well as the
manifold aspects of the one being who is praised by this music (Estrella becomes
Aurora, Pallas, and Flora, according to the praise bestowed on her in the songs
of the birds, the salvos, the perfume of the flowers; Krenkel's commentary has
nothing to say about this passage except: "C. braucht wilkürlich lateinische u.
griechische Götternamen neben einander"; but there is as little arbitrariness
in the fusing of the two classic worlds as there is in the fusing of the cosmos).
I had pointed, in *Roman. Stil- und Literaturstud.*, II, 202–3, to the "statisch
vor uns aufgerichteten Gesamtkunstwerk der Welt," but I had not at that time
recognized the *musical* character of this static Calderonian world harmony
which Tieck must have sensed, since he calls the Spanish poet (quoted *loc. cit.*,
p. 193): "O Calderon, du hier schon Gottheit-trunken, Herold der Wonne,
Cherub nun im Chore"—and static the Calderonian world harmony is, not
only because the world appears to be directed by stable laws, and the chants
and responds could as well resound in antiquity as in Calderón's times, but
also because these are in fact basically unaltered: they are the chants and responds
of Pythagoras and Ambrose.   The completeness of the world is always suggested
by the Calderonian world harmony.   Thus when one of the "musicians" in
the concert is mentioned, the others are *ipso facto* associated.   In *El Mágico
prodigioso*, II, 832–50, the beloved woman is (statically) composed of sun,
brook, rose, carnation, snow, bird, etc. (i.e., she is a microcosmos reflecting the
macrocosmos).   The bird is described as "veloz cítara de pluma / Al órgano de
cristal"; the "cristal organ" being the brook on whose bank the bird sings
(Krenkel quotes as parallels [from *Ni amor se libra de amor*]: "el cristal cuya
asonancia[!], / Tal vez instrumento á quien / Trastes de oro y lazos de ambar /
Son las quijas"; [from *Polifemo y Circe*] ". . . Desta apacible fuente, / Que es á
la solfa de la primavera [the troubadour motif] / Instrumento sonoro / Con
cuerdas de cristal y trastes de oro"); the carnation "en breve cielo es estrella de
coral," i.e., it is a microcosmic star contributing its coral color to the microcosmos
of the lady.   In the great monologue, Segismundo, following an Augustinian

trend of thought, compares man to the other creatures and, in his enumeration of the different realms, says of the brook (*La vida es sueño*, I, 153–60):

> Nace el arroyo, culebra
> Que entre flores se desata,
> Y apénas sierpe de plata,
> Entre las flores se quiebra,
> Cuando *músico* celebra
> De las flores la piedad,
> Que le da la majestad
> Del campo abierto á su huida.

Here the one word *músico* places the brook once more within the concert of nature, from which man seems to have been exiled; and this music is in praise of the *piedad*, of the love of the flowers; music—grace—nature are again intertwined. (As Curtius, *Rom. Forsch.*, L, 89, and I myself, *Neuphil. Mitt.*, XXXIX, 369, have stated, Calderón, in his theoretical treatise on painting, subordinates music to painting, the Renaissance art par excellence which had to please a playwright: "a no menos acordes cláusulas [que la Música] le *suspende* la Pintura con las ventajas que lleva el sentido de la vista al del oído"; nevertheless the musical references in his plays are neither fewer nor less important than are the pictorial ones.)

8. We saw in Calderón a "concert" (*asonancia, solfa*) given by the brook. With Góngora we have the same concert, called, in the classical manner, *concento* (this word, which is correctly translated by Dámaso Alonso as "concertada harmonía," occurs, according to the same critic, much later [in 1606] in Góngora than does *armonía* [which appears already in 1584]; the same temporal relation may be seen in the contemporary dictionaries: 1616 vs. 1570; these dates indicate the growing tendency in Góngora toward linguistic sophistication); *Soledades*, I, 343–8:

> el ya sañudo arroyo, ahora manso:
> merced de la hermosura que ha hospedado,
> efectos, si no, dulces del *concento*
> que, en las lucientes de marfil clavijas,
> las duras cuerdas de las negras guijas
> hicieron a su curso acelerado . . .

(I accept the explanation given by Dámaso Alonso in note 16 of his second edition, rather than that implied by his translation): The brook is a stringed instrument plucked by the black pebbles, and the ivory *clavijas* are the limbs of the mountain girls bathing in the brook (cf. 550: the *concento* of the *sirenas de los montes*, i.e., of the mountain girls; 585: the *concento cristalino* of a fountain; 706: *la dulce de las aves armonía*; 276–7: *el oido de métrica armonía* of a rustic concert; 590: the *músicas hojas* of a tree [musical, as Alonso explains, because

of the wind which stirs them, or of the nightingales which nest in them—
evidently a parallel to the *músico arroyo* of Calderón]). We see the brook and
the birds engaged in a concert in the *Soledad segunda*, 349-58:

> Rompida el agua en las menudas piedras,
> cristalina sonante era tiorba,
> y las *confusamente acordes* aves . . .
> muchas eran, y muchas veces nueve
> aladas musas, que—de pluma leve
> engañada su oculta lira corva—
> metros *inciertos sí, pero süaves,*
> en *idiomas* cantan *diferentes.*

The concordant strife of the birds rivaling with the Muses is probably at the
bottom of such a highly traditional, but conceptistically developed picture.
From all these examples we can draw the conclusion that the "conceptismo"
of both Góngora and Calderón is in our cases a deliberate attempt to establish
connections (audible, visual, and mental) between the manifold participants in
the world concert: the world cithara is ever at hand, into which any transient
phenomenon in nature may be transformed (brook, pebbles, bathing women,
birds).

9. It has not yet, to my knowledge, been pointed out that there is a similar
passage in Fénelon's *Télémaque*, Book 7 (ed. Cahen "Les gr. ecrivains de la
France"; Paris, 1920, I, 313-14), which, evidently, is in no way influenced by
Cervantes. The Phoenician Adoam has a magnificent meal served to Télémaque and Mentor, after which "tous les plaisirs dont on pouvoit jouir" are
enjoyed by the guests: perfumes, flute-playing, singing, dancing. The singer
Architoas, whose name reminds us of Archytas, by means of "les doux accords
de sa voix et de sa lyre, dignes d'être entendus à la table des dieux et de ravir
les oreilles d'Apollon même," attracts, Orpheuslike, the Tritons, Nereids and the
sea-monsters: "De temps en temps les trompettes faisoient retentir l'onde
jusqu'aux rivages éloignés. *Le silence de la nuit, le calme de la mer, la lumière
tremblante de la lune répandue sur la face des ondes, le sombre azur du ciel semé de
brillantes étoiles,* servoient à rendre ce spectacle encore plus beau." Since the
whole epic of the preceptor Fénelon is destined to warn the young duke of
Burgundy of "plaisirs qui . . . vous amollissent," Télémaque is shown hesitating
before the pleasure of music; he is encouraged, however, by Mentor, who
himself outdoes Architoas in a religious song (of his own): "Mentor chanta
ces vérités d'un ton si religieux et si sublime, que toute l'assemblée crut être
transportée au plus haut de l'Olympe, à la face de Juppiter," he is declared by
the assembly to be "Apollo himself." And then the host Adoam is asked to
tell about the primitive people of Baetica and "l'aimable simplicité du monde
naissant." In contrast to the scene of Cervantes, the emphasis here is on
"solemn," religious music, which, as is so often true in the seventeenth century,
is didactically opposed to worldly, effeminating music. But, just as in *Don*

Quixote, so, in the *Télémaque*, we have the ensemble of starry night, silence, beauty, music—and the Golden Age of primitivism. In Fénelon there still appears a faint reflection of world music, e.g., in the description of the Elysian Fields (Book 14; II, 350); of the immortal, good, and virtuous beings he says: "Je ne sais quoi de divin coule sans cesse au travers de leurs cœurs, comme un torrent de la divinité même qui s'unit à eux; ils voient, ils goûtent, ils sont heureux, et sentent qu'ils le seront toujours. Ils chantent *tous ensemble les louanges des dieux*, et ils ne *font tous ensemble qu'une seule voix*, une seule pensée, un seul cœur : une même félicité fait comme un flux et reflux dans ces âmes *unies*." This is a Christian (Ambrosian) musical atmosphere transferred to the pagan Elysium; it is even imbued with the mystical flavor of Fénelon's contemporary and friend Mme Guyon (*le torrent de la divinité* recalls her *Torrents spirituels*, 1683).

10. The history of the French word family *concert* (*concerter*) is clear. The word, in the meaning "(to put in) agreement," came to France from Italy in the sixteenth century, as Pasquier states (also to England, 1598: "to concert and agree"). Latin may have contributed its share: Michel de Tours' translation of Suetonius contains a *concerter* which clearly means "to vie" ("les musiciens, cest à savoir ceux qui *concertoient et contendoient* à l'honneur"). The idea of world harmony is perhaps latent in a passage from D'Aubigné (*Tragiques*, II, 869–72): "La *discorde* couppa le *concert* des mignons [of Henri III], / Et le vice croissant entre les campagnons / Brisa l'orde *amitié*, mesme par les ordures, / Et l'*impure union* par les choses impures" [here we have an ironic description of a world in reverse: the *concert des mignons* is a parody of concord, "friendship," and "pure union"]. In the seventeenth century it is the idea of "agreement" that prevails. Bossuet: "Ce qu'un sage général doit le mieux connaître, c'est ses soldats et ses chefs. Car de là vient ce *parfait concert qui fait agir les armées comme un seul corps*" [=a well-tempered body]; "Tout cela est l'effet du secret *concert* que vous avez mis entre nos volontés et les mouvements de nos corps"; "[the Sorbonne Professor Cornet] connaissait très parfaitement et les confins et les bornes de toutes les opinions de l'Ecole; jusqu'où elles concouraient, et où elles commençaient à se séparer. . . . C'est . . . du *concert* des meilleurs cerveaux de la Sorbonne, que nous est né cet extrait de ces cinq propositions, qui sont comme les justes limites par lesquelles la vérité est séparée de l'erreur . . ." Corneille: "Mais j'aurais souhaité qu'en cette occasion / L'amour *concertât* ["harmonize"] mieux avec l'ambition." We may see the influence on *concert* of the rationalistic and voluntaristic trend of the French seventeenth century: "elle est concertée en sa contenance"; "faire qch. *de concert*"; "Le Cardinal de Retz est tous les jours *en concert et en cabale*[!]." The mechanics of the century bring about *concerter une machine*, "to devise"; and *une machine bien concertée* could easily be *déconcertée*. Fénelon: "La transpiration, facilitée ou diminuée, *déconcerte* ou rétablit *toute la machine du corps*." Bossuet: "Que verrons-nous dans notre mort . . . que des esprits qui s'épuisent,

que *des ressorts* qui *se démontent et se déconcertent*" [a Ciceronian sequel of prefixes]. La Bruyère: "La raison ... est ... *déconcertée* ... par le désordre de la machine" (passages cited by Littré and Cayrou, *Le fr. classique* ... [Paris, 1924]). Because of this emphasis on "regularity," *concert(er)* suggests the contrary of "chance"; thus Bossuet, at the end of his *Discours sur l'histoire universelle*, proclaims: "C'est ainsi que Dieu règne sur tous les peuples. Ne parlons plus de hasard ni de fortune. ... Ce qui est hasard à l'égard de nos conseils incertains est un dessein *concerté* dans un conseil plus haut, c'est-à-dire dans ce conseil éternel qui renferme toutes les causes et tous les effets dans un même ordre."

It is not difficult to find passages throughout the seventeenth century in which the meaning "musical concert" is imminent, not only in the verb (La Fontaine, *Fables*, IX, 160: "La musique en sera d'autant mieux concertée"), but in the noun; cf. for example the lines of Boileau (*Sat.* VI, 23):

> Tandis que dans les airs les nües émües,
> D'un *funèbre concert* font retentir les nües,
> Et se mêlant au bruit de la grêle et des vents,
> Pour honorer les morts, font mourir les vivants.

Here, however, the chimes offer not a concert in the modern sense, but rather "concert their bells" with nature: an echo of world harmony as reflected by the chimes. And with Rotrou (*St. Genêt*, IV, 5: "Sans interruption de *vos sacrés concerts* / A son aveuglement tenez les cieux ouverts") as well as with Molière (*Les amants magnifiques* [premier intermède]: "Allons tous au-devant de ces divinités / Et rendons *par nos chants* hommage à leurs beautés / ... Redoublons *nos concerts* / et faisons retentir dans le vague des airs / Notre réjouissance ..."), and Racine (*Esther*, III, 2: "Les compagnes d'Esther s'avancent vers ce lieu, / Sans doute leur *concert* va commencer la fête"), the word *concert* refers to vocal music, to choirs.   It should be noted that when the musicmaster of the *Bourgeois Gentilhomme* (II, 4) advises him to follow the mode of offering a concert at home once a week, the term used in reference to this technical concert (as late as 1670) is *concert de musique* (as in Cotgrave); thus it is clear that we would not be entitled to translate, in the passages just cited, the simple *concert* by "concert." There is a scene in Fénelon's *Télémaque*, Book 1, where, after a meal with the nymph Calypso, four young nymphs, accompanied by the lute, sing to Télémaque of mythical subjects and of his father (in imitation of the scene in the Odyssey where, at the table of the Phaeacians, a bard sings to Odysseus of the hero's own exploits); the *Grands écrivains* edition (I, 20) comments on the passage: "On notera encore ici la manière dont Fénelon modernise les données d'Homère.   Dans Homère, le chant du poète est une monodie, qu'il accompagne lui-même de sa lyre; Fénelon présente au duc de Bourgogne un 'concert,' semblable à ceux qu'il a pu entendre lui-même dans les divertissements de la cour: il est composé de quatre chanteuses, chantant en quatuor ou l'une après l'autre, et soutenues par un accompagnement instrumental." In the text, however, the word *concert* is not used: either in order to respect the ancient *décor*, or because the term was not yet sufficiently current.

In the prefaces of the *Harmonie universelle* (1637) of Mersenne one can see how the idea of world harmony and of religious music that celebrates it is still prevalent: "[he would not, as a theologian, have written the treatise on chord instruments] si je n'auois quarante et quatre mille Saints pour mes garans, qui chantent tous les jours de nouveaux Cantiques, et des Airs ravissans et mesmes avec celle de Dieu. . . . *La lettre de leurs Concerts* nous est aussi propre comme à eux, puis qu'elle consiste à dire: 'O Seigneur, que vos œuvres sont admirables . . .'; [his book will bring about the concurrence of heavenly with human music] . . . que l'Eglise Militante face *un mesme Concert* avec la Triomphante, et que nous en commençons les recits par ses paroles: Cor meum et caro mia exultaverunt in Deum unum. . . . C'est Monsieur ce que je souhaite . . . pour tous ceux qui se serviront seulement de l'Harmonie pour loüer *le souverain Maistre* du grand Concert de l'Univers." But in another passage he speaks polemically of *assemblees de concert* that last two to three hours and are devoted only to world music which should, in Mersenne's opinion, be replaced by *airs spirituels*. Only in this last passage, *concert* (in the phrase *assemblees de concert*) seems to be equal to "concert."

With the pre-Romantics and the Romantics something of the French classical tradition is still perceptible, e.g., in Fontanes' pre-Romantic poem, "Le jour des morts dans une campagne," where the "mixture" of (gloomy) nature and (gloomy) songs in honor of the dead is emphasized:

> Nos chants majestueux, consacrés au trépas,
> Se mêlaient à ce bruit précurseur des tempêtes;
> Des nuages obscurs s'étendaient sur nos têtes;
> Et nos fronts attristés, nos funèbres concerts
> Se conformaient au deuil et des champs et des airs.

The phrase *funèbres concerts*, and the idea of the accord of the death bells with nature may be borrowed from Boileau.

In Lamartine's "Isolement" the Romantic poet hears the sounds of the church bells against the panorama of mountains and evening:

> Cependant, s'élançant de la flèche gothique
> Un *son religieux* se répand dans les airs,
> Le voyageur s'arrête, et la cloche rustique
> Aux derniers bruits du jour *mêle* de saints *concerts*.

Here, *mêle* is reminiscent of Latin *temperat*; and yet it must be noted that, of the world harmony, only the harmony between the mood (> *Stimmung*) of nature and of man, or between the music of the bell and of the air, survives; there is no longer the serenity of a universal order.

In other poems of Lamartine, the "concert" is placed within the ego of the poet, and the world concert disappears, e.g., in "Invocation" (1830): "Je n'ai point entendu monter jamais vers toi / D'accords plus pénétrants, de plus

divin langage, / Que ces concerts muets qui s'élèvent en moi ... / Mon âme
[ne sera] qu'un cantique, et mon cœur qu'une lyre, / Et chaque souffle enfin
que j'exhale ou j'aspire, / Un accord à ton nom." The concert is, then,
replaced by "harmonies" (in the plural); the definition of a "harmony" in
Lamartine's introductory letter to M. d'Esgrigny is utterly lacking in clarity:
any *Stimmung* of the soul seems to be accepted as such (and the feeling for
God is only one of those polytheistic "harmonies"): "Rien ne peut mieux
expliquer ce que c'est qu'une *harmonie*: la jeunesse qui s'éveille, l'amour qui
rêve, l'œil qui contemple, l'âme qui s'élève, la prière qui invoque, le deuil qui
pleure, le Dieu qui console, l'extase qui chante, la raison qui pense, la passion
qui se brise, la tombe qui se ferme, tous les bruits de la vie dans un cœur sonore,
ce sont des harmonies. Il y en a autant, qu'il y a de palpitations sur la fibre
infinie de l'émotion humaine" (*Harmonies poétiques et religieuses* [Paris, 1914],
p. xxxiv).

The orthodox Christian idea of the world concert has been restored by
Chateaubriand in *Le génie du christianisme*, especially in Book V where music is
said to sing eternal praise of the Creator (cf. K. Döhner, *Zeit und Ewigkeit bei
Chateaubriand, Bibl. d. Arch. Rom.* I, 17).

11. The idea of loving rivalry in music can be seen in Tintoretto's painting,
"Women Playing Music," in which De Tolnay has recognized the relationship
to world harmony: the six women, each playing a different instrument, probably
also symbolize the six musical tones. The group sways as if floating in air,
"upheld merely by the attraction that one exerts upon the other," each figure
seeming "to be animated by a rotating movement" as if according to "rules
governing the movement of celestial bodies" (*Journal of the Walters Art Gallery*,
6 [1943], 101). It is music itself that supplies the atmosphere in which they
move, and the rhythm by which this movement is directed. Each figure is
turned amicably to the other, though their particular musical tasks cause their
bodies to be twisted into individual postures, and the circle which they form
(this representing, no doubt, the perpetual recurrence in any piece of music
of the same tones of the scale), though not entirely closed in the foreground
(thereby, perhaps, including the spectator [and listener] into the group?),
tends in this direction, for the legs of the two contrapostal figures almost touch:
the attitude of *con-* is as strongly stressed as is that of *certare*.

This is a typically baroque painting: not only is the dynamism of the figures
so strong that, at any moment, the law of the "concentus"–*concerto* seems in
danger of being broken (a danger never realized), but we have also a cosmic and
metaphysical thought portrayed in the beautiful flesh of the six triumphant
female figures.

12. The epithalamium sonnet of Andreas Gryphius (1643), "Eliae Aebelii und
Jungfr. Barbarä Gerlachin Hochzeit" (ed. Julius Tittman, "Deutsche Dichter
des siebzehnten Jahrhunderts, 14" [Leipzig, 1880], p. 35), offers a paraphrase
of marital love in the form of a "concerto of Viadana." The bridegroom, who

first sings alone in *basso ostinato*, is joined, successively, by the instruments (viola, lute, organ), by the "tenor" of the bride, and by the "treble and alto" (that is, the lonely voice is joined by three instruments and by three companion voices)—which cannot fail to bring forth the concerto of happiness. Notice, too, the *Stellt lange Pausen ein*, which = the continuity of singing, characteristic of the concert of Viadana:

> Bissher hört' ich allein, mein werther Freund, euch singen,
> Wofern es singen heisst, wenn nicht Gefährten sind:
> Schaut, wie der Himmel euch zu neuem Dank verbindt,
> Der zu Viol' und Laut' die liebe Braut muss bringen.
> Wol, lasst die Balge gehn! Nun wird die Orgel klingen!
> Stellt lange Pausen ein, singt hurtig, nicht zu lind
> Den euch bequemen Bass. Wo ihr Tenor sich findt,
> Wird leichtlich der Discant sich in die Tripel zwingen.
> Der Alt, so itzt noch ruht, und was die kluge Welt
> Vor Stücklein mehr erdacht, drauf man so trefflich hält,
> Wird schon zu rechter Zeit sich ins Concert aufmachen.
> Wol dem, der also singt! . . .

13. The *concerts champêtres* of the eighteenth century (which we know from Watteau) were given under the starry sky but at sunset, a time at which the sharp contrasts seen in daylight are blunter and dimmer, in the worldly setting of a *jardin d'amour*, which had the sensuous beauty of Tasso's enchanted garden (cf. De Tolnay, *op. cit.* p. 100).

14. The worldliness to which the concert had descended in his time is well expressed by Goethe in *Bekenntnisse einer schönen Seele* ("Goethes Werke," 22 [Weimar, 1899], 341), where his mystic protagonist tells of Latin *a cappella* chants, evidently *concerti* with four or eight voices, sung as a "solemn music" (to express "eine feierliche Stimmung"): "Ich hatte bisher nur den frommen Gesang gekannt, in welchem gute Seelen oft mit heiserer Kehle, wie die Waldvögelein, Gott zu loben glauben, weil sie sich selbst eine angenehme Empfindung machen; dann die *eitle Musik* der Concerte, in denen man allenfalls zur Bewunderung eines Talents, selten aber, auch nur zu einem vorübergehenden Vergnügen hingerissen wird. Nun vernahm ich eine Musik, aus dem tiefsten Sinne der trefflichsten menschlichen Naturen entsprungen, die durch bestimmte und geübte Organe in harmonischer Einheit wieder zum tiefsten besten Sinne des Menschen sprach und ihn wirklich in diesem Augenblicke seine Gottähnlichkeit lebhaft empfinden liess." We find here the Augustinian opposition of artistic music to the music of well-meaning but untutored nature, but there has developed in the eighteenth century a third variety: the vain virtuosity displayed in worldly concerts.

We find, however, in the eighteenth century, an example of a village being made to resound with simple, popular music, in praise of God, thanks to the endeavors of the music-loving, pietistic teacher, Heinrich Jung-Stilling (in

Heinrich Stillings Junglingsjahre: "Dadurch [by the singing of spiritual chorales in four voices] wurde nun ganz Preisingen voller Leben und Gesang. . . . Wenn dann der Mond so still und feierlich durch die Bäume schimmerte und die Sterne vom blauen Himmel herunter äugelten, so ging er mit seinen Sängern heraus an den Preisinger Hügel, da setzten sie sich ins Dunkel und sangen, dass es durch Berg und Thal erscholl; dann gingen Mann, Weib und Kinder im Dorf vor die Thür, standen und horchten; sie segneten ihren Schulmeister, gingen dann hinein, gaben sich die Hand und legten sich schlafen" (*Deutsche National-Litteratur*, ed. Kürschner, vol. 137, p. 107). As if to teach us that the "night concert" is a reflection of world harmony, the next paragraph, dealing with Stilling's fondness for painting sundials, tells us that his favorite motto was: "Coeli enarrant gloriam Dei."

15. From the moment when Fr *concert* took on the fixed meaning "concert" (possibly at the time of Rousseau), there were two homonyms at hand in the language—for the older meaning, "order, device," still continued—and the two could be telescoped. When we read in Diderot: "Des sensibilités diverses qui *se concertent* entre elles pour obtenir le plus grand effet possible, qui *se diapasonnent*" (quoted by Brunot, *Histoire de la langue française*, VI², 1, p. 1394), we have a real pun.

The Concert of The Hague in 1710 between England and Holland and the *concert européen* of the treaty of Chaumont in 1814 (already in 1804, Czar Alexander I of Russia had proposed to England a "concert of powers" for the purpose of balancing the power of Napoleon [communication of Prof. Eric Vögelin]) suggested a peaceful co-operation for the settling of differences between the powers, instead of following the more mechanically devised Russian policy of balance (of power) in Europe (the expression "balance of power" is attested for 1677 and 1701). Obviously, it is the idea of the "purposeful device" or "teamwork" which prevails in such an expression as "concert of powers"; but who would insist that, in the "European Concert," the idea of a musical concert, even of a fugue performed by the different powers, is to be excluded, or that the Holy Alliance did not wish to emphasize the earthly political reflection of a musical world harmony? At any rate, the ambiguity of the term lent itself at all times to punning. In the German political review *Kladderadatsch* of 1856 (the year of the Treaty of Paris), Müller explains to Schultz the change which has come about in the "world orchestra": "Jetzt tauschen sie die Instrumente [pun on instruments of peace and musical instruments]: jetzt wird Frankreich die erste Violine spielen, England an die Pauke kommen, Deutschland wird sie was blasen, Russland pausieren und der Türke flöten gehn" (quoted by Ladendorf, *Schlagwörterbuch*, p. 76). And in André Gide's "Réflexions sur l'Allemagne" (in *Morceaux choisis*, p. 55), Germany is given, in the "concert of European nations," the *instruments de cuivre*, the brasses.

Still more recently, we find in the *New Yorker* (of January 26, 1946) the idea of the teamwork of nations developed humorously in musical terms:

At their earliest convenience the delegates to the United Nations Organization should form an orchestra. . . . Once a week all deliberations, all matters of state, should be put aside and the public invited to the assembly hall to hear that rarest of sounds—the concord of nations. . . . There is, in fact, great need that the U.N.O. delegates find some human activity or pastime which will illustrate people's ability to lose themselves in a universal theme, to harmonize, and to create beauty by following a single score rather than fifty-one scores. . . . Imagine a Gershwin morning in the assembly hall, with an all-world symphony group playing music written by an American of Russian-Jewish extraction about Negroes whose ancestors had come from Africa in slave-ships!

16. Throughout the following passage, which represents one of the most beautiful expressions of the Romantic German feeling of world harmony, one may sense a consciousness of the original impact of *certieren* in *Konzert*. Bettina von Arnim (*Goethes Briefwechsel mit einem Kinde*, "Bettina von Arnims Sämtliche Werke," III [Berlin, 1920], 385–6) speaks of the heroism of Andreas Hofer and his companions in their resistance to Napoleon in 1809:

Gedanken machen mir Schmerzen, und so zaghaft bin ich, dass ich ihnen ausweiche, und alles, was in der Welt vorgeht, das Geschick der Menschen und die tragische Auflösung macht mir einen musicalischen Eindruck. Die Ereignisse im Tirol nehmen mich in sich auf wie der volle Strom allseitiger Harmonie. Dies Streben mitzuwirken ist grade wie in meinen Kinderjahren, wenn ich die Symphonien hörte im Nachbarsgarten und ich fühlte, man müsse *mit einstimmen, mitspielen*, um Ruhe zu finden; und alles Zerschmetternde in jenen Heldenereignissen ist ja auch wieder so belebend, so begeistigend, wie *dies Streiten und Gebären der verschiedenen Modulationen, die doch alle in ihren eigensinnigen Richtungen unwillkürlich durch ein Gesamtgefühl getragen*, immer allseitiger, immer in sich konzentrierter in ihrer Vollendung sich abschliessen.—So empfinde ich die Symphonie, so *erscheinen mir jene Heldenschlachten auch Symphonien des göttlichen Geistes*, der in dem Busen des Menschen Ton geworden ist himmlischer Freiheit. Das freudige Sterben dieser Helden ist wie *das ewige Opfern der Töne einem hohen gemeinsamen Zweck, der mit göttlichen Kräften sich selbst erstreitet*; so scheint mir auch jede grosse Handlung ein musikalisches Dasein; so mag wohl *die musikalische Tendenz des Menschengeschlechts als Orchester sich versammeln* und solche *Schlachtsymphonien schlagen* . . .

Here Bettina sensed the essential principles of a symphonic concert: the portrayal of the totality of the universe and the subordination of the willful individual voices of the orchestra to the "sacrifice," the "collaboration" of the whole; moreover, she is able to see in any tragic happening of world history a Beethovenlike "Schlachtsymphonie" composed and "resolved" by the Divine Spirit itself. And yet, there is absent with this dithyrambic poetess the concept of laws, of *numeri*, of divine clarity: in fact, she confesses that her tragic musical conception of the world is an escape from intellectual clarity ("Gedanken machen mir Schmerzen"). Her tragic gods, impersonated in music, live for strife, for the assertion of vitality, for sensuous self-expansion, and Minerva is presented as only one deity among many, along with Mars, Bacchus, etc. Before Nietzsche, she was able to sense in music the dionysiac element: after listening to Marcello's arrangement of the Psalms, and the duets of Durante, with their startling "harmonic disharmony," she writes: "Auf Apollos hohen Kothurnen schreiten, mit Jupiters Blitzen um sich schleudern, mit Mars Schlachten liefern, Sklavenketten zerbrechen, den Jubel der Freiheit ausströmen, bacchantische Lust ausrasen, mit dem Schild der Minerva die anstürmenden Chöre zusammendrängen, ihre Evolutionen ordnend schützen, das sind so einzelne Teile dieser Musik . . . Musik wirkt sinnlich auf die Seele . . . die scheinheiligen, moralischen Tendenzen seh' ich so alle zum Teufel gehen mit ihrem erlogenen Plunder, denn nur die Sinne zeugen in der Kunst wie in der Natur, und Du weisst das am besten" (ibid., p. 403).

(In regard to the adoption of the German word *Konzert*, it may be noted that the term, first limited to a musical reference, came to be used of "concerted teamwork" in general, if we may judge by Jean Paul's *Titan* (III, 21, 90). Here, a rehearsal of Goethe's play *Tasso* is called a "poetisches Konzert" in which one of the participants has "mit der Ripienstimme mitgesprochen."

17. The nineteenth-century physiologist, T. Billroth (*loc. cit.*, p. 153), whose approach to music, as we shall see later, was predominantly pantheistic, denies the existence of any such entity as "religious music": it would be quite possible for a piece of music, with the so-called *religiöse Stimmung*, to be devoted to a beloved person or to an ardently-espoused ideal.   Moreover, our modern tendency to associate religious music with such an instrument as the organ, or with music of the old style, is, according to Billroth, only a symbolical device derived from common historical associations.   But these remarks, while quite correct as far as concerns his appraisal of the factual situation of today (note also his excellent description, p. 167, of the motives of a modern public for attending a concert), merely show how far we have come from the time when any "solemn music" was necessarily religious, and when (contrary to Billroth's statement) "love music" was influenced by ecclesiastical music.

18. What became of the concerts of the starry night sky, in the eighteenth century, that period of demusicalization, in which the "concert" developed into a technical term of musicology?   For this, Kant may be a witness who writes, at the end of his *Kritik der praktischen Vernunft* (1788):

Zwei Dinge erfüllen das Gemüth mit immer neuer und zunehmender Bewunderung und Ehrfurcht, je öfter und anhaltender sich das Nachdenken damit beschäftigt: *der bestirnte Himmel über mir und das moralische Gesetz in mir*.   Beide darf ich nicht als in Dunkelheiten verhüllt, oder im Überschwenglichen, ausser meinem Gesichtskreise, suchen und bloss vermuthen; ich sehe sie vor mir und verknüpfe sie unmittelbar mit dem Bewusstsein meiner Existenz.   Das erste fängt von dem Platze an, den ich in der äusseren Sinnenwelt einnehme, und erweitert die Verknüpfung, darin ich stehe, ins unabsehlich Grosse mit Welten über Welten und Systemen von Systemen, überdem noch in grenzenlose Zeiten ihrer periodischen Bewegung, deren Anfang und Fortdauer.   Das zweite fängt von meinem unsichtbaren Selbst, meiner Persönlichkeit an, und stellt mich in einer Welt dar, die wahre Unendlichkeit hat, aber nur dem Verstande spürbar ist, und mit welcher, (dadurch aber auch zugleich mit allen jenen sichtbaren Welten) ich mich, nicht wie dort in bloss zufälliger, sondern allgemeiner und notwendiger Verknüpfung erkenne.

And Kant goes on to say that, just as this sidereal world has been explained, not by superstitious astrology but by mathematics (he is evidently thinking of Newton), so the moral world should keep free from superstition and *Überschwenglichkeit*, by separating, as in chemistry, the rational from the empirical: "science . . . is the narrow door which leads to philosophy."

Here, love is replaced by ethics (Jean Paul has pointed out the absence of love in the "revolutionary" system of Kant): the visible (sidereal) cosmos and the invisible world (identified, narrowly, with the moral world) are accessible only to analytical science, not to the synthetic sense of world music as the expression of divine love. (We shall deal later with the dissolution of Catholic world harmony by Protestantism; here, it need be stressed only that the Protestant mind, at its most rigid, sees an inexorable order within and above man, without the fusion of the two worlds as we have seen it with the Spanish writers.)

This profession of faith, dualistic and "transcendentalistic," a faith in the separateness of science and faith, conditioned by the supposed rift between *mundus sensibilis* and *mundus intelligibilis*, between *Sein* and *Sollen*—this has been considered so characteristic of Kant's mature thought that it has been allowed to figure in the epitaph on the grave at Königsberg. But, as R. Unger has shown (*Aufsätze zur Literatur- und Geistesgeschichte* [Berlin, 1929], p. 42), Kant had not always conformed to such dualistic rigor. In his juvenile *Allgemeine Naturgeschichte und Theorie des Himmels* of 1755, Kant wrote of the night concert of the stars: " . . . so gibt der Anblick eines bestirnten Himmels bei einer heitern Nacht eine Art des Vergnügens, welche nur edle Seelen empfinden. Bei der allgemeinen Stille der Natur und der Ruhe der Sinne redet das verborgene Erkenntnisvermögen des unsterblichen Geistes eine unnennbare Sprache und gibt unausgewickelte Begriffe, die sich wohl empfinden, aber nicht beschreiben lassen." In this passage, then, the metaphysical faculty is represented as enabling man to sense an unanalyzed ("unausgewickelt") unity; and such terms as "edle Seele," "unnennbare Sprache," "verborgene Erkenntnisvermögen des unsterblichen Geistes" are reminiscent of the Klopstockian (that is, Miltonian and Platonic) hymnic language. And in 1764, in *Beobachtungen über das Gefühl des Schönen und Erhabenen*, the Sublime is symbolized by "night," and the Beautiful, by "day": "[by the starry night] Gemütsarten, die ein Gefühl vor das Erhabene besitzen, werden . . . allmählich in hohe Empfindungen gezogen, von Freundschaft, von Verachtung der Welt, von Ewigkeit" (p. 42); slowly, the starry night creates a *Stimmung*. It was in the period between 1764 and 1788 that Kant acquired his horror of metaphysical speculation unsustained by natural sciences, his aversion to the eudaemonistic "sensuality of imagination," and had developed an urge for critical "purity" of thinking, as we find it in his *Critique* of 1788; here, where he speaks in terms of the two irreconcilable worlds, we must recognize a continuation of Cartesian thought (he states outspokenly in 1793 that a "denkende Materie" is an impossible concept) which, as we shall show later, was in part responsible for the destruction of the concept of world harmony.

What Unger has failed to point out in his study of the genesis of Kant's profession of faith is the Platonic model for the sentence, quoted above: "Zwei Dinge erfüllen das Gemüth mit . . . Bewunderung und Ehrfurcht . . . : der bestirnte Himmel über mir und das moralische Gesetz in mir." The Platonic source, which has been discovered by A. Rüstow, *Das Versagen des Wirtschaftsliberalismus als religionsgeschichtliches Problem* (1945; note to p. 8), is to be found at the end of the *Laws* (XII, 966, d–e), just as the passage of Kant belongs to the last pages of the *Critique*: "There are two things that lead to the belief in the gods: first what we said of the soul . . . secondly the regularity of the movements of the stars and of all that is subjected to the domination of reason, of that reason that has given the universe its order." But, while the Platonic influence is unmistakeable, I might point out that, with Plato, the observation concerning the two worlds is put into the service of a theodicy!

In his comments on the text of 1755, in which Kant meditates on the night concert, Unger had occasion to mention certain of the German philosopher's predecessors: Wieland, Klopstock, Haller—and Edward Young. In the latter, we have a link between the extreme Protestant dualism of Kant and the unity of the baroque concept concerning the world concert. In the *Night Thoughts* of the English pre-Romantic poet Young (which foreshadow the "Meditations," the "Contemplations" of later Romantic poets), the concert of the night, that message of divine love ("the song of Angels, all the melodies / Of choral gods are wafted in the sound") is still heard against the background of silence ("Silence how dead! and darkness how profound! / . . . Silence and Darkness! solemn sisters! twins / From ancient Night who nurse the tender thought / to Reason . . ." [lines 21–30]). The "night poetry," the "graveyard poetry," is still within the tradition of the Spanish baroque age—a tradition which could be summed up in Young's lines: "True taste of life, and constant thought of death." This baroque tradition is modified, with Young, by a certain narrowing of the world stage, and by a much greater emphasis on the didactic; nevertheless the continuity is unmistakable—a fact which is ignored by comparative historians of literature, who are more interested in the concurrence of poetic motifs in the literatures of a given period, than in the preceding traditions, of which this concurrence may be so largely a continuation (in this regard, Unger [*ibid.* p. 28] says only: "Der innige Zusammenhang des Geheimnis- und des Demütigungsmotivs in Youngs Gedankengang und die mehrfache Wiederkehr beider in der empfindungsvoll weichen Nachtstimmung unter dem unermesslichen Sternenhimmel . . . bezeugen . . . die Abkunft dieses religiösen Antirationalismus . . . aus der Sphäre religiös ergriffener Empfindsamkeit"). Van Tieghem, *Le préromantisme* is more concerned with the migration, from England to the world at large, of the themes "night" and "graves," than with the *genesis* of these themes. In regard to the latter, he offers only vague references to the Middle Ages, as well as some remarks on the graphic art peculiar to the English in their treatment of death (e.g., the gravedigger's scene in *Hamlet*). In such melancholy themes I see rather the fusion of a typical baroque motif (Shakespeare: "Imperious Caesar, dead, and turn'd to clay . . ."; Young: "An heir of glory! A frail child of dust! / Helpless immortal! insect infinite! A worm! a god!") with the Ciceronian idea of the world harmony of night: what is man, this transient inhabitant of earth, in comparison with the eternal night concert of the universe?

When the Romantic Musset borrowed from Young the title and setting of his *Nuits*, he introduced into his poems an optimistic element: the ultimate transiency of human sorrows, the healing of scars, the inner rebirth that comes to man, even as nature and love are born and die and are again reborn within the cycle of the year (May—December—August—October).

19. The same is true of the metaphor "the concert of the birds": what was primary has become secondary.   A poem, found in a textbook for German grade schools, plays, with a certain *préciosité*, on the theme: "Konzert ist heute angesagt [!] / Im frischen grünen Wald; / Die Musikanten stimmen [!] schon, / Hei, wie es lustig hallt! / Das musiziert und jubiliert, / Das schmettert und das schallt . . ." (there follow stanzas on the different bird-musicians).

20. But the "night concert" can always be revived.   When, to the 75,000 Americans assembled before the marble steps of the Lincoln Memorial to hear Marian Anderson sing, Harold Ickes introduced the singer, he spoke the following words: "In this great *auditorium under the sky*, all of us are free.   When *God gave us this wonderful outdoors and the sun and the moon and the stars*, He made no distinction of race or creed or color. . . .   Today we stand reverently and humbly at the base of this memorial to the Great Emancipator, while glorious tribute is rendered to his memory by a daughter of the race from which he struck the chains of slavery."

While Luis de Léon would stress the laws governing the universe in the concert of stars, the American statesman—somewhat in the Kantian tradition— stresses the freedom of justice; but, with him, too, the idea of the concert of the night sky has been re-enacted.

21. One must remember that a return of Orpheus (that is, of harmony) to this world was conceived by the Renaissance thinkers and poets as a corollary to the idea of "renaissance" itself: the rebirth, in their own time, of the ancient civilization.   De Tolnay quotes in this connection a passage from the *Alter- cazione*, Chap. II, of Lorenzo de' Medici: "I thought that Orpheus returned to our world, so sweet was the music from the lyre which I seemed to hear him playing.   I said 'Perhaps the lyre which was formerly among the constellations has fallen from heaven.' "   A similar idea may be underlying the name "Uranio" given by Sannazaro in his *Arcadia* to his divinely singing shepherd: Uranio evidently suggests a reincarnation of the muse Urania in the shepherd whose music is described as divine harmony: "Mentre il mio canto e 'l murmurar de l' onde / s' accorderanno; e voi di passo in passo / ite pascendo fiori, erbette e fronde. / Io veggio un uom . . . el par che sia / Uranio, se 'l giudizio mio non falle. / Egli è Uranio, il qual tanta armonia / ha ne la lira et un dir sì leggiadro, / che ben s' aguaglia a la sampogna mia."

22. This uninterrupted popularity of the opera in Italy has, incidentally, had the result of checking the development of the (psychological) drama, with its emphasis on the rational element, which leads to (dramatic) conflict with feeling. A musicalized Faust or Hamlet is no more a dramatic one.   Even the *Barber of Seville* suffers by the transposition from drama to opera: in Rossini's

work this figure has only a fixed role to play and sing; he is no longer a
"character."

23. "Musical" is thus loosely used for "harmonious." The classical painter
Holanda, a friend of Michelangelo, applied the term *desmúsico* to the Flemish
and German painting which emphasizes (in landscapes) "the accidental, the
national and the exterior" (Borinski)—thereby establishing the arbitrary
equation "harmonious = classical," and overlooking the "musical," the *Stimmung*
which permeates precisely the Northern school of painting.

"Music" as a synonym of "harmony" and "blissfulness" is attested in several
German baroque writers in whom a Romance influence made itself felt:
Schulz-Basler quote the following passage from Guarinonius, *Die Grewel der
Verwüstung menschlichen Geschlechts* (1610): "unnd sie das schöne mittel unnd
so *fürtreffliche Musik* verloren"; Albertinus Aegidius, *Lucifers Königreich und
Seelengejaidt* (1616): "Wie Nabuchodonosor *in seiner glori und music* in ein
unvernünfftiges Tier verkehrt ward."

In the lines from the *Viaje del Parnaso* in which Cervantes describes his
own poetry ("Que a las cosas que tienen de imposibles / siempre mi pluma se
ha mostrado esquiva; / las que tienen vislumbre de posibles, / de dulces, de
suaves y de ciertas / explican mis borrones apacibles. / Nunca a *disparidad* abre
las puertas / mi corto ingenio, y hállalas contino / de par en par la *consonancia*
abiertas") as well as in those from *Persiles y Sigismunda*, where he postulates
verisimilitude for a story to the extent "que a despecho y pesar de la mentira,
que hace *disonancia* en el entendimiento, forme una verdadera *armonía*," we
find the musical terms used in exact correspondence with this same ideal of proportion and clarity. He seems to think (as may be gathered from the epithets
dulces, suaves, ciertas) that deviation from the objectively, rationally possible,
from the "likely," interrupts the quasi-musical flow of a tale. Cervantes starts
from a classical aesthetic doctrine, though his aesthetic practice is often baroque.
His classical approach is borne out also by his attitude to music which is revealed
in *Don Quixote*, II, 26, where the protagonist and the puppeteer give the
following advice to the boy whose role it is to accompany the puppet show with
a story which he himself has put into words: "Niño, niño, seguid vuestra historia
línea recta, y no os metáis en *las curvas ó transversales* . . . Muchacho, no te
metas *en dibujos* . . . ; sigue tu canto *llano*, y no te metas *en contrapuntos*, que
se suelen quebrar de sotiles. . . . *Llaneza*, muchacho: no te encumbres, que
toda afectación es mala." Contrapuntal adornments are here "affectation."
That *armonía* means to Cervantes simply "order" (with no implication of music)
may be seen from the passage of the *Don Quixote* (I, 36) in which he describes a
rowdy tavern scene: the brawling confusion caused by the protagonist's mad
fancies, the sensuousness of the Asturian maid Maritornes, and the jealousy of
the mule driver, the sleepy fisticuffs of Sancho and the final misguided judgment
of the innkeeper—all this is ironically summed up as *toda aquella armonía.*

24. Hans Pfitzner, in accordance with his German romantic aversion against

progress in art—an aversion shared by the Thomas Mann of 1920 (*Betrachtungen eines Unpolitischen*)—represents, in his opera, *Palestrina*, the master of the Mass rather in the light of a conservative who preserved medieval figural music against the political will of Counter Reformation councils while younger disciples were endorsing enthusiastically the modern artistic developments. The feeling of this German conservative prewar artist is full of pessimism, resignation, and nostalgia, which, projected into the past, makes Palestrina's work appear rather as an end than as a beginning of Church Mass art. But there is one highly effective scene, in the first act of the opera, which portrays on the stage (as Browning had done in a poem, "Abt Vogler") the influence of religious world harmony on the artist himself: no better description can be offered than that given in the words of Thomas Mann (p. 414): "Sie [the predecessors seen by Palestrina in a vision] schwinden, aus Not und Finsternis schreit der Einsame noch oben, da schwingt die Engelsstimme sich erschütternd im Kyrie empor, die Gnadenstunde des Müden bricht an, er neigt sein Ohr zum Schattenmunde der verstorbenen Geliebten, die Lichtgründe öffnen sich, die unendlichen Chöre brechen aus in das *Gloria in excelsis*, zu allen ihren Harfen singen sie ihm Vollendung und Frieden." This is indeed "ein wahres Festspiel zu Ehren schmerzhaften Künstlertums und eine Apotheose der Musik."

25. The same title is borne by a work inaccessible to me: Georgius Fr. Venetius, Minoritanae familiae: *De harmonia mundi cantica tria* (Venice, 1525), translated into French by Guy Le Fevre de la Boderie, *L'Harmonie du Monde divisé en trois cantiques* (Paris, 1578).

26. On this synesthetics is based our modern feeling, prompted especially by Bach, that music is comparable to architecture: hence the architectural similes in Browning's "Abt Vogler," and Goethe's reverse conception of architecture as "frozen music."

27. Again, Wellek writes (p. 557-8):

Seine Haltung zur Sphärenharmonie ist mit der Fludds sehr nahe verwandt. . . . Es ist ein vollständiges Sammelsurium alter musikalischer Mythen, was Kircher hier bietet, vorwiegend ins Anekdotische verzerrt und oft stark entstellt und widerspruchsvoll; selbst die "harmonische Disposition der Climaten" nach Vitruv und die Harmonie des menschlichen Leibes—in Anschluss an Dürer—fehlt nicht.   Gott heisst immer wieder "der ewige Archimusicus," dessen harmonische Wunderwerke "wir bis auf den heutigen Tag mit Verwunderung anhören müssen." Die sechs Tagewerke werden, sogar auch in einer Abbildung, den sechs Hauptregistern einer Orgel verglichen, wobei z.B. von den Gestirnen und ihren Umläufen als von "harmonischen Melodien" gesprochen wird, "so unter dem grossen Zeitconsono und dissono, das ist, dem Tageslicht und Nachtschatten verborgen gelegen."

Paul Friedländer has quoted to me the final prayer of the *Musurgia Universalis* (1650): "O magna Harmonia, qui omnia in mundo numero, pondere et mensura disponis, dispone animae meae monochordon juxta divinae voluntatis beneplacitum"; where the biblical and Augustinian words clearly point toward *Stimmung*.

Here we should mention also the aeolian harp whose inventor is Athanasius Kircher. Romantic poetry has celebrated this musical instrument on which nature herself seems to play without any intervention of man.

INDEX

www.ingramcontent.com/pod-product-compliance
Lightning Source LLC
Chambersburg PA
CBHW022005080426
42733CB00007B/487